GANGLAND

Paul Williams

What they say about *Gangland*

'Written with pace and a forensic attention to detail'
Irish Independent

'Few journalists have the guts to trawl the dark underbelly of
Irish society like Williams' *Irish Independent*

'In the best traditions of investigative journalism'
Irish Independent

'Williams again comes up trumps with his depiction of the
evil men who control Dublin's gangs'
Evening Herald

'Williams does a fine job' *Sunday Tribune*

'This book must be read' *Kerry's Eye*

'Compelling, chilling and unputdownable' *Garda News*

'Racy and riveting, you'll be instantly buttonholed'
Books Ireland

'A racily written account of the failed lives of men who chose
crime as the way to rise out of the Republic's social and
economic underclass'
The Irish Times

PAUL WILLIAMS is Ireland's most respected crime journalist. A qualified criminologist, he works with the *Sunday World* newspaper. He has won several awards for journalism, including the National Media Award for Outstanding Work in Irish Journalism, the citation for which states: 'The name of Paul Williams has become synonymous with courage in crime reporting and campaigning.' His first book, *The General, Godfather of Crime*, is a No. 1 bestseller and has been made into a major award-winning feature film, directed by John Boorman.

Other books by Paul Williams
The General, Godfather of Crime

GANGLAND

PAUL WILLIAMS

THE O'BRIEN PRESS
DUBLIN

First published 1998 by The O'Brien Press Ltd,
20 Victoria Road, Dublin 6, Ireland.
Tel: +353 1 4923333; Fax: +353 1 4922777
E-mail: books@obrien.ie
Website: www.obrien.ie
Reprinted 1998, 1999, 2003.

ISBN: 0-86278-576-6

British Library Cataloguing-in-Publication Data
Williams, Paul, 1964-
Gangland
1.Organised crime - Ireland 2.Gangsters - Ireland
I.Title
364.1'06'09415

4 5 6 7 8 9 10
03 04 05 06 07 08

Typesetting, editing, layout and design: The O'Brien Press Ltd
Cover design: Designit
Printing: Cox & Wyman Ltd

Acknowledgements

Writing about so many underworld figures, some of whose careers span four decades, would have been impossible but for the assistance, patience and good will of a great many people. I want to thank all those involved in the law-and-order business, from both sides of the thin blue line, for their help, advice and information. None of you, for various good reasons, wanted to be identified and I appreciate that. One of these people is an elusive character who can only be referred to here as the 'fortune teller'. He has been a great friend over the past few months.

My gratitude also goes to my equally patient editor and friend, Colm MacGinty, for allowing me the time to complete the book, and North Leitrim's finest, Big Mick McNiffe, who has always been there to watch my back. Also my thanks and congratulations to *Evening Herald* crime man and friend, Stephen Rae. During these long months, we kept each other going with words of encouragement while trying to finish our respective books. Thanks to *Irish Independent* librarian Lorraine Curran, *Sunday World* picture editor Gavin McClelland and the staff of the RTÉ library. A special word of thanks to Sarah Hamilton for the amazing amount of work she did in order that I could finish the project on time. Also to legal mastermind Simon McAleese, of Matheson Ormsby Prentice, who, after four years in the *Sunday World*, probably knows more about villains than most of the criminal Bar put together. Finally, thanks to Michael O'Brien and his staff at The O'Brien Press. Our relationship could at times be described as stormy, but in the end he was the only publisher in Ireland with the courage to enter uncharted waters and publish *The General* – and now *Gangland*.

Dedication

To my family and friends

Contents

Introduction

An elusive brutal world called Gangland has existed in Ireland for over a quarter of a century. It is the criminal underworld, a parallel society which thrives on fear, death and dirty money, with its own codes of conduct and behaviour. It is the underbelly of the Celtic Tiger. Here, some of the most successful and respected citizens are killers, robbers, fraudsters, fences, extortionists and drug dealers.

This book pieces together the story of Gangland through the life and crimes of its better-known residents. These are the godfathers and gangs who have influenced the underworld over the past twenty-five years, and whose crimes have both outraged and fascinated. *Gangland* is the story of the struggle between the forces of law and disorder. Here are the people who have made their mark on underworld history. It is the story of the horrific violence of PJ Judge, the appropriately nicknamed Psycho; the meticulously planned heists associated with Gerry Hutch, The Monk; abhorrent young drug dealers like Thomas Mullen, The Boxer, who brought misery to his own neighbourhood by supplying heroin; the pitiable figure of former armed robber Paddy Shanahan, who was murdered because he wanted to cut his ties with the mob; the colourful and dapper Christy 'Bronco' Dunne, who once headed the country's most notorious crime gang; and the extraordinary real-life cops and robbers drama of the so-called 'Athy gang'.

The story is also about the appalling experiences of the innocent victims of gangland. The story of a courageous wife and mother called Jennifer Guinness, kidnapped by the Cunningham brothers who wanted to hit the 'big time' no matter what it cost anyone else. The gruesome murder of a small-time crook and Walter Mitty character, William Jock Corbally, who was tortured to death before being dumped in an unmarked grave. And the reign of terror wrought by a ruthless one-man crime wave called Mickey Boyle across Wicklow and Dublin.

Gangland did not exist before the late 1960s. Ireland was a sleepy place in the days before the outbreak of war in Northern Ireland and the mayhem which spread south of the border as a result. The economic boom of the 1960s also played its part in the transformation which was to come. In a few short years, petty crime became much more serious. The burglars and the pickpockets of the 1960s became the armed robbers of the 1970s. And, in turn, a lot of the robbers became the drug barons of the 1980s and 1990s. Drugs, in the words of one criminal interviewed for this book, destroyed the old ethics of so-called Ordinary Decent Criminals. As in every other country in the western world, drugs became a source of vast wealth for organised crime. Ironically, the people who have suffered most from the drug epidemic were the gangsters' old neighbours and friends, the downtrodden and forgotten working classes of the sprawling suburbs and inner-cities, where the Celtic Tiger's largesse is out of reach.

Drug dealing brought death and devastation to the streets. It also created a new Gangland phenomenon – the contract murder. Since criminals moved into the narcotics trade, dozens have been executed in feuds fed by greed, their names added to Gangland's roll of dishonour. In practically every Gangland murder case, the victim was a player in what Martin Cahill liked to refer to as 'the game' that is crime.

During the 1970s and 1980s, the slow and inadequate response of both the Gardaí and the legislature effectively gave Gangland its independence and the godfathers established its borders. Lack of resources or strategic planning, and a disorganised, plodding criminal justice system helped to facilitate the much more organised crime wave. Gang bosses and their hoods, flush with the millions their rackets had earned, began to think of themselves as untouchable and above the law.

Never was that more brutally illustrated than on 26 June 1996, when a gunman cold-bloodedly shot journalist Veronica Guerin five times, at point-blank range. The outrage was a chilling wake-up call from the gangsters to the establishment. Guerin was shot simply because she had tried to do an interview with the 'main man'. The gang boss who organised the killing was warning the establishment that anyone who crossed him or his cronies was fair game.

But, when he sent his hitman out to work on that sunny summer afternoon, he also made a devastating miscalculation. It led to a counter-offensive against organised crime, which turned the tables in favour of law and order for the first time in over two decades.

As a crime journalist with the *Sunday World* for over a decade, I have written about all the shady characters in this book and reported on their exploits. Some of them I have known on first-name terms. Others were not as friendly. One even planned my murder, until an unknown assassin indirectly spared me by taking him out of the picture first.

As a study, I have always found crime a fascinating subject. What are the factors which help create a serious criminal and what motivates him to continue committing crime no matter how many times he has been inside? The study of crime gives an insight into a much bigger picture, which a lot of our social leaders through the decades have preferred to ignore. Crime causation tells us as much about the fundamentals of our society and, indeed, ourselves as any other study. It illustrates social dysfunction – in other words the failure of our systems of education, welfare, employment and justice. Crime is about the gulf between the haves and the have nots. The vast majority of our criminal population grew up in deprivation, on the wrong side of a social and economic boundary wall. Behind this wall exists a sub-culture where the norms of the middle class mean little. Here it is survival of the fittest, and gangsters tend to be the more nimble ones. Achievement in the underworld is pulling off the big crime and getting one over on the cops. Why have our socially-minded commentators never questioned why so-called Ordinary Decent Criminals are often the heroes of their local communities? In October 1998 the Garda Commissioner, Patrick Byrne, warned that the intervention of the police in social disorder should be a last resort. He argued that social and economic reforms were vital if crime was to be reduced.

Crime journalists are regularly criticised for glamorising crime. When I wrote *The General*, I was asked by one individual: 'Why write about that dirty bastard? He was only a scumbag, and you're glorifying him.' The reason that book was written is the same as this one – that Cahill and his underworld cohorts are as much a part of our social history as anyone else. They have had such a profound effect on the national psyche that it would be wrong to ignore them. It is neither glorifying nor glamorising. It is informing the public of what is going on around them. Crime will always be a feature of society, however 'civilised' we are supposed to be. In the midst of Ireland's unprecedented economic boom, we are creating the next generation of criminals, as the socio-economic boundary grows higher and more impregnable.

The psychologist Carl Jung once wrote of the public's fascination with crime: 'With what pleasure we read newspaper reports of crime. A true criminal becomes a popular figure because he unburdens in no small degree the consciences of his fellow men, for now they know once more where evil is to be found.'

Welcome to Gangland.

Paul Williams
October 1998.

The Kidnappers

John and Michael Cunningham, like most hoodlums, were ambitious criminals who dreamt of the 'big one', the crime which would set them up for the good life. They craved an epicurean existence of long holidays in the sun, big houses, flashy cars, expensive suits, champagne and women. But it was the Cunningham brothers' pursuit of the great 'underworld dream' which would earn them an unenviable place in the history of organised crime.

The brothers came from Ballyfermot in west Dublin and were part of the new breed of criminals who emerged in the 1970s and ushered in an era of organised serious crime. At the time, the police were putting most of their limited resources into tackling the IRA, who were financing their war by robbing banks throughout the country with apparent impunity. Meanwhile, the new young generation of petty thieves was learning from the paramilitaries and exploiting the lack of police attention.

The Cunninghams, along with the other notorious families on the south side of the River Liffey, the Dunnes and the Cahills, quickly learned their trade and became professional armed robbers. By the early 1980s they were among the underworld's trend-setters – swaggering, cocky crooks, giving the two fingers to the police. Those were the days when a hoodlum could drive a Jaguar and live in a mansion and still be entitled to collect his unemployment benefit down at the Labour Exchange before collecting more money in the bank around the corner with the help of a sawn-off shotgun. Today older criminals reminisce with affection about those halcyon times when organised crime was still a relatively new phenomenon in Ireland.

The Cunningham brothers came from a family of seven children. Their father, Frank, from County Clare, had been a soldier and their mother, Lily, was from County Mayo. When the children were small the Cunninghams, anxious to give their children a decent upbringing, moved from the slums of Blessington Street in the north inner-city to Le Fanu Road in Ballyfermot, one of a number of sprawling suburbs where the Government built thousands of new houses in a bid to give the working-classes better living conditions. But they would become notorious breeding grounds for the new generation of ruthless hoodlums.

Michael Joseph Cunningham, born in 1949, was the older of the two brothers. John was born two years later. Michael qualified as a plasterer but gave it up in 1971 for a more lucrative career in crime. John worked for a short time as a metal worker and gave it up for the same pecuniary reason. John Cunningham was the leader of the criminal enterprise. He received his first custodial sentence in 1966 at the age of fourteen for house breaking and larceny. He was given a two-year sentence and sent to Daingean Industrial School, a notorious institution run by religious brothers. It was in institutions such as Daingean where most of gangland's future godfathers got their first brutal experiences of incarceration.

Over the next twenty years, John Cunningham would accumulate another twenty-seven criminal convictions, for larceny, receiving stolen goods, assault and malicious damage. Michael Cunningham, on the other hand, was slightly more successful at avoiding the attentions of the police. His first conviction was for larceny, which he received in 1963, on the day of his fourteenth birthday. He was fined £1. Between 1963 and 1986 he received another eight criminal convictions for larceny, receiving stolen goods and malicious damage.

In the meantime, John and Michael's older brother, Fran, nicknamed the 'Lamb', was making a name for himself as a big-time fraudster. Fran the Lamb, a smooth-talking conman, used his charm to rob banks instead of his brothers' preferred tool, the sawn-off shotgun. He teamed up with two other notorious con artists, John Traynor and Sean Fitzgerald, to organise all kinds of elaborate fraud scams, netting them huge sums of cash which were blown on wine and women.

From an early age, Michael and John Cunningham were close

associates of Martin Cahill and some of his brothers. Cahill was the same age as Michael. He was serving two years in Daingean for burglary when John Cunningham was sent there in 1966. The two were to remain close friends. The Cunninghams were also closely associated with the notorious Dunne brothers – Christy, Henry, Larry and Shamie. These three groups of hot-headed young thieves were to become the most prolific robbers in the country.

The Cunninghams began featuring in Garda intelligence reports as suspects for a string of armed robberies around Dublin from the mid-1970s. In 1976 John was jailed for eighteen months for an armed hold-up at his local post-office in Ballyfermot. On another occasion he and Michael were arrested at a party in a house at Scholarstown Road in Rathfarnham after an armed robbery from the Carlton Cinema. The guns and cash from the heist were found in the house. John Cunningham was also questioned about the murder of a security guard during a raid at Clery's Store in central Dublin in 1982. And that same year both Michael and John were suspected of taking part in a £120,000 robbery from a post-office in Mallow, County Cork, with Martin Cahill.

John Cunningham also participated in the robbery which was to establish Cahill as a major-league criminal godfather – the O'Connors jewellery heist in July 1983. The 'stroke' netted the gang £2 million in gold and diamonds and earned Cahill the nickname 'The General' for his meticulous militaristic planning. After the heist Cunningham was given the nickname 'The Colonel'. On the night following the robbery Martin Cahill and Cunningham collected the van they had used to transport the huge haul to a lock-up garage where the loot was split fourteen ways.

The two hoods drove the van to Poddle Park in Crumlin to burn it and whatever forensic evidence it contained. They threw in petrol bombs to start the fire. As Cunningham was about to throw one of the bombs, it ignited prematurely in his hand. He was wearing a rubber glove which melted onto his hand in the flames. The General helped his pal to a waiting car driven by another gang member.

They took Cunningham to his home in Tallaght, where he soaked in a cold bath and had the wound dressed by The General. Two days later Cunningham was treated for the burns at a Dublin hospital. The injuries were consistent with a plastic object melting on his hand. Later, he claimed that he had received the injury when a chip-pan caught fire in his home. A subsequent search of his home by the Gardaí found no evidence that there had ever been a fire of any kind.

The Cunningham brothers loved the high life their criminal activities paid for. Like the Dunnes they wined, dined and partied in all the city's best restaurants, pubs and clubs. They drove fast cars and enjoyed lavish holidays abroad in places like Barbados, Florida and Spain. Michael and John also shared the same interest in women. In 1978 Michael separated from his wife Anne, with whom he had a son and daughter, and began living with Patricia McCormack in Clondalkin. At the same time, John started a relationship with Patricia's sister Mary, who was also separated. She had a twelve-year-old daughter, Caroline, whom Cunningham treated as his own child. In 1981 he bought a bungalow for his new family in Tallaght, Dublin.

But the high life was a big drain on money and took a lot of armed robberies to sustain. John Cunningham wanted one big 'job' which would earn himself and his brother enough money to sit back for the rest of their days. He decided that the most effective way was kidnapping a member of a family worth millions. By 1986 the IRA had been responsible for a number of high-profile abductions, most notably that of supermarket executive Don Tidey in December 1983, which resulted in the murder of a Garda and a soldier. Earlier that year, Gardaí arrested four members of the IRA in a shoot-out when they tried to kidnap Galen Weston, another supermarket millionaire.

But while the Gardaí had succeeded in rescuing the hostages in the reported cases, Cunningham was interested in the number of kidnappings which were never reported. As in the case of armed robbery, Dublin crime gangs were taking their lead from the Provos and looking at abduction as a means of making easy money. The most notable of these kidnappers was Mickey Boyle from Bray, who was well known to the Cunninghams. (See chapter 6, 'The Hitman and the Penguin'.) Boyle had been caught following two kidnaps in County

Wicklow in 1984. But John Cunningham knew that Mickey Boyle had got away with several other such abductions. The super-confident crook reckoned that he and his sibling could do a better job than the IRA or Boyle.

In early 1986 the Cunninghams began looking for a target. They had decided to go it alone because Martin Cahill was involved in his own rackets. They did not agree with The General's methods, which invariably involved large teams. They wanted to divide up the loot among the smallest number possible. At the time the Cunninghams were working with Anthony Kelly from Tallaght. Kelly was born in 1943 in Dublin but moved to live in Leeds in Yorkshire at an early age. He had been in trouble with the police from the age of eleven, accumulating thirteen convictions for larceny, forgery and burglary for which he received a total of over seven years behind bars.

In 1975 Kelly absconded to Dublin while awaiting trial on robbery charges in Leeds. A warrant was issued for his arrest. When he came back to Ireland he got involved with the underworld, and met the Cunninghams. In 1980 his marriage broke up and his wife and children returned to live in England when he began living with a seventeen-year-old street trader called Julie Lyons.

Like the Cunninghams, Kelly liked the high life. He had developed a taste for expensive wines, liked to wear flashy 'Miami Vice' suits and holiday in the Bahamas. He also bought a house with cash in Clondalkin. He paid for his lavish lifestyle by taking part in armed robberies in England with Dublin-based criminals, including the Cunninghams. The police in Leeds set up a special team to track down the gang, which commuted between England and Dublin to do 'jobs' and were suspected of robbing in the region of £1 million over a three-year period up to 1984. Their targets were mainly banks and security vans. Often the gang would fly from Dublin airport, do a robbery somewhere in the north of England and take a return flight to Dublin the same evening.

In October 1984 the Dublin-based gang were the prime suspects for the murder of police sergeant John Speed who was shot dead during a chase in Leeds. After that the gang discontinued their day trips to England. Early in 1986 the West Yorkshire police informed the Gardaí in Dublin that, among others, they wanted to extradite John and Michael Cunningham and Tony Kelly to face charges. The three crooks were tipped off that the Gardaí were to be asked to arrest them for the purpose of extradition to England and were advised to keep their heads down. They decided to bring their kidnap plans forward. If they were going to face a jail stretch in England, they wanted to ensure that their families had enough money to keep them going. They hastily drew up a shortlist of possible hostages. Among these was Susan, the first wife of Independent Newspapers proprietor Dr Tony O'Reilly. Also on the list was Guinness heiress Miranda Guinness and Norma Smurfit, the former wife of business tycoon Michael. However, neither Miranda Guinness nor Susan O'Reilly were in the country and Norma Smurfit was too well protected by private bodyguards to get near.

Eventually, they decided on the family of John Guinness, the millionaire chairman of the Guinness Mahon bank. The fifty-one-year-old banker, a former officer in the Royal Navy, was married to Jennifer, who also came from a wealthy family background. The couple had three grown-up children – Gillian, Tanya and Ian. The family lived in a splendid period mansion, Censure House, at Baily, near the fishing village of Howth in north County Dublin. John and his forty-eight-year-old wife were a very close, happy couple who shared the same passion for yachting. They were well-known in the sailing world and regularly participated in high-profile races such as the Round Ireland yacht race. Jennifer, a very strong and resilient woman, also did a lot of charity work in her spare time. Cunningham had read a feature about the family in a glossy magazine and decided that they would have little difficulty in raising the ransom money.

In March 1986 the gang started making preparations for the abduction. Because of the extradition threat the crooks all moved off-side and went into hiding at the beginning of the month. They carefully began watching the house and generally building up a pattern of the family's movements. Cunningham solicited the help of Brian McNichol, a drinking acquaintance of his. The Derry-born forty-nine-year-old former businessman had lived in Dublin since 1965. McNichol was a shady, small-time con artist who Gardaí would later describe as a mystery man. He had worked in the demolition business in Dublin until 1984. McNichol and Cunningham had had some dodgy dealings. He was not known to the Gardaí and had not been in trouble with the law except for a few drink-related minor offences. McNichol, who had lost an eye in a mugging incident, had been married but was now separated. He spent most of his time with a girlfriend who lived at Waterloo Road in Ballsbridge.

The gang agreed that they would abduct either one of the family's daughters or Jennifer Guinness herself. John Cunningham was confident that if they convinced the family they were the IRA the police would not be alerted and the money would be paid over within a few days. Their plan was to then skip the country for a far-flung hot spot where there were no extradition arrangements with Ireland or England. Because time was against them they decided to do the job on the afternoon of Tuesday 8 April. They would demand a ransom of £2 million for the safe return of the hostage. Tony Kelly took on the job of finding safe houses where they could hold their hostage.

On Good Friday he rented a fisherman's bungalow near Drumconrath in County Meath. The house was quiet and private. He paid the rent up front in cash, and told the owners he wanted it for two weeks from 1 April. Along with a woman who was never identified, Kelly also rented a flat above a shop in Arbour Hill in Dublin up to 17 April at £20 per week. On 1 April Kelly also hired a green Opel Kadett hatchback car from Liffey Car Rentals in Dublin's city centre. At the same time John Cunningham collected the gang's arsenal of weapons.

Since the West Yorkshire police had begun their investigation into the Speed murder in Leeds, a special surveillance team attached to the Garda Central Detective Unit had been keeping tabs on the Cunninghams and Kelly. Under the command of Detective Inspector Gerry McCarrick, the squad had been set up in 1982 to target major organised crime figures in Dublin and liaise with other police forces in targeting international crime networks involving Irish hoodlums.

McCarrick and his tight-knit team had been hugely successful, as a result of using what were considered at the time to be radically new undercover methods.

The squad tailed one of the city's underworld gun-hire merchants to a meeting with John Cunningham in the car park of the Submarine pub in Crumlin, Dublin, in late March. They had been watching the illegal gun dealer as part of an operation code-named 'April'. Cunningham had paged the dealer, asking him to meet 'Jack'. McCarrick was convinced that Cunningham and his team were getting ready for a major crime, possibly a kidnapping or a robbery. Intelligence sources revealed that the gang planned a major crime during the June bank holiday weekend. A number of potential targets were placed under Garda protection.

Cunningham obtained a hand-grenade, a replica Uzi sub-machinegun and three hand-guns for the kidnapping. He also made up two devices which would look like bombs, complete with 'remote control' detonators. Bombs with electronic detonation devices tended to scare people out of their wits and focus the mind on paying up, Cunningham believed. On the afternoon of the kidnapping the gang planned to use a battered old car belonging to an associate of McNichol to abduct their victim. Michael Cunningham and Kelly would conceal themselves in the back seat. The car would then be used to bring the hostage to a pre-arranged spot where the green Opel hire car would be waiting for the change-over. Everything was ready. The Cunninghams were about to etch their names in gangland history.

At 3.30pm on Tuesday, 8 April, Jennifer Guinness took the family's two dogs for a walk, as she often did in the afternoon. As she returned to the house around 4.15pm, a battered old car pulled into the driveway. She could see that the driver was the only occupant, a respectable-looking man, smartly-dressed and wearing a blue felt trilby hat. There were sheets in the back covering what she would describe as something bulky. One of the dogs began barking wildly and she restrained it, apologising to John Cunningham as she did so.

'You have come to collect the books?' Jennifer asked Cunningham, who smiled and replied, 'Yes.' A half-hour earlier a bookshop owner, Simon Nelson from Schull in County Cork, had arranged to call and collect some sailing directories and she assumed that he was the man in the car. Jennifer Guinness was the secretary of Irish Cruising Club Publications Ltd., and the club's headquarters was at the house. Sailing enthusiasts regularly called to collect books from her at Censure House. The gang could not have timed their arrival any better.

Jennifer turned and walked up to the front door. Cunningham followed. She pushed open the door, walked over to a hall table and picked up the stack of books she was holding for the bookshop owner. When she turned to hand them over Cunningham was standing behind her with a .45 pistol in his hand. 'Don't be so stupid ... you've got to be joking,' she exclaimed in surprise at the sight of the weapon. 'Oh, no, it's not a joke. Keep your hands on the table,' Cunningham replied in a sinister tone.

By now Kelly and Michael Cunningham, who were both wearing balaclavas, had jumped out of the car and were running into the front hallway. They rushed past the 'Colonel', who also pulled a mask over his face, and into the kitchen. The housekeeper, Patricia Coogan, and Jennifer's daughter Gillian were sitting at the table. The criminals pointed their guns at the heads of the two women and ordered them not to move. One of the kidnappers grabbed the housekeeper and brought her to fetch her fifteen-year-old daughter, who was watching TV in a flat adjoining the main house. When they returned they marched the four women into a television room adjoining the hallway.

The three kidnappers demanded to know the location of any panic buttons. There were none. They also asked what time John Guinness was expected home and who else was expected to call. The phone lines in the house were ripped out. The men gave their terrified captives the impression that they were paramilitaries by referring to the 'organisation'. They said they were following orders because the organisation needed money and that if everyone behaved themselves no-one would be shot. Michael Cunningham and Kelly made a point of calling John 'Colonel'. In turn Michael was called 'Sergeant'.

John Cunningham announced that they intended taking Gillian Guinness as a hostage and that they wanted a ransom of £2 million paid for her safe return. Then he ordered Jennifer out to the hallway where he quizzed her about where her jewellery was kept. He also demanded to know which paintings in the house were valuable. He was abusive and pointed the gun at her head. She took him around the house, explaining the value of each painting. Jennifer showed him the family's most valuable piece, an Osborne painting of her grandmother-in-law. She explained to the 'Colonel' that it was too well-known in the art world, as it had been on exhibition in Dublin, and was therefore worthless to a thief.

As they walked through the house, Cunningham demanded to see the safe. When she opened it and showed him her collection of Victorian jewellery Cunningham demanded to know where the 'real safe and real jewellery' were. Jennifer Guinness tried to explain that the gang had targeted the wrong family. 'Do we look like people who have an enormous amount of money?' she asked him. Cunningham and his brother took whatever jewellery was there. It was worth just over £50,000. They ransacked every room in the house looking for valuables.

At one stage, the 'Sergeant' found Jennifer's Irish passport and declared, 'We don't shoot Irish people,' to substantiate their claims of being paramilitaries on a 'fund-raising mission'. Jennifer, a strong-willed, courageous woman, was determined to do everything in her power to prevent the gang taking her daughter. She was terrified of what the masked thugs could do to a defenceless young girl. From the beginning of her nightmare ordeal she steadfastly refused to show fear in front of her captors. She pleaded with John Cunningham to take her instead of Gillian. 'No, you would be better because you would make sure that everybody would stay quiet. I want you to stay and put pressure on John to pay the money quickly,' Cunningham replied.

About twenty minutes had now passed since the kidnap gang entered the Guinness home. Around 4.30pm Simon Nelson arrived in a white van. The book dealer knocked on the door. Jennifer Guinness answered and invited him in. A masked gunman emerged from behind the door and held a gun to his head. Jennifer explained to Cunningham that this was the man she had been expecting to call for the books. A short while later, the family butcher called to deliver meat, as he did twice a week. The gang waited with their guns cocked as he walked around to the kitchen door, placed the meat in the fridge and left again, totally unaware of the unfolding drama in the house.

Nelson was taken out of the room by the 'Colonel' and questioned about his family and where he came from. Cunningham held a grenade in front of the petrified man and told him that he had been unfortunately caught up in something which was not his business. If he talked about what happened to anyone then they, the organisation, would find him no matter where he tried to hide.

Then a woman delivering census forms called to the door. One of the gang members held Jennifer's arm behind her back and a gun to her head. She opened the door slightly and accepted the form. The census enumerator was nervous about dogs and got the impression that Jennifer was holding one of them behind the door. She promptly left, suspecting nothing.

At 5.30pm John Guinness's silver-grey Mercedes car drove up the driveway to Censure House. He first tried to use the front door, which he found locked. He walked around to the back of the house and entered through the kitchen door. As he walked from the kitchen into the hall, he was stunned to see his wife standing near the TV room door with a masked man who was pointing a gun in his direction. 'What's all this about?' he gasped in amazement. Jennifer told him that it was all 'for real' and that the gang had the rest of the household at gunpoint in the TV room.

John Cunningham, who was also holding the replica Uzi, ordered John Guinness to sit down on the sofa in the hall and face the opposite wall. Jennifer was put back with the rest of the hostages. Cunningham and his brother frisked the banker. They told Guinness that they were kidnapping both Jennifer and Gillian and that they wanted a £2 million ransom. When he was asked if he could raise that sort of cash

John Guinness said he did not think so. He was ordered into the dining room, where he was made to sit down.

Michael Cunningham brought in two hold-all bags. He unloaded them, taking out the two fake bombs and transmitters that they had prepared beforehand. He also placed the live hand-grenade on the table. John Guinness was under the impression that the gunmen were going to blow him and his family up. He spotted the Uzi on a sideboard near where he was sitting. While John Cunningham was fiddling with the 'bombs', Guinness jumped up and grabbed the weapon. Cunningham immediately pointed his pistol into the banker's face and ordered him to put down the weapon, which he did. The 'Colonel' held the gun to Guinness's temple and told him that that had been a stupid thing to do and accused him of being unco-operative. He would later tell detectives that he left the gun beside the banker to 'test him'.

Cunningham punched his victim hard into the ribs with his left fist. Then he punched him in the left eye and pressed the gun against his forehead. Cunningham cocked the revolver and held it to his victim's ear as he was hunched over in pain from the blows. John Guinness thought that he was about to be either executed or kneecapped. Cunningham squeezed the trigger but the weapon failed to fire. John Guinness heard the click and the barrel revolving. He froze in terror. Cunningham cocked the gun again and fired a shot past the banker's head. He beat Guinness around the head and face with the gun.

Cunningham then told his victim that he would not allow him to see the 'bombs' being assembled. He said the two devices were to be strapped to Jennifer and Gillian and could be detonated by remote control from a quarter-mile away. He repeated his demand for £2 million, which he said he wanted in sterling and US dollars. He warned several times of the dire consequences which would result from calling in the Gardaí. Cunningham asked John Guinness how long he thought it would take for him to gather up the ransom money. He said about a week. Cunningham said that was OK and that he would ring him in a week at his home, but then changed his mind and said he would call on the following Friday, 11 April, using the code-word 'Jackal'.

Across the hall in the TV room everyone had heard the shot and the commotion. Jennifer Guinness was terrified that her husband had been hurt or even murdered. She heard the gang members shouting and hurling abuse. A few minutes later, to her relief, John was led back into the room by the Cunninghams. He was bleeding heavily from cuts to his nose and a gash under his eye. One of the gunmen walked in with a bundle of ties which they used to tie up everyone except Jennifer and her daughter.

John Cunningham ordered Jennifer and Gillian to get ready to be taken away. Gillian was suddenly overcome by the brutal ordeal of the past ninety minutes which had turned her family's life into a nightmare. She broke down and sobbed uncontrollably. For her mother, whose courage and strength would astonish even her captors, it was a blessing in disguise. She could now convince her abductors that it would be more logical just to take her and not Gillian. Two hostages would be much more trouble to a kidnap gang, she reasoned with the gang leader, especially if one of them was so scared and distressed.

John and Michael Cunningham discussed it momentarily and agreed with Jennifer. They sent Gillian back into the room and tied her up with the others. Michael Cunningham went upstairs with Jennifer, who picked out some heavy clothes and washing materials. John Guinness asked one of the gunmen if he could see his wife before she was taken away. Jennifer was brought back into the room. She was wearing heavy clothes for the outdoors. She gave her husband a hug and reassured him that she would be fine. Her husband said that he would do everything he could to see that she was rescued.

At this stage, John Cunningham's demeanour changed from being aggressive to appearing considerate. He asked if anyone wanted a drink before the gang left and if they were comfortable enough. He also assured John Guinness that his wife would be looked after and that they would arrange for her to phone him when they reached their destination. This appeared odd as the gang had ripped out the phone lines. Jennifer Guinness looked around the room, gave them a reassuring smile and said goodbye to her family. Then she bravely walked out of her home with three armed and masked men on a dreadful journey into the unknown.

Outside she was bundled into the back seat of the car and covered over with a rug and a sheet. She had a loose pillow-case on her head but could still see out. Michael and John Cunningham sat in the front and Kelly sat on her legs in the back. The gang drove down to Sutton Cross and out across north County Dublin, towards the bungalow Kelly had rented at Drumconrath. They were driving for over an hour-and-a-half. On the way one of the men got out of the car, leaving two gang members with the hostage. They stopped a second time on a rough lane with trees and hedges on either side. Here they changed transport and got into the hired Opel Kadett. Jennifer was placed in the compartment behind the back seat of the hatchback car. She was given a pillow and covered with a rug. A third person again joined them and they drove for another hour. The kidnappers stopped a number of times to make phone calls along the way.

Back at Censure House, Gillian Guinness freed herself within ten minutes. She then released the rest of the captives. Everyone in the house was extremely distressed. When they discovered the phone lines were ripped out, John and Gillian Guinness drove off to the home of a neighbour, Liam McGonigle. When they arrived at the house, they were agitated and upset. John Guinness very quickly explained what had happened and wondered what they were to do. John and Gillian returned to their home ten minutes later. McGonigle, a solicitor by profession, decided to call the Gardaí.

When the neighbour called, Detective Garda John O'Mahony answered the telephone in the offices of the Central Detective Unit in Harcourt Square. Forty minutes later detectives met with John Guinness and a huge police hunt got underway. From an incident centre set up at Raheny Garda station in north Dublin, scores of detectives from throughout the city were alerted, along with specialist squads from the Serious Crime Squad and the Special Detective Unit. A pre-arranged plan called the 'National Cordon', to set up security checks throughout the country, was put into operation. It had been devised after previous kidnappings. The media agreed to a total news blackout for the next forty-eight hours to convince the gang that the Guinness family were complying with their wishes. Senior officers also needed time to consult with various detective units and intelligence sources to compile a list of possible suspects.

As the Gardaí were beginning their investigation, the kidnappers arrived at the bungalow with Jennifer, who was still hooded. The gang members removed the pictures on the walls in each room and anything else which might have given her a clue as to the location of the house. The gang were wary of their hostage because she had been so calm and in control since her ordeal began. She was also very agile and they were scared that she might try to escape. That night she was handcuffed to Tony Kelly, who lay on a single bed beside her and snored. At one stage Michael Cunningham came into the room and pushed a second single bed over to the one Jennifer was lying on. She now had a bed to herself although she remained handcuffed to Kelly. She was unable to sleep.

The following morning, Wednesday 9 April, Raheny Garda station was the venue for the first major conference of the investigation. The station was filled to capacity with detectives gathered for the mammoth enquiry. Officers from all the force's main units and district detective squads were present. Squads involved in armed response, surveillance, organised crime and anti-terrorist operations had been called in overnight. Many of them had experience in kidnap operations in the previous few years, including the rescue of Don Tidey and the attempted abduction of Galen Weston.

The officers in overall charge of the operation were local superintendent Tom McDermot and Detective Superintendent Hubert Reynolds of the Investigation Section in Garda HQ. Chief Superintendent Edward O'Dea of the Special Detective Unit at Harcourt Square and Detective Superintendent Michael Maguire of the CDU, both of whose units were deeply involved in the case, also liaised with the Guinness family and would meet them at their home every day. The three objectives of the investigation were outlined to the assembled team. They were the safe return of the hostage, the identification and capture of the gang members and the prevention of a ransom payment. Officers from various districts were asked to nominate suspects and a plan of action was drawn up to place them under immediate surveillance.

A kidnap investigation is one of the most difficult any police force has to deal with. Investigators must move quickly but carefully, because the life of a hostage is in the balance. In the case of a major robbery or murder detectives can take more time to accumulate evidence and clues. It is also accepted that kidnappers are extremely dangerous, volatile individuals. They know the consequences of such a serious crime and are prepared to take drastic action to prevent capture. Ransom demand deadlines are invariably short. The abductors just want to take the money – a lot of money – and run, which places an extraordinary strain on the police charged with their capture and the safe return of the hostage.

In the initial stages the investigation chiefs discounted the involvement of a terrorist organisation, because the intelligence services had no indication that the Provos or INLA were planning such a crime. Also, the initial abduction was not characterised by the kind of professionalism associated with subversive crime, although they could not rule out the involvement of individual members of these groups.

The main suspect was a criminal figure from Santry, also in north Dublin, who had links with a gang of north-side hoodlums involved in major armed robberies over the past year. An informant with paramilitary links was already feeding information to the investigation squad about this team. The other obvious choice was Martin Cahill, The General, who by now was the country's most wanted criminal. He had the capacity, the personnel and the resources to pull such a crime. But not everyone was convinced of his involvement.

One of the officers at the conference was Detective Inspector Gerry McCarrick. He immediately nominated The General's close associates, the Cunningham brothers and their sidekick Tony Kelly, as the prime suspects. He told the conference of his belief that they had been planning a kidnapping and may have recently hired weapons. Other officers, however, felt that they should first eliminate the local north-side suspects. Throughout the country, hundreds of searches were carried out in vacant farm buildings and rented accommodation. Across the border in Northern Ireland the RUC were also on alert.

While the massive security operation to find her was getting underway, Jennifer Guinness was offered breakfast, papers and magazines by her captors. She had been refusing to co-operate with them and wanted concessions in return for her silence. They asked what she wanted. She said a radio and some books. A short time later one of the gang handed her a radio and a bunch of cheap paperbacks. Michael Cunningham was doing the cooking and tried to make her eat. He cooked steak for her supper that evening and eventually she managed to eat something.

That night the gang chained Jennifer to the bed. The chain was two feet long and held by a padlock, which she would later recall was a lot better than being handcuffed to a snoring ruffian. She slept through the night. The following day, Thursday 10 April, Michael Cunningham gave her breakfast, including grapefruit and apples, which she managed to eat. At one stage his hostage even praised his cooking.

But her fear and apprehension were never far away. Up to now there had been no mention of her abduction on the news. Her abductors seemed relaxed and were friendlier towards her. She was able to have a bath and relax somewhat. But she feared that her husband was going to pay the ransom. She would later recall how appalled she would have been had the thugs been paid. 'It wasn't the amount of money but the thuggery – that this could happen in Ireland. It would have encouraged other such crimes,' she later said.

Jennifer Guinness did not have long to wait to find out what was going on in the world outside her prison. At 10.45am that morning the Gay Byrne radio show was interrupted by a news flash about the kidnapping. That morning the Gardaí had agreed to lift the news blackout, much to the annoyance of Jennifer's family. Details were given of the number of gang members involved and that a nationwide manhunt was in operation throughout the country, north and south of the border. The Gardaí appealed for information to help in tracking down the kidnappers. After that the abduction became the main topic of every news programme.

The Irish public was stunned and shocked at yet another kidnapping. But what made it all the more shocking was the fact that the victim was a defenceless, middle-aged woman. The investigation team felt that the publicity would help them force the kidnappers out into the open. Jennifer was startled by the broadcasts. She knew that her abductors had not yet heard the news. At this stage, there was only one gang member, Michael Cunningham, with her and he was in the kitchen. Kelly had gone to the shops for more groceries. John Cunningham was away making arrangements with Brian McNichol. She knew all hell was about to break loose.

When they heard the news, the Cunninghams were furious that the Gardaí had been alerted. They began to panic. One of them horrified Jennifer when they said they would have to move and she would have to be buried. Then she was reassured that they were only going to hide her in the woods. She was ordered to put on all the clothes she had brought with her, including a number of jumpers and two pairs of jeans. The kidnappers were jumpy and aggressive. She was frightened that they were going to harm her. They drove in the Opel Kadett through back-roads and up a bumpy track into a forestry area.

It was around 2pm when they left the car and marched Jennifer Guinness into a thick pine wood. They tied the chain around a tree and handcuffed her to it. She was also hooded. Michael Cunningham remained with her while John Cunningham and Kelly went off to make arrangements for their next safe house. Cunningham now began to play mind games with his hostage. He fancied himself as an actor and began putting on a Northern accent to give the impression that there was a fourth member of the gang present. The accent was also intended to convince her that they were part of an IRA team. Jennifer and her captor stayed shivering in the forest until around 11pm when the car returned with one of the gang members. She had been told that they might have to spend the night out in the open and that they might have to take her across the border into Northern Ireland. She was now totally disorientated, frightened and extremely tired.

The car drove for over an hour, arriving in Dublin around 1am, although Jennifer didn't know where she was. She was bundled into the dreary ground-floor bedsit Kelly had rented earlier at Arbour Hill. The gang told Jennifer that she was in the North and that they were across the road from an RUC station. The accommodation consisted of one room, with a sink, a gas heater, one bed, a cupboard and a small TV. The decor was just as bleak, with damp, peeling wallpaper and a boarded-up window. The toilet was a single bucket in the corner of the room which everyone had to use. It was an appalling experience.

Jennifer insisted that they leave the heater switched off because she thought it better to be cold rather than sick from gas fumes in such a stuffy atmosphere. She was kept in this room from the early hours of Friday 11 April until late on Saturday night. At all times there was one masked member of the gang in the room. Again she had to sleep hand-cuffed to Kelly, the snorer.

Meanwhile, at the investigation headquarters in Raheny, officers were becoming concerned at the lack of contact with the kidnappers. Around 10.28am on Friday morning they received an anonymous call purporting to come from the 'Colonel', demanding the payment of the £2 million ransom by the following Tuesday, 15 April. But Gardaí had no way of knowing whether the call was genuine.

John Guinness and his three children were still anxiously awaiting news. They were all deeply distressed as each day went by without any news or contact from the kidnappers. John engaged the services of the London-based security firm Control Risks, which specialises in kidnap negotiations. The Guinness family decided they were able to pay a ransom in the region of £300,000 for the safe return of their loved one although the Government and the Gardaí insisted that they were totally against such action. The Gardaí leading the hunt made it clear that they disapproved of the presence of representatives of Control Risks, who stayed at Censure House. There was also some friction and internal jealousies between some of the police units called in on the case. Four days into the drama there was still no sign of a significant breakthrough. The tension was mounting. Time was running out.

Detective Inspector McCarrick and his team took on the task of tracking down the Cunninghams. They had not been seen for several days and McCarrick was still convinced they were the prime suspects. Most villains are creatures of habit and John Cunningham was no exception. Every Saturday he went to lay bets in a bookmaker's shop on Middle Abbey Street in central Dublin. On Saturday 12 April, the fifth day of the kidnap drama, Cunningham turned up at the bookie's.

Detective Garda James Mitchell, a member of McCarrick's surveillance team, spotted his target. As he left the shop, the undercover cop followed the 'Colonel'. He walked around the corner to a carpark off Liffey Street and got into the passenger's side of the green Opel Kadett hire car, which immediately took off. The detective could not see who was behind the wheel. Mitchell took down the number and traced it to Liffey Car Rentals. Because it was late on Saturday, a check could not be done on who had rented the vehicle until after the weekend. The information was passed back to the investigation headquarters in Raheny, along with scores of other leads, all of which would have to be checked out individually. No-one yet realised just how significant this latest piece of information would be in the coming days.

Before he took time out for his habitual flutter, Cunningham was busy keeping his plan together. He and the rest of the gang were becoming frustrated that the pay-off hadn't yet been arranged. The gang needed another safe house. John Cunningham met Brian McNichol to discuss where they would move next. The Derry man had a place in mind. That evening Cunningham and McNichol went looking for Fergus Kerrigan, an acquaintance of McNichol, who lived in a south Dublin suburb. The house, McNichol explained, was the perfect place to keep their hostage. It was a spacious house at the end of a quiet cul-de-sac.

Kerrigan was a father of four grown children, who had once been a successful businessman. But a serious drink problem and financial hard times had resulted in the collapse of the business and now he was selling double-glazed windows. His wife had left him and his grown-up daughter, Daryl, lived with him occasionally. On the previous Thursday, 10 April, she had left Dublin and travelled to the west of Ireland with her boyfriend for a long weekend. McNichol had been in the house when she left. He had given her a lift to a car rental office and knew that Kerrigan would be on his own for the weekend.

John Cunningham had met Kerrigan in various pubs around the city in the company of McNichol. McNichol introduced Cunningham as John Doherty. Kerrigan was the perfect patsy, down on his luck and wide open to exploitation by ruthless men like McNichol and Cunningham. After visiting several pubs, the kidnappers finally met up with Kerrigan in the Tuning Fork pub in Rathfarnham. McNichol told Kerrigan that they wanted to use his house until Sunday night and they would pay him £10,000 for his trouble. McNichol gave him £50 to pay for a hotel room for the night and arranged to meet him the following morning in a pub on Baggot Street. Kerrigan felt that 'something funny was going on' but asked no questions. He was frightened for his safety and needed the money, so he handed over his keys.

McNichol and Cunningham then drove back to Arbour Hill and bundled Jennifer Guinness into the car. McNichol drove the car to Kerrigan's house. Jennifer would later recall how a 'horrid little man' came on the scene on the Saturday of her ordeal. McNichol was abusive towards her. He wanted to tie her up in the garage of the house and leave her there but the other gang members allowed her to use a bedroom upstairs.

The following morning the gang members began pressurising Jennifer for the names of people they could contact to arrange the payment of the ransom. They were now desperate for some kind of pay-off. She was reluctant to give them any names, hoping that in the absence of contact the gang would give up and release her. Eventually, however, she suggested the number of a family friend. A member of the gang called, but there was no reply. Later that evening,

Jennifer asked Tony Kelly to call another friend in order to get a message through to her husband that she was all right. Kelly relayed the message as requested. It was the first time that the Guinness family had got a firm indication that Jennifer was still safe.

The same afternoon it was decided that they needed another location to hold their hostage. This time McNichol, who was in regular touch by telephone with Cunningham, suggested the house of his girlfriend, Clora Lenehan, at Waterloo Road in the Ballsbridge area of south Dublin. The house was a two-storey over basement terraced Georgian building. Clora had been going out with McNichol for over eighteen months and had given him the keys to her home. The forty-three-year-old company secretary who was separated from her husband knew very little of McNichol's past except that he was in the demolition business and was married. He was secretive about certain aspects of his life and had led Clora to believe that he was a businessman.

McNichol came up with a plan to lure Clora away from the house. That same afternoon he brought her to meet Kerrigan for a drink in a pub on Baggot Street, near her home. While there he suggested that she go away with him the following morning, Monday 14 April, for a few days in the country. When she agreed he was delighted. He said he was going to spoil her. McNichol and Kerrigan went off drinking on their own for the rest of the evening. At one stage Kerrigan, who was getting drunk, demanded to know when he could go back to his house. McNichol told him that he could have his house back the following day, Monday. When Kerrigan asked who was staying in the house, McNichol told him: 'Mrs Guinness is in your house.' Kerrigan became anxious and demanded that she be taken out of the house. McNichol told him that the woman would not be harmed and if he told anyone about it he would be dealt with. Kerrigan was now in fear for his life.

By Monday morning, John Cunningham was desperate to make contact with the family to secure the ransom money. He had been reading the newspaper reports about the involvement of Control Risks and decided to make contact with them. He was aware also from the reports that the Government and Gardaí did not want the company involved. But he realised he could not call the Guinness home as the line would be tapped. They would have to go about it another way.

At 9am Jennifer was taken downstairs to the telephone. She was hooded and a gun was held to her head. Cunningham dialled the London number of Control Risks and handed her the phone. To her utter amazement the kidnap victim was put on hold by the company which was working to secure her release. A receptionist told her: 'Hold on, I'll come back to you.' Four times the gang hung up, re-dialled the number and put the receiver to Jennifer's ear. Each time she got the same response and the kidnappers grew more frustrated. Eventually she got through to someone. 'This has to do with the Guinness kidnapping. Please will you give me a number to contact in Dublin?' Her voice trembled as the extraordinary pressure began to show. Incredibly, the man on the other side replied: 'I am awfully sorry. I cannot help you.' The line went dead.

The strain was now beginning to take its toll on Jennifer. She began to shake and grew weak. The gang gave her water. When she got herself together again she gave Cunningham the name and telephone number of her brother in London, George Hollwey. When Jennifer called the number her brother was not there, nor was he at home. An hour later she was brought to the phone to try again and got through. She handed the phone to Tony Kelly who spoke to Hollwey. Jennifer felt a sense of relief.

Negotiations began and the family told the gang they were prepared to pay a ransom. The money was to be sent from London in a briefcase and picked up by a friend of the family at Dublin airport. The ransom, which was believed to be in the region of £300,000, would be left at a pre-arranged location on Tuesday evening, 15 April, or in the early hours of the following morning. Jennifer would be released near a Garda station. The Cunninghams had decided to drop her in Herbert Park in Ballsbridge.

The police were fully aware of the plan and advised against it. But in the absence of any strong leads in the case John Guinness and his family were not prepared to prolong Jennifer's trauma any longer. A special team of heavily-armed surveillance officers was put on standby to monitor any ransom hand-over. The cops were not going to let the gang get away with it. In the meantime, however, the drama was about to take a new twist.

Fergus Kerrigan spent most of Monday drinking with Brian McNichol. That evening they drove to Waterloo Road to pick up Clora Lenehan. She was packed and looking forward to her surprise trip to the country with McNichol. Later they went to a pub in Rathmines where they met John Cunningham, who had arranged to meet McNichol there. The two men left the bar together for a while and returned for another drink. Cunningham then left on his own. McNichol and his girlfriend drove Kerrigan back to his home.

Daryl Kerrigan and her boyfriend had returned from their short holiday around 4.30pm. The green hire car was parked outside, and she noticed that all the blinds were down in the windows. When she walked into the front hall she was startled by the sight of three men who emerged simultaneously from three rooms on the ground floor. One of them went upstairs. The Cunninghams and Kelly had been in the process of getting ready to move to Waterloo Road.

Daryl asked the men what they were doing in her home. They said they were friends of her father and that he had allowed them to use the house as a favour because he was in financial debt. As she tried to walk up the stairs, she was told: 'No. Don't go up the stairs, come into the living room and we'll explain what's going on.' Neither she nor her boyfriend was allowed to go upstairs by the gangsters.

Later, Daryl again asked if she could go upstairs to her room. One of the men insisted on accompanying her. At the top of the stairs the man behind her ushered her past her father's bedroom. This was the room where Jennifer Guinness was being held. In her own bedroom she saw a masked man standing with his back to her. She became frightened and ran downstairs crying. John Cunningham told her not to worry. 'It has nothing to do with you. You just walked in on it.' Michael Cunningham made tea and asked the couple about their trip. After a while, John Cunningham left the house to meet with Kerrigan and McNichol in Rathmines. He came back an hour later.

Shortly after Cunningham's return, Kerrigan arrived into the house. He was drunk and in high spirits although he broke down at the thought of what he had got himself involved in. He sat down beside his daughter and her boyfriend. Upstairs, Kelly moved Jennifer Guinness to another room and chained her to a radiator. She still had a mask on.

At that moment, there was a knock on the front door. Fergus Kerrigan answered it. Detective Garda Aubrey Steedman from Rathfarnham station was standing outside. The station had received a report that a number of strange men had been observed going in and out of the house and he asked Kerrigan if everything was all right. Kerrigan, slurring his words and unsteady on his feet, said everything was fine. He invited the cop in to see for himself.

In the room, Michael Cunningham, showing no sign of worry, sat down in an armchair and poured himself a drink. Kerrigan introduced him to the detective as a friend of the family and then fell over the coffee table. At this stage in the kidnap investigation, police stations around the city had not been issued with a list of suspects to watch out for. Michael Cunningham smiled at the detective, who felt there was something familiar about his face. Kerrigan showed no sign that there was anything wrong and the detective left again.

Just as the police car pulled out of the estate, John Cunningham appeared. The two Cunningham brothers pushed Kerrigan, his daughter and her boyfriend up the stairs and into one of the bedrooms. They were told not to move for ten minutes. One of the brothers said to Kerrigan: 'The first half of the deal is done.' Jennifer Guinness was taken out of her room and carried downstairs and into the garage. She was put into a large cardboard box which was placed in the back of the car. The gang drove to Waterloo Road and carried the box into the house. Jennifer was taken out and chained to a fireplace in an upstairs bedroom.

After the gang had left the Kerrigans' house, Daryl found a woman's clothes strewn around her father's room. Later that night Fergus Kerrigan went back to the pub. While there he met two off-duty Gardaí and told them he was in danger, but he would not elaborate. They arranged to go to see him the following day. The next morning, Tuesday 15 April, Daryl Kerrigan rang the incident room at Raheny Garda station. From the events of the previous night and the few pieces of information she had got from her father, she had come to the conclusion that the house had been used in the kidnapping. It was the breakthrough which had been so desperately awaited.

That evening, Fergus Kerrigan also made a statement to investigating detectives, which convinced them that Jennifer Guinness had been held in Rathfarnham. Based on what he disclosed about McNichol it was also likely that she had been moved to Waterloo Road. The car being used by the gang, as described by Kerrigan and his daughter, matched the description of the vehicle spotted by Detective Inspector McCarrick's surveillance team the previous Saturday, carrying John Cunningham. At the same time, a check with the rental company showed that the car had been hired by Tony Kelly, the Cunningham brothers' partner in crime. It was booked to be returned that same day and the car rental company was placed under surveillance. During the day, Kelly called to say that he wanted to hold onto the car for another two days. The investigation team now knew the identity of the kidnap gang.

Detective Inspector McCarrick and his team were dispatched to watch the house at Waterloo Road. At 9.30pm the team spotted the green Opel Kadett car parked along Waterloo Road. The information was relayed back to the investigation centre in Raheny. A top-level conference was called. It was presided over by Deputy Commissioner Eamon Doherty, and all the senior officers attached to the local district, the Technical Bureau, the SDU and the CDU were present. It was decided to surround the house at Waterloo Road immediately.

Meanwhile at Waterloo Road, Jennifer Guinness was settling down for what she believed would be her last night in captivity. Just then the Cunninghams came bolting through the door and ordered her to dress quickly. They had received a call from an unknown individual who warned them that the Gardaí knew their location and were about to surround the place. They taped up Jennifer's eyes and put dark glasses on her. She was taken downstairs and put sitting on a chair in the hall while they started to clean up the house.

Outside, the surveillance team saw Kelly walk out of the house and get into the hire car. He reversed the car up to the front door and got out, leaving the car doors slightly open. He tapped on the front door and went back inside. McCarrick and his team got ready to rush the house but they were ordered back. A large team of detectives armed with revolvers and machineguns began moving into positions around the house. At 1.23am Detective Inspector Bill Somers, Detective Sergeant Dermot Jennings and three other members of the Special Detective Unit knocked on the front door of the house.

The Cunninghams and Kelly spotted the police at the front and bolted out the back. Kelly jumped through a back window with Michael Cunningham behind him. Detective Garda Tony O'Donnell, who had taken up a position along the rear wall, spotted them and shouted: 'Stop. Gardaí. Stop.' Michael Cunningham fired a shot. The detective heard the bullet whizzing past his head. He returned fire with one shot. At the same time, Detectives Tom Kelly and Aidan Boyle fired bursts at the kidnappers from their Uzi sub-machineguns. On hearing the shots, the Cunninghams retreated back into the house.

Jennifer Guinness was now in danger of being caught in the crossfire. The police were at the front, the gang were at the back. She lay down on the floor. Michael and John Cunningham came racing up from the basement, grabbed her and ran upstairs. Jennifer got down under a bed for cover. The Cunninghams were panicking and she feared that they were about to throw the grenade. John Cunningham shouted down at the detectives. 'We have that woman up here and we will blow her fucking head off if you don't get out of the house.' Detective Inspector Somers, a trained hostage negotiator who had also been involved in the Tidey kidnapping three years earlier, shouted back that he would guarantee their safety if they released the woman unharmed and came out with their hands up. John Cunningham was holding a gun and standing at the window which he smashed so that he could communicate with the cops below.

When Somers again asked them to give themselves up,

Cunningham replied: 'No way are we going down for thirty years. You will shoot us if we come down like you did our friend.' Somers told them that Kelly was alive and well. Cunningham said he didn't believe the policeman. Somers said he would get Kelly so they could see for themselves. The police negotiator then asked how Mrs Guinness was. She appeared at the window and told Somers she was in good form and had been well treated. She disappeared from the window again.

At the back of the house, Tony Kelly had given himself up and was taken into the basement flat. He was shaking and very nervous. Detective Garda Kelly asked him why had he taken part in the kidnapping. 'I needed the money. John organised it and Michael. I didn't fire any gun. We were going to release her tomorrow. We were going to take her to Herbert Park, leave her at the bottom of the road and give her £5 for a taxi home.'

Detective Inspector Somers and Detective Sergeant Jennings quizzed him about what firepower the Cunninghams had in the house. Kelly lied. 'Don't go up there. They will blow you away. There is enough explosives to blow you to Kingdom Come. They have black plastic explosive, the bomb is already made up and probably strapped to her and they have a remote control switch. John has the switch and he is mad enough to use it.' Kelly was asked what had he hoped to get out of the kidnapping. 'I won't get anything now, will I?'

At 3.05am Somers took Kelly out to the front of the house so that he could talk with his pals. It was raining heavily outside. Michael and John Cunningham were now at the window. They laughed nervously at Kelly. John Cunningham spoke first. 'Tony, did they bash you?' Kelly replied: 'No, no, I'm all right. They didn't go near me,' and then added cryptically, 'I just want to say one thing to you, remember the Pud.'

Kelly was brought back into the house next door and put on the phone to John Cunningham. 'I'm fucked. Straightforward cop, no other way ... listen to sense, no heroes, no heroes, reality, reality, I got a bit of a roll around but it's the wrong time for heroes. There's no other way out,' Kelly told his friend. 'I feel that Somers and Jennings have the woman's interests at heart more than anything else. If she comes out it will go a long way. I wouldn't like sending flowers to you, we are all grown men. I will give you half-an-hour to think about it.' The phone went dead.

Inside the house, Jennifer sat on the floor. John Cunningham paced up and down the room, chain-smoking. He still held a gun and the grenade in his hand. He seemed unbalanced and said he couldn't take what was waiting for him outside. Michael Cunningham was more relaxed and calm. They allowed Jennifer to call her husband and John Cunningham rang his wife Mary. Then Cunningham went off the rails again. 'I'm not going out there. I couldn't do it.' He seemed prepared to go out fighting or even to take his own life. Michael then said that if his brother wasn't surrendering then neither was he. They talked about killing themselves. Jennifer was now very scared. She knew that there could easily be a bloodbath on Waterloo Road if the Cunninghams decided go out in a blaze of glory, in a showdown with the scores of armed police outside.

The Cunninghams made several emotional calls to their wives and families. Bill Somers continued to talk up to the brothers. It was now approaching 5.50am. Jennifer Guinness and Michael Cunningham sat on the floor. There were long silences as John continued to pace the floor. Then both Michael and his hostage tried to persuade John to surrender. She decided to let them talk it out between them. Their family were on the phone pleading with them to give it up. Jennifer walked to the the window and told Somers that things were looking good. Dawn was breaking.

John Cunningham shouted out to the police negotiator that he would come out after he phoned his wife. Mary Cunningham was due to give birth at any time to the kidnapper's first child. In an emotional conversation she told him to think of his unborn child and to give himself up. Michael Cunningham rang his solicitor. Somers instructed the Cunninghams to put all their weaponry on the floor in the middle of the room and to come out unarmed. Inside, Jennifer helped her captors to put the stuff together. The Cunninghams unloaded their pistols. They both shook hands with their hostage and each other. Michael handed her back the jewellery they had taken during the first horrific hour of her ordeal a week earlier. Then he smiled to Jennifer, opened the door for her and said, 'Ladies first'.

At 6.24am on the morning of Wednesday, 16 April, the Guinness kidnap drama ended, and so too did the Cunningham brothers' aspirations to the big time. John Cunningham opened the front door and stepped back with his hands in the air. Bill Somers walked into the house and took the hostage by the arm. He led her down the steps where his boss, Chief Superintendent Ned O'Dea of the Special Detective Unit, was waiting. O'Dea brought her beyond the cordon of detectives still training their weapons on the house and reunited her with her husband. They hugged each other and thanked the Gardaí for their work.

At 6.25am Detective Sergeants Jennings and Rice moved into the hallway and arrested Michael and John Cunningham under Section 30 of the Offences Against the State Act. They were brought to a convoy of waiting police cars and whisked across the city to Santry Garda station. As he sat in the back of a squad car sandwiched between two officers, John Cunningham was asked if he really thought he could have succeeded in his crime. 'We wouldn't have done it if we didn't think that we were going to get the money. Two million was only a starting figure. We thought it would only last about two days. Five more minutes and we were gone. It was going to be the big one but it all went wrong.'

Later, Cunningham broke down and cried when his wife visited him in custody. 'My life is shattered. I will say my piece to the judge when the day comes. I will plead to it. I am caught bang to rights. It could be worse. There was no-one hurt. I suppose it was worth the chance.' When he was asked how Mrs Guinness behaved during her ordeal he said: 'She is a tough lady. I told her not to worry, that it was a new experience for her and that she could write a book about it. That's life. Whatever will be will be.'

While Michael Cunningham was being driven to the police station, he described to detectives what it had been like inside the siege house. 'It was pretty tense in there. John is a bit hot-headed. He was on for ending it all there. She'd be gone and we'd be gone too. John wouldn't give a fuck, he'd throw a grenade down on top of you. Today was to be pay-day. Fuck ye anyway.'

Later his wife, Patricia, came to see him. She asked him why he had kidnapped Jennifer Guinness. He shrugged his shoulders. 'It doesn't matter much now. We were only a few hours from collecting the money.' Then he revealed that he had thought of taking his own life at the end of the siege. 'What would that have solved?' Patricia asked him. 'It just seemed like an easy way out,' he replied. Then he described the drama when the cops moved in. 'They shot at us and we shot at them. It was like the Wild West.'

Brian McNichol returned to Dublin on Wednesday afternoon with Clora Lenehan. He was now fully aware of what had happened on Waterloo Road. While he had been away he had called to the home of an acquaintance in County Westmeath and confessed to the man that the kidnappers 'were my boys ... I'm in terrible trouble'. McNichol also assumed that Fergus Kerrigan had been the one who called the police. On his way back to Dublin he phoned Kerrigan's number and threatened the person on the other end of the line: 'We are coming to get you.' Unfortunately for McNichol, the person on the other end of the phone was a detective. It was not going to be a good day for him.

Shortly after 7pm on 16 April he arrived at Waterloo Road with Clora Lenehan. She was shocked to discover what had happened there that morning. Detectives had been on the lookout for McNichol and couldn't believe their luck when he turned up, trying to pretend he was a totally innocent party. He was immediately arrested.

On the evening of Thursday, 18 April, John and Michael Cunningham and Tony Kelly were driven to Dublin District Court 6 in a convoy of unmarked police cars with sirens blaring. They were led into the court in handcuffs and each one stood as the charges were read out. They were charged with the false imprisonment of Jennifer Guinness by unlawfully detaining her against her will. They were further charged with being in possession of firearms with intent to endanger life at Waterloo Road.

The following night Brian McNichol made his debut in the same court. He was charged with the false imprisonment of Jennifer Guinness and with having possession of a firearm for an unlawful purpose. Detectives recovered the pistol in a follow-up search of his house in Rathfarnham. The next day John Cunningham's wife gave birth to a baby girl in the Coombe maternity hospital in Dublin. A nurse was her only company during the birth. Mary Cunningham would later describe it as the loneliest day of her life. John Cunningham would first meet his daughter in a visiting room in Mountjoy prison.

While the Cunninghams were on remand, their father Frank died. There was a huge security operation as the brothers attended the funeral handcuffed to detectives. Before they were allowed to pay their final respects to their father, officers searched the coffin for concealed firearms. A month after their capture, their old friend, Martin Cahill, pulled off one of the biggest art heists in the world when he made off with the Beit art collection. If they hadn't decided to go their own way, the Cunninghams would probably have been admiring the collection of priceless masterpieces.

On 24 June 1986 the two brothers pleaded guilty in the Circuit Criminal Court to the kidnapping charges. During the short hearing a senior Garda officer revealed that there had been thirty-seven cases of false imprisonment in Ireland in the previous year. In 1986 there had been fourteen, including the Guinness kidnapping. The court resolved to send a stern message to any other crooks hoping for the elusive 'big one'. John Cunningham was given seventeen years for his role as the leader of the gang. Michael got fourteen years. They served their sentence together in Limerick prison along with the Dunne brothers, Larry and Henry, and several more of their once-swaggering contemporaries who were also caught while in pursuit of easy money. The West Yorkshire police applied to extradite all three kidnappers upon their release in Ireland. Subsequently, however, the English case was dropped when another criminal confessed to the murder of Sergeant Speed.

On 5 November of the same year, Tony Kelly was jailed for fourteen years for his part in the crime. His young wife told his hearing,

'He is the best husband. I love him very very much. When I heard he was involved in the kidnapping, I thought it was the end of my life. I was in despair and still am.' Jennifer Guinness was forced to relive the trauma of her kidnapping in the same month, when she gave her evidence in the trial of McNichol in the Circuit Criminal Court. He had denied the charges. It took the jury one hour to return a unanimous guilty verdict. He was jailed for twelve years and nine months.

The courage and resilience of Jennifer Guinness during and after her kidnapping captured the hearts of the Irish public and she became a household name overnight. On the Thursday after her ordeal had ended, and while her captors were still being questioned, she gave a press conference in Dublin surrounded by her family. Hugging her husband, she thanked the Gardaí for their professionalism in rescuing her and also the many thousands of well-wishers. She said she did not hate her captors, although she was never in any doubt that her life had been in danger. The next night, she appeared on Gay Byrne's *Late Late Show*. A few weeks later, she and her husband were back on the high seas, attempting to set the Round Ireland yacht record. But two years later, in February 1988, tragedy struck the happy couple and their family. John Guinness fell to his death while mountain climbing in Wales. He was fifty-three years old. Since then Jennifer Guinness has immersed herself in helping other victims of crime to cope with their trauma. She became chairperson of the Irish Association of Victim Support. But she was still not allowed to forget her ordeal.

In September 1996 John Cunningham bolted from the Shelton Abbey open prison, where he was serving the last two years of his sentence. He had already been granted temporary release to attend the wedding of his adopted daughter, Caroline. She was eleven years old when he was first sent down. Two weeks before the wedding, Cunningham made a run for it after he and a member of the General's gang, Eamon Daly, were spotted drinking in a pub in Wicklow. As a punishment he and Daly were to be sent back to an enclosed prison. Cunningham said he felt he had served his debt to society and skipped. His brother Michael, who was released in early 1996, had to stand in for his brother and give Caroline away at the wedding. John

Cunningham, the man who always wanted to pull off the big one, is still in hiding. A number of Dublin criminals who once worked with him have paid for his new life. He has vowed never to set foot in Ireland again.

Bronco's Last Ride

The dapper, grey-haired man, with his matching grey beard, had the appearance of a wealthy businessman as he sat alone in Circuit Criminal Court number 14. In his expensive suit and hand-made Italian leather shoes, he exuded the self-confidence and aplomb of a senior counsel as he flicked through a sheaf of legal documents. When the jury returned, however, Christy 'Bronco' Dunne's face paled to the same shade as his neatly-trimmed beard as he stood up to hear their verdict.

His eyes narrowed and he folded his arms as if bracing himself for what was to come. Then he heard the words he had successfully avoided for many years: 'You have been found guilty as charged.' Fifty-three-year-old Bronco Dunne, who once compared himself to Wild West outlaw Jessie James, had just enjoyed his last ride in gangland.

During the 1970s, before big gang bosses took over the crime scene, Christy Dunne was one of the Dublin underworld's most colourful crooks. Tall and handsome, with a glib tongue and a good command of English, he was an incorrigible womaniser with the airs and graces to charm the ladies and the bravado to attract the admiration and respect of the rest of the city's criminals. He looked down his nose at so-called 'ordinary decent criminals' and set out to make a name for himself as a gang boss.

In the early 1970s Christy Dunne introduced most of his younger brothers to a new type of crime – armed robbery. The Dunnes were gangland's first big family-based firm of armed robbers and played a major role in ushering in a new era of serious crime in Ireland. It was the gang of Christy and his brothers Shamie, Larry, Robert, Henry, Vianney, Mickey and Charlie who transformed a small-time thief called Martin Cahill into a clever criminal mastermind known as The

General. In their heyday Christy Dunne described himself and his gang as serious professional robbers, highly-skilled craftsmen who were the cleverest crooks in town.

In the days before heroin became his family's stock-in-trade, Bronco relished the media hype which their activities attracted and the kudos associated with being the head of a mafia-style crime syndicate. But the true story of Christy Dunne and his family is anything but romantic. For Bronco was no Don Corleone. His family did achieve notoriety – but not the type Bronco had intended for them. In the 1980s many of his brothers became the country's most infamous criminals for their involvement in unleashing the monstrous heroin plague which destroyed the lives of thousands of young people. They helped to create a social disease which would eventually destroy them too.

Christy Dunne was born on 10 October 1938. He was the first child of Christy senior and Ellen. The couple, both from the inner-city, had married two years earlier. Dunne senior, nicknamed 'Bronco' after the cowboy Bronco Bill, was twenty-two and Ellen, who worked on a second-hand clothes stall, was fifteen. Over the next two decades or so Ellen Dunne endured twenty-two pregnancies, from which sixteen children survived. When she wasn't expecting, Ellen Dunne tried to scrape a few shillings together to feed her large family by running her small stall in the Iveagh Market, off Francis Street, in the Liberties area of south inner-city Dublin.

For his part, Christy senior was a hard drinker who stumbled from one job to another. As a youngster he had been in and out of trouble with the law but had not done time behind bars. After their wedding the couple first rented a run-down tenement flat in Kildare Street before moving to a house at New Street. In 1939 Bronco Dunne senior was convicted of manslaughter. A drinking buddy of his had reportedly hit his mother (Christy junior's grandmother) in a pub brawl and he decided to do something about it. He found the man at his home in York Street and punched him hard twice about the head. The man fell back, cracking his skull on the floor. He went into a coma and died a week later in hospital. Bronco senior was jailed for eighteen months and sent to Portlaoise prison where, over thirty years later, most of his sons would also take up residence for much longer periods. By the time his father was sent down, Christy junior was almost two years old, there was another baby in the increasingly crowded house and a third one was on the way.

Bronco senior's reputation as a violent hard man was consolidated by the death of the man he would later describe as 'my so-called friend'. He showed no remorse for the crime and told his young sons that he killed the man to defend the honour of his family. When he got out of prison he went to work in wartime Britain but was deported twice because he didn't have a permit to work there. When he came home he got a good job in Guinness's brewery but lost it when the stout-making business became another economic casualty of the war.

The lack of work and the inevitable hardship it brought on his family did not interfere with Bronco senior's drinking habits. During a boozing session in a pub on Braithwaite Street he took a revolver from another customer. The following night when he was drunk again old Bronco, in an act of typical Dunne bravado, fired off a shot in the pub, hitting a whiskey bottle across the counter. He was jailed for six months in Mountjoy prison as a result.

It was against this backdrop that Christy Dunne and his siblings were reared. In 1951 the ever-increasing Dunne family were moved to a new Corporation house at Rutland Avenue in Crumlin as part of the Government's slum-clearing programme in the inner-city. But the new house changed little.

The children's mother simply couldn't cope and their father was rarely there. The neglected children began running wild around the streets and stole or begged for food to eat. Many of them, including Christy junior, were reared by their grandmother, Nellie O'Brien. At home violence was a way of life. The children watched Bronco senior beating their mother when he fell in from the pub. Old Dunne would also beat manners into his children and when he wasn't around Ellen beat them in a vain attempt to control them. They were left alone for long periods without either parent. An old family friend recalled visiting the house and seeing Christy standing in the middle of a room with no furniture dishing out stew from a pot to eight of his hungry siblings. Before they were ten years old, most of the young Dunnes were out robbing. Christy, Shamie, Larry, Robert, Henry, Vianney, Mickey, Hubert and Charlie all began their criminal careers as young tearaways.

Years later, when many of her sons were being blamed for flooding their native town with heroin, Ellen Dunne talked about them during a television interview. 'My sons were all gentlemen, beautiful men, beautiful manners, beautiful bodies. I never knew they were on drugs. I had to get work and I never had it easy with my husband either, son. I could never lay down and have my children in comfort. I lay down with black eyes. Now that's the truth, so don't talk to me about drugs son,' she told the interviewer.

Christy Dunne junior was the first member of the family to become involved in crime. He once boasted that by the time he was ten he was robbing more than some men earned in a week. He picked pockets and stole food from the shops and coal from the dockyard to bring home. He would get up early from bed and bring his younger brothers, Shamie and Johnny, to school. The boys would often bunk off and Christy would bring them on mini-crime sprees. After a while they quit going to school altogether. Over thirty years later Christy Dunne went on national radio and in his inimitable style took responsibility for introducing his brothers to serious crime. 'I felt along with my younger brothers that if we ever did anything together, which we have done, it would be a closely-kept secret. We knew we could depend on one another.'

In the Dunne household, a hunger for food surpassed any appetite for education and one by one, as the children got older, they dropped out of school. Neither of their parents seemed to care. The kids ran wild in the streets of Crumlin and increasingly got more involved in criminal activity. But they never bothered anyone in Rutland Avenue. Christy junior and his siblings adhered to the few family precepts which had been beaten into them. They were to be courteous, take pride in their appearance and, above all, never steal from their own people. Many of the Dunnes spent much of their childhood in and out of the notorious industrial schools for a variety of offences, from truancy to theft.

Christy was the first to be incarcerated. When he was twelve he was sent to the Carriglea industrial school on Rochestown Avenue in Dun Laoghaire for truancy. He later described the place as something from a Dickensian novel: a miserable existence of constant beatings and hard physical work. Christy decided that he wasn't prepared to take any more abuse. He ran away and hid in the home of his grandmother, who had always done her best for the Dunne children.

A year after that, young Bronco took the boat to England, where he worked in a coalmine and laboured on building sites. He was a big lad for his age and no-one seemed to notice that he was under fifteen. In 1955 he received a blunt telegram message from his father: 'Come home, Hubert's been drowned.' His fourteen-year-old brother had drowned while swimming at the coast near Upton industrial school in County Cork, where he had been sent along with his brother John. After the funeral Christy decided to stay at home. Shortly after Hubert's death, Ellen Dunne gave birth to her youngest child, Gerard. She now had fifteen children, ranging from seventeen years down. Bronco senior took off for England looking for work.

In the meantime, Christy junior got back to doing what he did best – thieving. When he was sixteen he was sent to Marlborough House, a remand home in Dublin, after being convicted of burglary. The judge in the juvenile court told him he was a rogue and a pest. Dunne was rather flattered. He wanted to become a major-league villain and had notions of one day becoming Public Enemy Number One. He longed to be older so that he could do big heists and have his mugshot on the wall of every police station in the country.

By the time he was eighteen, he claimed he had done more than 200 burglaries. He was regularly before the courts and served short sentences in Saint Patrick's Institution for young offenders where he was respected by the other juveniles as a serious criminal. When he got out, he teamed up with two other associates and they specialised in travelling to the country to rob shops and pubs along the way. He would later write in an unpublished autobiography called 'Wildfire':

'I never thought of reforming. I just wanted to rob and achieve a sense of importance.'

By the time he was twenty-two, Bronco Dunne was achieving his goal. He liked to do something unusual during the commission of a crime and then read about it in the newspapers. He craved recognition. One day he was recognised by a Garda who spotted him behind the wheel of a judge's car he had just stolen. Bronco ended up in Mountjoy Prison.

Here he developed his own theories about why he was a criminal. Bronco blamed society for making him that way. He commited crimes out of economic necessity, in order to feed and clothe his family. In a corrupt capitalist society the working class had been left to live in squalor, without jobs, education or self-esteem. Crime, Bronco declared, was the only way of fighting back against the system. He blamed the police, the politicians, the judges and everyone else in authority for his predicament. The Dunnes were as much victims as the people they robbed.

After this short stretch in Mountjoy, Dunne was once again in trouble. This time he had been charged with robbery. Bronco sought the assistance of Father Michael Sweetman, a Jesuit priest who campaigned on behalf of the under-privileged and deprived in society. Fr Sweetman had also taken a genuine interest in trying to help young offenders like Bronco Dunne to reform. He had first met and befriended the aspiring gangster while he was in Marlborough House.

Sweetman was one of the first people to listen sympathetically to the young, confused Bronco and treat him like a human being. The pair formed a strong bond of friendship and the priest has remained close to the rest of the family ever since. Over two decades, Fr Sweetman appeared as a character witness for the Dunne brothers at several trials. Each time he would explain to the judge the circumstances of the family and plead for a chance to help them reform. In his book Bronco wrote of Fr Sweetman: 'He was a priest, a father, a friend and a teacher. I always felt I really wanted to keep out of crime after talking with him. He was the only one to make me keep from crime.

He took time and great patience to help and teach me. He showed me the way of God.'

Fr Sweetman looked after twenty-three-year-old Dunne for six months in 1961, during which time he wrote the book 'Wildfire'. A journalist who read the unpublished manuscript described it as 'sometimes cruel and harsh, sometimes fragile and sensitive, reflecting the contradictory instincts of its author.' During his stay at the Jesuit retreat house in Clontarf, Dunne attended daily mass with the priests and worked hard. He also convinced his mentor that he had changed. In his book he wrote about his salvation from crime. 'I knew I had passed the stage of being drawn back to my old environment. How I wish men could see how stupid a life of crime is. I always knew I would have to answer to God for the wrong I had committed, but still I could not lead a decent life. I felt I was owed something from somebody.'

Fr Sweetman made approaches to the Justice Minister, Charles Haughey, the Attorney General, Andreas Ó Caoimh, and Assistant Garda Commissioner William Quinn to give Christy a chance. They were told that Dunne had made a serious decision to go straight. Haughey remarked at the time that six months lying low in a Jesuit retreat house was 'as good as any jail sentence'. But Commissioner Quinn had a better knowledge of the Dunnes than Haughey. 'You'll never be able to reform any of that family,' he warned prophetically.

When he got his reprieve, Dunne made an attempt to go straight. He married Jeanette Bermingham, an attractive young woman from the south-side, with whom he had four children. Fr Sweetman officiated at the ceremony. Christy worked for a while as a taxi-driver before starting his own building firm, C and J Dunne Construction, at Patrick Street in Dublin. In 1966 his aspirations towards respectability and social elevation got him involved in the presidential election campaign of Fine Gael candidate Tom O'Higgins. Dunne was attracted by the liberal wing of the party which espoused a vision of a more egalitarian society, where the working class got a bigger slice of the cake. Dunne supplied a lorry during the campaign in Dublin from which several prominent members of the party made speeches on behalf of the candidate.

But Bronco soon got bored with respectability. He was self-conscious about his criminal background and felt that the middle-class party membership were sneering at his social pretensions. At the same time his business foundered and shut down. Again Bronco blamed police harassment for his failed attempt at honest business. He never for a moment thought it had anything to do with the rather questionable quality of the building work.

His political interests led him into more dubious company. Dunne, now espousing a hard-line Republican ideology, began running with a quasi-political group called Saor Éire. This maverick collection of Republicans was a cross between a paramilitary group and a criminal gang. Saor Éire was a flag of convenience with no political ideology to speak of. Through his criminal and family links in England, Bronco ran a lucrative racket supplying the Saor Éire mavericks with pistols stolen from the British Small Arms factory in Birmingham.

Saor Éire robbed financial institutions throughout the country with apparent impunity. Every Thursday and Friday, the days when wages were paid and banks were flush with cash, the Saor Éire gang struck. The takings from each heist were divided between the 'cause' and the patriotic robbers' own pockets. More often than not their pockets benefited more than the cause. They would take over a village or small town in the style of a highly-disciplined military operation, wearing combat uniforms and brandishing rifles, and rob the local banks at will. At the time they met with little opposition and the pickings were easy. Up to the late 1960s violent crime was practically non-existent in Ireland, but Saor Éire changed all that. They were the first armed robbers in the country and introduced criminals like Christy Dunne to a new source of easy, ready cash. They also paved the way for the IRA, who would finance their war in the North through what they euphemistically referred to as 'appropriations' from southern banks. The troubles had begun in Northern Ireland and the Republic's overstretched Gardaí were caught on the hop. They were not prepared, equipped or trained to deal with this new kind of serious crime. Between 1967 and 1969 there was a total of eighteen armed robberies in the Republic. By the early 1970s the annual average was over 150.

Saor Éire's reign of terror was relatively short-lived. In April 1970 the group disbanded after they shot dead an unarmed Garda, Dick Fallon, during a bank robbery in Dublin. Six months later, the founder member of the gang, Liam Walsh, who had introduced Christy Dunne to the organisation, was blown up while transporting explosives. With Saor Éire effectively disbanded, Walsh's funeral gave Christy a chance to grab the limelight. He was one of the main organisers of the paramilitary-style funeral on Saturday, 17 October 1970. His friend Fr Sweetman officiated. The funeral procession stopped outside the GPO on O'Connell Street and a number of speakers, including Christy, ranted on about the need to reunify Ireland at any cost.

But not content with enthralling the mourners with his passion for Republican politics, attention-seeking Bronco fired a shot in the air to prove his dedication to the cause and he was subsequently charged. In February 1971 he was acquitted of the firearms offence in the Dublin district court. But Bronco, ever anxious to consolidate his growing notoriety, jumped up and hit the judge who had just set him free. He was given six months in Portlaoise for his efforts. In November 1972 he was caught again and sentenced to two years for receiving stolen goods.

After he was released, his marriage to Jeanette broke down and she left with their four children. Like his father before him, Christy had neglected his wife and children as he pursued his dream of gangland infamy. He was also fond of drink and gambling, which often left him penniless and his family wanting. But the charming gangster wasn't alone for long. He met and fell in love with Mary Noonan, an attractive seventeen-year-old girl from Coolock in north Dublin. The couple had three children together.

Christy began organising robberies with his brothers Shamie, Henry, Robert and Larry. Most of them had gone to England in the 1960s. Gradually they came home to join the well-organised family business. They were a highly effective team of 'blaggers', or armed robbers. They had their work down to a fine art, doing a heist within three minutes. They were the first gangsters to begin hitting big cash vans. Henry, who once held the title of the most competent robber in the country, came up with the idea: 'Why should we be hitting individual banks when we could hit the money from ten of them in the back of a van?'

Bronco made sure that any 'outsiders' who were brought on heists were carefully screened before being accepted into the fold. After a 'job', it was the brothers, and not their associates, who counted and divided up the loot. They distributed the money equally between them. They also ensured the rest of the family were looked after financially.

But with their success came the attentions of the police. The Dunnes were the talk of the town. They were confident, flamboyant and seemed untouchable. Christy and the gang reckoned they were running rings around the police – and they were, for a while at least. Christy used to look down his nose at the cops who followed them. To Bronco they were poorly-paid 'culchies'. In the clubs he would often send over an expensive bottle of champagne to his Garda watchers. After a big heist the Dunnes were never shy about flaunting their new-found wealth. While criminals like The General kept a low profile, the Dunnes bragged openly about their prowess and exploits.

They wined and dined in the best clubs and restaurants in Dublin. One of their favourite haunts was a club on Nassau Street called 'Vile Bodies'. The Dunnes would turn up with their wives, girlfriends and associates and take over the place, ordering the best champagne in the house and buying drinks for everyone. They wore Armani suits and expensive jewellery and drove fast flashy cars. Their women were equally well turned out. For the Dunnes these were the halcyon days. The brothers were the princes of the city, and Christy was king.

On 10 February 1975 six armed men burst into the home of Robert Halpin, the manager of West's jewellers in Grafton Street, Dublin. West's is one of the longest established jewellers in the capital. The gang held the manager and his family at gunpoint through the night and the following morning brought him to the store. They took over £170,000 worth of gems before making off. At the time, it was one of the biggest jewel robberies ever.

Following the robbery, one of the Dunne brothers had arranged for a 'fence' to collect the loot within a few days, but Bronco disagreed. As the head of the 'firm', he insisted that he would dispose of the jewels himself. Within a month, word reached the Central Detective Unit in Harcourt Square that a man high on their wanted list was trying to fence the loot from the West's robbery. Detective Superintendent Mick Sullivan had suspected Christy Dunne was behind the job but had nothing to go on until now. Sullivan set up a sting operation to trap Dunne. He used a dodgy businessman with whom he had had 'dealings' in the past to set up a meeting with Bronco with a view to buying the stolen jewellery. The first meeting took place on 13 March 1975. Dunne offered the jewellery for a bargain price of £45,000. The businessman said that he might be able to set up a deal with an American buyer.

The following day Bronco brought the businessman to a field outside the city. Two other members of the Dunne 'firm' produced two bags containing the West's loot. He continued to bargain with Dunne and a maximum figure of £37,000 was agreed. On the following day, St Patrick's Day, the businessman who was working for the Gardaí went with Bronco to the Dunne family home on Rutland Avenue. There were two gang members in the front of the house and two more at the back as security. Upstairs it took the businessman over two hours to sort through and value the haul from West's.

Later that night, the businessman met with Detective Superintendent Sullivan and his team. Afterwards, when the businessman arrived at his home in Tallaght, Bronco was waiting for him. He ordered the businessman to take the jewels and store them in his house. The businessman agreed to hold the loot and Dunne left. He immediately called his police handlers and the house was placed under surveillance. Bronco was walking into the trap.

The following afternoon, Dunne arrived at the businessman's house to help him bury the loot. As Dunne placed the jewels in the boot of the Garda agent's car, Detective Superintendent Sullivan and his men swooped. They had caught Bronco red-handed. He was even wearing one of the solid gold bracelets taken from West's. He was charged with the West's robbery and receiving the stolen jewellery. Bronco was released on bail.

One evening in January 1978, a month before his trial for the West's heist, Christy and some of his brothers were working. Shortly after 8pm a post-office van carrying a consignment of cash and jewellery from the Munster mail train was stopped on the North Wall Quay in Dublin by what appeared to be a uniformed Garda. The Garda, an armed robber called Paddy Shanahan from County Kildare (See Chapter 5, 'The Builder'), produced a gun and pointed it at the driver. Christy Dunne, who was also armed, appeared and ordered the driver into the back of the van. Then he and Shanahan jumped into the van and drove into a disused storage yard where Larry and Shamie Dunne were waiting. The gang took all the bags carrying registered mail and drove off.

Later, Christy and Shamie took the cash and selected packages from the mail bags to the rear of a pub near Dublin airport to sort through the loot. Shamie threw a large number of small brown envelopes away. Most of the cash in the haul was worthless because it was being returned to the Central Bank to be burned. The notes had been taken out of circulation and perforated. Christy and the gang were disappointed with the takings. But a few days later the newspapers reported how over £100,000 worth of industrial diamonds stolen in the post-office van robbery had been found in a skip. Shamie, who could not read or write, hadn't bothered to ask Bronco to read the words 'Industrial Diamonds' which were written on the little envelopes.

Christy and his brothers were luckier in a heist at Brereton's jewellers and pawn shop in Capel Street in the city. This time the gang made off with almost £60,000 in jewellery and cash. During the robbery the owner of the shop, John Brereton and his son John were badly beaten by the gang. John Brereton needed thirty stitches and his son sixty-five. None of the haul was ever recovered, but a sizeable quantity of forensic evidence was found in the homes of Shamie, Robert and their parents. Christy and Larry Dunne provided alibis for their brothers. The only one to be charged with the crime was Robert, and he was eventually acquitted.

Bronco's trial for the West's robbery was due to start on 23 February 1978, but he didn't turn up. He had gone on the run. The following day, West's was robbed for a second time. Detectives uncovered evidence linking a close associate of the Dunnes with the heist. He was Eamon Saurin, a violent armed robber and hash dealer from Liberty House in the inner-city. Both Saurin and Dunne were sharing the same safe house in Crumlin. Saurin was already wanted for the murder of an elderly pensioner in England. Dunne had at last achieved his ambition. His name and photograph were circulated to every police station in the country.

The following month, despite Bronco's difficulties with the law, the team were back in action. This time the Bank of Ireland in Finglas was relieved of almost £20,000 in cash. Henry Dunne was charged with the heist but the case was subsequently dropped. In June Bronco decided to give himself up. He had been writing to several journalists in Dublin to ensure he got the maximum publicity when he did. One letter he wrote to *Sunday World* journalist Sean Boyne was headed: 'Christy Dunne on the run, 9 April, 1978.' In the letter Bronco alleged Garda corruption. He claimed that a detective had spotted him and would have shot him, but bystanders got in the way. He never offered any proof to back up his claims.

At the trial in the Central Criminal Court, Mr Justice Finlay directed that the robbery charge be dropped for lack of evidence. Bronco Dunne now faced only a charge of receiving the stolen jewellery. It was decided by the Director of Public Prosecutions not to call the businessman who had acted as an agent for the Gardaí for fear that his life might be at risk. Dunne's defence put forward a convincing case that he could not be accused of receiving the stolen jewellery because it was already in the businessman's car when the Gardaí swooped. A jeweller gave evidence that the bracelet Dunne was wearing at the time of his arrest could have been bought in ten other jewellery shops around Dublin. The jury found Dunne not guilty. He was ecstatic.

A month after his acquittal in July, Christy, together with Henry, Shamie and another associate, Joe Roe, broke into the Antigen drugs factory in County Tipperary and stole over £300,000 worth of palfium, a powerful painkiller. Henry bought the consignment from the rest of the gang members, including Bronco. He re-sold the drugs for a huge profit. It was to be the turning point for the Dunnes.

Following the West's case, Bronco fell out of favour with many of his brothers, who blamed him for losing the jewels. There were accusations that certain members of the family were not contributing enough to those who needed support. And there was division over who should be in overall control of the armed robbery operation. The brothers broke up into different teams.

At the same time, Henry, Shamie, Larry, Robert, Vianney, Mickey and Charlie were gradually being enticed into the drug business. At the turn of the decade a glut of high-grade cheap heroin came on the market and the gang simply couldn't resist. Through their many underworld contacts in England, most of whom had already moved full-time into dealing heroin, they realised the huge profits which could be made. With a highly-addictive drug like heroin, also known as 'gear' or 'smack', supply creates a rapid and escalating demand. Dealing in it was more lucrative, and certainly less risky, than holding up banks. They were on the slippery slope to disaster and devastation.

Not all of the brothers got involved simultaneously. They operated independently of each other, each with his own 'patch'. Whenever the Drug Squad relieved a family member of his supply the others would lend him money and heroin to get him off the ground again. Most of the brothers became extremely wealthy. Larry was the largest supplier of the drug in Dublin and the richest. He bought a large split-level mansion in the Dublin mountains, overlooking the city. Within a few short years, the areas where the Dunnes had grown up were in the grip of the drug. As one observer once put it, they did for smack what Henry Ford did for the motor car: made it available to the working man and woman, even the kids on the dole, even the kids at school.

The working-class people of the inner-city ghettos blamed the Dunnes for what was happening to their children. The drug dealers in the family, true to Bronco's form, blamed the system and social deprivation for making them what they were. But time was running out for the Dunnes.

The last time the entire family got together was at the wedding of Christy's daughter Jacqueline, in January 1983. Bronco pulled out all the stops for a lavish celebration which would have put any high-society bash in the shade. It was also the last time the family actually enjoyed their celebrity status. Over 400 guests attended the wedding ceremony at Mount Argus church, and Fr Sweetman officiated. The family's growing status as Public Enemy Number One was also evident. A television crew and photographers turned up to watch the jewel-laden, designer-clad underworld come out to play. The Gardaí, who were now openly targeting the entire family, were also there with their cameras.

Over the next few years, the cops went to war with the Dunnes, their attentions resulting in the imprisonment of most of Bronco's siblings. The crackdown would effectively end their reign as a crime family. Larry, Mickey, Robert, Gerard, Charlie, their sister Colette and Shamie's wife, Valerie, were all jailed for various drug offences. Henry was given ten years for possession of firearms. Shamie was charged with possessing almost £500,000 worth of heroin, but he was not convicted, and he fled the country before the State had time to re-enter the case. He moved his operating base to London, where he still lives. Some of the Dunne children had also become chronic heroin addicts themselves. The dream for Christy Dunne was over. He was on his own.

Bronco steered clear of the heroin trade. He prided himself on the fact that he was neither a user nor a dealer, although he was involved sporadically in the distribution of hash. He remained in the background as most of his family raced to their downfall. He did, however, attempt to help them out from time to time. In 1984 the Provos began conducting their own investigations into the drug business in Dublin. At the time they were well-established within the ranks of the

Concerned Parents Against Drugs movement. They arranged a meeting with Bronco Dunne. Bronco's support for the Republican movement, his brief involvement with Saor Éire and the fact that he was not involved in the drug trade made him a respectable source of information. Dunne, an impressive spoofer, convinced the Provos that there was nothing going on in the underworld that he didn't have a handle on.

He gave the Provos a list of the names of twenty known criminals who he insisted were now dealers. There was little or no evidence against most of the people on the list, other than that they had fallen out with Bronco. And nowhere did his list include the name Dunne. Significantly, at the top of his list was the name of Martin Cahill, The General. The General had recently pulled off the £2 million O'Connors jewellery heist and the Provos wanted a slice of the action. There was also speculation that Cahill and his men would turn the loot into heroin. That led to a confrontation between The General and the IRA which almost ended in all-out warfare.

While the conflict between Bronco's family, the cops, the Provos, The General and the ordinary citizens of working-class Dublin continued, he went about his business. Dunne and his old friend John Cunningham, The Colonel, were arrested and charged with an armed robbery at a pub in Julianstown, County Meath, on 21 November 1983. The charges included stealing almost £3,000 from the pub owner, Patrick Farrelly, imprisoning the publican's wife and possession of a firearm. A few weeks later, the pair were charged with falsely imprisoning another man during a second armed robbery. In February 1984 Dunne and Cunningham went before Judge Frank Martin in the Central Criminal Court. During the trial there were allegations of intimidation of witnesses and the judge complained of receiving threatening phone calls. As a result, both the judge and the witnesses were given police protection. In the end, both gangland chums were acquitted.

After his series of close shaves with the law and his family's continuing problems, Bronco decided that it was time for himself and Mary Noonan to take a break in the sun. On 3 June 1984 he flew to

Majorca on his own. Noonan, who was expecting their second child, and their two-year-old daughter Jessica were to join him a week later. They planned to stay for a month, and Bronco talked about starting a new life on the island.

At the same time, an old enemy of the Dunnes, Detective Inspector Jim McHugh from Pearse Street station, was making headway in an investigation into a major armed robbery at the American Express office in Grafton Street. In March of that year, five armed and masked men, one dressed as a Garda, had held the family of the office manager hostage overnight. The following morning, the gang had gone with the manager to the office, tied up the staff as they arrived for work and made off with £500,000 in traveller's cheques. The *modus operandi* was the same as in the West's job. In the months that followed, £150,000 worth of the cheques had been cashed in various European cities.

On the morning of 18 June, Detective Inspector McHugh arrested a nineteen-year-old girl in connection with the heist. She admitted to burying £130,000 worth of the stolen cheques, as well as fifteen Irish passports, on waste ground near the holiday resort of Illetas in Majorca. The woman claimed that Bronco Dunne had given her the parcel to bury. On 20 June the young woman travelled back to Majorca in the company of McHugh where they were met at the plane by Spanish police. Later that day they recovered the parcel and its contents. The following morning, police raided Dunne's apartment and arrested Bronco, Mary Noonan and former international soccer player Tommy Carroll. A year earlier Carroll, from Coolock in Dublin, had been convicted of forging traveller's cheques valued at £3,300. Bronco explained that he and Carroll had just bumped into each other while on holiday.

The three adults and the toddler were held in the Centro Penitenciario near Palma. After two days Mary Noonan, who had fallen ill as a result of the primitive conditions in the prison, was removed with her child to a local hospital for treatment. Three days later, she was released without charge and allowed to return to Dublin. Dunne and Carroll appeared before a Palma magistrates court on 24 June. They were both remanded in custody without charge.

In September Bronco Dunne was charged with altering his passport and driving licence. In December he was further charged with cashing some of the stolen traveller's cheques in Majorca. Bail was set at £5,000 but Dunne didn't have the money to pay it. He sent messages to his family back in Dublin to bail him out, but they were ignored and Christy was left in jail. It was reckoned at the time that the family was punishing their older brother for turning his back on them when they were in trouble. During his incarceration Dunne sent a blizzard of mail to influential figures in Ireland protesting his innocence. He wrote to the Irish consul and Amnesty International and gave interviews to the Irish media.

In one of those interviews Dunne claimed he had been set up: 'I am a big fish according to the Irish police. They could never put me in this position but relied on innuendo and rumour as evidence against me.' On 30 April 1985 Dunne's trial took place in Palma. It was short and sweet. He was asked if he had altered his passport and he replied that he had. He was then asked by the magistrate was he a member of an international gang responsible for large-scale robberies. Bronco said he wasn't. Nevertheless, he was convicted of cashing the cheques. On both charges he was jailed for two years and eight months.

Bronco Dunne, who was almost forty-eight years old, was desparate to get out. He even considered the possibility of going on hunger-strike. He began reading up on Spanish law in his quest for a way out. Back in Dublin, Mary Noonan had given birth to a son and due to her poor financial circumstances had been forced to move out of Dunne's luxury apartment in Clontarf. She had since been given accommodation by Dublin Corporation.

In an interview conducted with an Irish journalist in October 1985, sixteen months after his initial arrest, Dunne declared: 'I am going fucking mental in here.' He claimed that he was no longer involved in crime. 'Jessie James and the other outlaws didn't keep going until they were fifty,' he said. On 29 October 1985, Christy Dunne was suddenly released unconditionally from prison. He was given no explanation for the surprise move. Ironically, on the day of his release another armed gang held up the same American Express office in Dublin. When he came home from Majorca, the Gardaí did not interview him about the earlier robbery. They had just been happy that one of their more annoying gangland figures had been out of circulation.

Bronco's announcement that he was going to emulate his hero Jessie James and retire from crime was short-lived. Perhaps it was effects of the hellish heat in his Spanish prison cell that made him think seriously about going straight. But he was a devout recidivist and it wasn't long before he was up to his old tricks. Obviously it was easier for a criminal to go straight in the Wild West than it was in west Dublin, where Bronco now lived with Mary Noonan. Dunne also had two hobbies which put on a huge demand on his cash flow – drinking and gambling. He now began organising major robberies rather than actually participating in them.

Bronco Dunne did not approve of the straightforward armed robbery, where a gang burst in and took what they could within two minutes. It was too risky for the relatively small amounts of cash normally available. Dunne preferred targeting the family of the manager or owner of a financial institution or business. He terrorised them by holding the family hostage while the manager was brought to his office. The gang could take all the money at their ease and not have to worry about the alarm being raised. It was a nasty and vicious tactic used by many of Dunne's contemporaries.

At lunchtime on 26 August 1988, two men in overalls and caps walked into Dunne's Stores on North Earl Street in Dublin city centre. They stopped at the heavily-secured cash area and informed the staff inside that they were there to fix the telephone lines. A short time earlier a Telecom technician had knocked out the two lines to the office from a nearby exchange on the orders of Christy Dunne. Once they got inside, the two 'repair men' produced guns and took £21,000 in cash.

Sometime in November 1988, an old associate of Dunne's from Finglas came to him with a potential 'earner'. The target was to be the post office at Cardiffsbridge Road in the middle of the sprawling working-class suburb. On the morning of 15 December, almost £80,000 would be delivered to the post office under armed Garda escort. The delivery, double what it would normally be, was to pay the Christmas old-age pension bonuses and children's allowances. Armed with the background information, Bronco Dunne went to work on his plan. He had just turned fifty, the same age that Jessie James was when he hung up his boots.

Rocco Cafolla was the postmaster at Cardiffsbridge Road. The twenty-six-year-old, hard-working family man had been running the small post office for the past five years. During that period he had been the victim of several armed robberies, five in 1987 alone. Finglas at the time was considered a crime black spot. Cafolla had moved his post office branch into the rear of the Golden Fleece newsagents next door for better security. Every evening around the same time, he drove home to Swords. He lived with his wife Sharon and two children, a seven-month-old baby and a two-year-old boy.

Christy Dunne began putting his team together for the job. He recruited two of his nephews, Isaac Turner and Ryan Dunne. Turner was the eighteen-year-old son of Christy's sister, Anne. He and his older brother Abraham had been named after characters in the Bible. Both boys, like their mother, were heroin abusers. And, like most of his notorious uncles, Turner had been an active criminal with fifteen convictions. Ryan Dunne was the son of Bronco's brother, Robert, who at the time was serving a sentence for armed robbery. Like his cousin, seventeen-year-old Dunne was involved in crime and drug abuse. Both nephews looked up to their stylish uncle, Bronco. He had filled their heads up with nonsense about becoming members of the new Dunne family crime syndicate and was introducing them to the big time.

The third recruit was another drug addict, twenty-seven-year-old Raymond Roberts from Dolphin House flats. He had become a junkie when the Dunne family first flooded the area with heroin. A father of three children, Roberts had a string of criminal convictions for larceny, burglary and assault. He had just been released from prison after serving part of a six-month sentence. Like his two friends, Dunne and Turner, he was making his first move into the world of serious crime.

The fourth member of Bronco's team was thirty-year-old John Delaney from Mulhuddart in west Dublin. He was the Telecom technician who had knocked out the phone lines to Dunnes Stores the previous August, being paid £1,000 for the job. Dunne and Delaney had met three years earlier through their mutual addiction to drink and gambling. Delaney had suffered kidney failure as a result of his alcoholism and had serious financial problems. But he had never been in trouble with the police and Dunne saw him as a perfect accomplice.

In the weeks leading up to the Cardiffsbridge Road job, Dunne and his gang compiled detailed information about the Cafollas and their normal routine, both at home and in the post office. They knew the addresses of other members of the postmaster's family and memorised their telephone numbers. Dunne decided that they would hold Cafolla's family hostage on the night of 14 December. Posing as a terrorist gang, they would make up a false 'bomb' and strap it to the postmaster when they sent him to collect the money. The gang would show their innocent victims that they meant business. Bronco would stay in the background and co-ordinate what he described to his subordinates as the mission. Dunne was happiest when he was in control and giving out the orders from a safe distance behind the firing line.

Shortly after 2pm on the day of the job, Christy Dunne called to the home of Jimmy and Jean Galloway who lived around the corner from him in Monksfield Meadows, a private estate in Clondalkin. Dunne had befriended the Galloways a short time before this and Jean had agreed to lend him their car if he was ever stuck. This afternoon Bronco was stuck. He wanted to use their car to co-ordinate his crime. The Galloways were decent, obliging, law-abiding people, who were happy to help out. They had no idea what their smooth-talking, charming neighbour was up to.

At 4pm Dunne called to Isaac Turner's flat in Dolphin's Barn to pick up his team. Turner, Ryan Dunne and Roberts were waiting for him. 'Right, lads, we have work to do,' Bronco told them as they piled into the Galloways' car. On the way to Rocco Cafolla's home in Swords they stopped off and bought two candles and a bale of briquettes. When they arrived at Cafolla's home, Christy reminded Turner to keep the wife and children captive upstairs until her husband came home.

Sharon Cafolla was preparing dinner for her family when the doorbell rang. When she answered it, Ryan Dunne was standing there holding a cardboard box in his arms. 'Does Rockie live here?' he inquired. Sharon Cafolla was suspicious of the man standing at the door. He told her that her husband had won the 'hamper' in a pub draw. Rocco Cafolla did not drink in pubs. Sharon wanted to close the door but couldn't because her two-year-old son was standing in the way.

Suddenly Dunne pushed past the housewife. He grabbed her around the neck and dragged her into the kitchen. Turner and Roberts piled in the door after him. Sharon Cafolla screamed out: 'I want my children.' Dunne replied: 'I won't harm yer kids, don't look at me and you'll be all right.' Both of her little children were terrified by the commotion. She clutched them to her and tried to calm them down. Turner demanded to know where any panic buttons were located and what time she expected Rocco to return home. He threatened that her children would be harmed if she didn't co-operate. 'You are not going to harm my kids,' she said to Turner, who was wearing a balaclava like the others. 'No, we can't touch you or shoot your kids, your husband or yourself because if we do we will be shot ourselves or, if not, knee-capped. As long as you co-operate no-one will be hurt,' Turner replied.

Rocco Cafolla arrived home from work shortly after 6pm. As he walked in the front door two masked men grabbed him. One was armed with a knife, the other with a handgun. 'Say nothing, do nothing and your wife and children won't be harmed,' he was told as they bundled him into the sitting-room. He didn't know what was happening. The family were put together in the kitchen where they were ordered to have their dinner as normal. They were too shocked and distressed to eat. Then they were brought back into the sitting-room and Rocco and his wife were tied up. Later, Sharon was released to bring the children to bed, accompanied by one of Bronco's thugs. The couple feared that they and their children were going to be murdered.

At one stage Sharon Cafolla's sister rang the house. As Sharon answered the call, one of the gang members held a knife to her throat. At 11pm, according to plan, Turner told the Cafollas that he was going to 'receive further orders'. He left the house and met Bronco down the road. John Delaney was in the car with him. Dunne had picked him up earlier and offered him a small job for which he would be paid £1,000. He would have to 'pick someone up and drive from A to B and ask no questions'. Delaney agreed. The three drove back to the Galloways' house, arriving there after midnight.

The three men went into the house. Bronco introduced Turner as his son. While in the Galloways', Dunne told Jean Galloway that he wanted her car again the following morning and asked her to accompany him with her young son. When she refused, Dunne became nasty. 'If you want to see Jimmy and that little fucker of a son of yours upstairs, you'd better go with me,' Bronco snarled. Jean Galloway was terrified. She felt she had no choice but to agree.

Dunne left the Galloway home and drove his nephew back to the Cafollas'. On the way he dictated instructions on a tape-recorder which Turner was told to replay for their hostage. In the Cafollas' house Turner played Bronco's sinister message to Rocco who would recall that the voice was threatening and aggressive. The tape outlined Dunne's plan. The following is the text of that tape:

'These are your final instructions. The unit that is in your house are dedicated members. Do as they tell you or as your instructions on this tape tell you and nobody will come to any harm. Your wife and children – you know what I mean, Rocco. Tomorrow morning one of the unit will travel with you in the car. Go into your post office and wait for your delivery. Remember not to contact anybody, because we are watching and listening to you. When the van and the escort have left, and make sure they have left, put the bag unopened into the carrier-bag you have with you. Remember we know how much is in it, so don't open it, leave it intact. You should have about £9,000 in your safe. Leave £2,000 or £3,000 approximately so no-one notices when you are gone. Put £5,500 with the other bag into the carrier bag, go to your car and put it on the back seat. Drive to Cappagh Hospital, go in the main gate and park your car in the carpark on the right.

'Leave the keys in the ignition and go into the hospital. Go to the end of the main corridor. You will meet somebody you know. Ask them to help you. Just say "Will you help me?" This person, and you know them, Rocco, will unarm you. You can contact who you like now. You will find your car during the day and if everything is in order, your wife and children will be unharmed. P.S. We are watching you all the time. Don't do anything stupid.'

There was a short break in the taped message before Bronco's voice continued: 'I have just been informed that your wife works with you in the post office and your sister minds the children. I have never heard this through our intelligence and I suggest that you ring your sister and tell her that your wife and children have the 'flu or are sick. Don't try to say something stupid. Just organise it that it goes right, Rocco.' The tape ended. Turner replayed the tape a number of times for the postmaster, who was now convinced that he was a victim of the IRA or some other terrorist group.

Turner asked Rocco questions to check that he fully understood his instructions. Another member of the gang then gave him details of where his mother, father and sister lived and worked. The gangster could rhyme off their home and work telephone numbers from the top of his head. Bronco Dunne's plan to disconcert his victim was working.

The following morning, Isaac Turner strapped two candles to Rocco Cafolla's back. He told him it was a bomb and that if he followed his instructions to the letter he would be told how to disarm the 'device'. Shortly after 8am he accompanied the petrified postmaster in his car to the post office. Ryan Dunne and Raymond Roberts stayed with his wife and children. Sharon Cafolla was tied to one of her children's bunk beds and gagged and the two hoods left.

In Finglas, Turner got out of Cafolla's car a short distance from the post office. He told his victim: 'If you love your wife and family don't mess.'

Cafolla nodded nervously and opened up the post office. He had brought his baby's pink carrier-bag to hold the cash. He did as he had been instructed on the tape. At 9am a cash van arrived at the post office, escorted by two armed detectives attached to the Security Task Force. Cafolla signed for the £79,500 in cash and waited for the van and cops to leave.

At 9.45am Turner was picked up by Delaney in the Telecom Éireann van. At the same time, Christy Dunne was circling the area in the company of a very frightened Jean Galloway and her son. He was in contact with his nephew by walkie-talkie. Dunne was using the woman and child as cover in case he was stopped. The Telecom van was for the same purpose.

Meanwhile, Rocco Cafolla drove, as he had been instructed, into the carpark of Cappagh Hospital. He was followed by Turner and Delaney in the Telecom van. The postmaster ran into the hospital. While he went inside Turner jumped out of the van and grabbed the money from the car. As they drove off they signalled to Bronco that the plan had been executed. The car and the van drove back to the Galloways' house in Clondalkin. Meanwhile, the postmaster had met no-one in the hospital. He was shaking and sweating profusely. As far as he was concerned, he was a walking bomb. When he came out of the hospital, he saw that the money was gone. He drove back to the post office and raised the alarm. A local shopkeeper helped to remove the 'device'. Within minutes, the area was swarming with police units. Back in Swords, officers freed Sharon Cafolla and her children. They were unharmed.

As a major investigation swung into operation, Bronco Dunne and Isaac Turner were counting the money in an upstairs bedroom of the Galloways' home. There was £85,000 in total, including the money from the post office safe. After they had counted the loot, Turner got a taxi home. Bronco handed Jean Galloway £1,000 in cash and asked her for a lift to Monastery Road in Clondalkin. Dunne got out of the car, gave her one of his charming smiles and said thanks. She drove a short distance down the road and stopped her car. She was physically sick. She had been warned in no uncertain terms that the personal safety of herself and her family depended upon her remaining silent about her ordeal.

Within hours, a major manhunt was underway. Scores of detectives were drafted in from local units in Coolock, Blanchardstown, Swords, Cabra and Finglas. Detective Inspector Tony Hickey and a team of detectives from the Serious Crime Squad were also called in to assist. The first task for the investigators was to try to identify likely suspects for the horrific crime and whether it had been carried out by criminals or subversives. As the weeks went by, the investigation drew a blank. But then the team got a lucky break.

Detective Garda Tom Barbour from the Crime Task Force was on routine patrol on 3 January 1989 when he spotted Isaac Turner. Barbour knew Turner as a local heroin abuser. He was aware that there was an outstanding warrant with Turner's name on it. The young detective decided to pull him in for a drug search. In Kilmainham station he found sixty-five single £1 notes in an envelope in his pocket. He also found a building society book which showed a lodgement of £4,000 which had been made four days after the Cardiffsbridge Road robbery.

Turner was brought to the Bridewell where he was arraigned on the outstanding warrant. He was later released on bail. But Barbour decided to hang onto the money and had it checked to see if it had come from any of the scores of armed robberies occurring around Dublin at the time. The cash was traced to the consignment delivered to Rocco Cafolla. Although he had steered clear of his family's drug business, heroin was about to play a role in Bronco Dunne's downfall. The irony would be almost too bitter to contemplate.

On the morning of 16 January, Isaac Turner was arrested by detectives investigating the Finglas robbery and detained under Section 30 of the Offences Against the State Act. That evening the young drug addict made a full confession to Detective Sergeant Cathal Cryan, outlining his role in the crime and naming his accomplices. He fingered his uncle Christy Dunne as the leader and mastermind behind the crime. Turner also revealed to Cryan how his uncle paid him £24,000 three days after the robbery which he divided evenly between himself, Ryan Dunne and Raymond Roberts. He admitted being the one who had strapped the 'bomb' to their terrified victim.

On the same day that Turner was arrested, Raymond Roberts was also pulled in. His fingerprints had been found on adhesive tape used to strap the candles to Rocco Cafolla's back. The roll of tape had been left behind by the gangsters in the Cafolla home. The following day in Swords district court Roberts and Turner had four charges preferred against them as a result of the crime, including robbery, false imprisonment and possession of firearms. Ryan Dunne went on the run to England just days before the police called for him.

In line with standard investigation procedures, the Galloways were also briefly arrested, under Section 30 of the Offences Against the State Act. During their detention they revealed how they had been terrified to go to the police out of fear of Bronco Dunne. They gave the Gardaí full statements about what they had witnessed. Jean Galloway said she was glad to be able to clear her conscience. She and her husband had been sickened by the whole affair. The net was closing in on gangland's Jessie James.

Bronco Dunne was lifted within hours of his nephew's confession. True to form, Bronco denied all the charges. Folding his arms and sitting back in his chair, he told detectives: 'I know nothing about it [the robbery] ... what's this all about? I was never involved in violence in my life.' Bronco was charged the following day and remanded in custody.

On the evening of 18 January, John Delaney was arrested by Detective Sergeant Joe McGarty from Finglas Station. Delaney gave the Gardaí a full statement, admitting his involvement with Dunne and the crime. He also told them of his role in the Dunnes Stores heist. Delaney was charged with conspiracy to rob and with robbery.

Despite the mounting odds against him, Bronco Dunne was defiant. On 25 January, Detective Garda Jim Clinton took Rocco

Cafolla to the Bridewell station to see if he could identify the voice he had heard on the tape. He was placed in a room off the reception area to the station jailhouse. Several people passed through the reception area. At 11am Bronco Dunne was marched in on his way for a remand hearing. Rocco Cafolla recognised his voice. The postmaster felt sick and broke down. Dunne's voice brought back the terror he and his family had endured. Later Detective Garda Clinton brought Cafolla into the hallway to confront Dunne. Clinton told Bronco that his voice had been identified as being that on the tape and asked Cafolla again what he could say about Bronco's voice. 'I am satisfied that a voice I heard here this morning is the same voice I heard on a tape on the night of the robbery when I was being held hostage,' the postmaster said. Dunne dismissed Cafolla. 'I don't know what he is saying,' he replied. Rocco Cafolla was distressed. 'It was your voice I heard on that tape,' he told Dunne.

Bronco Dunne was eventually released on bail and it took three years before his case came before the courts. He used every delaying tactic possible and also tried to start a media campaign suggesting that he had been framed for the crime. In 1990 he approached Jean Galloway and tried to intimidate her into withdrawing her evidence. He was later charged with that offence as well.

In the Summer of 1989, both Isaac Turner and John Delaney pleaded guilty to their parts in the robbery. Delaney, who was awaiting a kidney transplant, was given a five-year suspended sentence on health grounds. He later left the country to live in England. At his court hearing, Judge Michael Moriarty said Turner's evidence might help to make 'a major professional criminal amenable to justice for this heinous crime'. Turner's defence counsel told the court that he had 'placed himself in danger from an evil and sinister person.' Judge Moriarty sentenced Turner to four years and directed that Bronco's nephew be afforded all possible protection while in prison.

In January 1992 Bronco Dunne went on trial. He appeared confident that he would again beat the rap. The Gardaí had been unsuccessful in tracing the whereabouts of John Delaney to give evidence against him. After four days, the first trial was aborted following a decision by the Supreme Court prohibiting some of the prosecution's evidence. But the following month Dunne was not so lucky. Detective Sergeant Cathal Cryan from Coolock station managed to locate Delaney in England and convinced him to return to give evidence against Dunne. His nephew, Turner, also told his side of the story. There was tight security around Circuit Criminal Court 14 throughout the trial, during which Bronco put on an impressive display to convince the jury he was innocent. But they didn't believe him. Christy Dunne was sentenced to ten years. The fifty-four-year-old criminal was shattered as he left the court in handcuffs.

Since then, Dunne has made several attempts to appeal his sentence. He says he is an innocent man, a victim of a nefarious plot by the police and others. In December 1992 Dunne was given an additional one-year sentence for attempting to intimidate Jean Galloway. During the case he told Judge Kieran O'Connor, 'If I don't get justice in this case I'll be leaving Portlaoise Prison in a coffin.' Bronco claimed he had been the victim of a campaign of vilification. At the time of writing, Bronco Dunne is sixty years old and still in prison. He is not due for release until the year 2002. He is the only member of the family he introduced to the big time still behind bars.

The Blaggers

The story of gangland is told through the exploits of the people who populate it – the godfathers, gang members and crime families – and their adversaries, the police. The deeds of the drug dealer, armed robber, kidnapper, hit-man, fraudster and cop are the cornerstones of this elusive underworld. It also has its physical landmarks – places where gangland's residents have participated in some dramatic, brutal event. Places which come to symbolise the conflicts either in gangland itself or with the law on the other side of its razor-wire fence. The unlikely setting of just such a conflict is a small provincial market town in County Kildare.

Athy is a typical country town, a bustling centre of commerce at the heart of a rich agricultural hinterland, forty-two miles from Dublin. It is a quiet, law-abiding place which rarely makes the national news. But it was here that a tense real-life cops and robbers drama reached its climax. The final bloody showdown could easily have been a scene in a modern-day crime movie like *Heat* or *Reservoir Dogs*. Athy provided the location for the final scene in the story of a ruthless professional Dublin gang of blaggers, whose illicit careers came to a bloody end at the point of several police guns. What happened here on a cold afternoon in January 1990 was to have a profound effect on gangland – especially on the criminals who specialised in well-organised armed hold-ups.

Thomas Tynan, Austin Higgins, Brendan Walsh, PJ Loughran and William Gardiner were a potent, deadly mixture of criminals and former Republican paramilitaries. They formed the nucleus of a team of nine, divided between the south- and north-sides of Dublin. All of them had gained experience operating with gangs on both sides of the Liffey. When they came together between late 1988 and early 1989 to form their own 'firm', it was considered an unusual mix in underworld circles. But it was also advantageous. It would take some time for the Gardaí to identify a new gang and for the Serious Crime Squad to give them their undivided attention.

The leaders of this motley crew were IRA-trained PJ Loughran and William Gardiner. Loughran, twenty-nine, was originally from Dungannon in County Tyrone. He had moved to live in Coolock, Dublin, to hide from the RUC, who wanted him in connection with terrorist offences in the North. Gardiner, thirty-seven, was from Cabra and had been an active IRA member. Although he had little 'form', he was an experienced armed robber. Both Loughran and Gardiner were suspected of being the ones who had got away following an armed robbery in September 1988 at the Navan Road Labour Exchange. Martin Cahill's older brother, John, had led the gang. He and three others were subsequently convicted.

Together Gardiner and Loughran recruited the team which would become known in underworld and Garda history as the 'Athy Gang'. Brendan 'Wetty' Walsh, thirty-four, from Ranelagh, south Dublin, and Thomas Tynan, twenty-nine, from Vincent Street flats off the South Circular Road were ideal candidates for membership to this exclusive den of thieves. Walsh and Tynan had both been in Martin Cahill's gang and were high on the Garda suspect list for several of The General's 'strokes'. Walsh had an impressive pedigree as a brutal hoodlum, with a long criminal record for armed robbery, violence and false imprisonment. Tynan was a heroin abuser with a record for violence, theft, burglary and drugs. But despite his problem with heroin, he was trusted by other criminals – he kept his mouth shut and he was an adroit robber. Austin Higgins, twenty-six, was the fifth member. He lived in Donaghmede in the north-city and was married with two small sons. Though he came from a respectable middle-class family, he had been attracted to the wrong side of the tracks as a teenager and had been involved in armed robberies for several years.

Tynan, Walsh, Higgins, Gardiner and Loughran made up what was referred to as the 'A' team in the 'firm'. The 'B' team was made up of four criminals, all in their twenties. One of them was a convicted robber from the Dolphin House corporation estate in south

Dublin. They took part in some of the robberies, but mainly played a peripheral role, organising stolen cars.

From the beginning of 1989, the 'Athy gang' went to work. Gardiner and Loughran used their IRA training to organise the gang like an Active Service Unit. Secrecy and meticulous planning of each 'job' were the hallmarks of their *modus operandi*. They began targeting banks, mostly branches of the Bank of Ireland, within a 120-mile radius south of Dublin. The gang believed that the chances of running into armed Gardaí in sleepy country towns was substantially less than in Dublin. Country cops were not as geared to the kind of rapid armed response as their city colleagues who were dealing with robberies every day. The maverick gang were soon making their mark with devastating effect.

Gardiner and Loughran would plan four or more heists in different counties at any one time. Detailed reconnaissance was carried out on each target and the gang familiarised themselves with the local network of country back-roads to travel to and from each robbery. The two former paramilitaries would not inform the team members of which bank they were going to hit until the morning of a heist, to prevent careless information leaks – and the prospect of a police welcome in the selected town. At any time, they would have a pool of four or more high-powered cars for getaways, juiced up and stashed in hotel and apartment-block carparks around the south-side of Dublin. They also had a large arsenal of firearms at their disposal, including a shotgun and a military assault rifle. They used scanning equipment to listen in on the local Garda communications frequencies.

The gang would arrive at the front door of a bank in a high-powered car with false number plates. Loughran was normally the 'wheels man' on each job and would stay in the car while the other four, wearing false beards and wigs, sprinted inside. The gang would burst in to the bank, shouting and ordering staff and customers at gunpoint to lie face-down on the ground. They roared abuse and threatened to shoot anyone who moved. Each member of the gang had a hold-all bag strapped across his body. Three of them would vault the security screens and empty the cash tills while the fourth covered the terrified occupants.

The sudden and violent nature of the raid ensured that the gang kept control of the situation. Tynan, Walsh, Higgins and Gardiner could be in and out of a bank in between two and four minutes. The getaway route was a back-road out of town. One or more of the other high-powered stolen cars would be parked within a ten-mile radius. Abandoning the first car, the team would split in two and make their way back to Dublin along separate routes using mostly back-roads to avoid Garda checkpoints. Gardiner or Loughran would stash the money and guns in a pre-selected hide *en route*.

During 1989, there was a total of forty-nine armed bank robberies in Ireland. The 'Athy Gang' were responsible for thirty-two of those heists, involving the withdrawal of over £300,000 from the teller desks of banks throughout the south-east. In the first eight months of the year, they had carried out twenty robberies and successfully made off with almost £200,000 in cash alone. Their technique made them one of the most prolific armed gangs ever and inevitably drew attention to them.

In Garda headquarters senior officers were in no doubt that the same gang was responsible for the spate of robberies. In each case the method was the same. It had become the gang's calling-card. It was decided that the Serious Crime Squad attached to the Central Detective Unit in Dublin would spearhead a major investigation to put the blaggers out of business. The head of the unit was Chief Superintendent John Murphy and he appointed his next-in-command, Detective Superintendent Noel Conroy, to lead the operation. Conroy, who was originally from County Mayo, had been a city-based detective for most of his career and was respected as a very capable investigator.

Conroy put Detective Inspector Tony Hickey in charge of the investigation on the ground. A Kerryman, Hickey was one of the force's most gifted policemen and on the way to the top of his profession. Conroy scheduled a special conference at the Serious Crime Squad offices in Dublin on the afternoon of 4 September, to launch an investigation to catch the mystery bank robbers. But just hours before the conference began the gang struck again, this time selecting the Ulster Bank in Edenderry, County Offaly. They hit the branch within minutes of its opening and were in and out in two minutes. As the gang members quietly slipped back into Dublin, the police team charged with catching them were plotting their campaign. The case file on each robbery with a similar *modus operandi* was scrutinised to build up a picture of the team. Every piece of information was painstakingly collated. The investigation, code-named 'Operation Gemini', was launched.

From the start, the Gardaí had no doubt that the gang was Dublin-based. Their disciplined method of working suggested paramilitary training, so they had to look closely at associations between ordinary criminals and subversives. Profiles of every known armed robber and paramilitary suspect in the Dublin area were studied. All available intelligence reports were consulted and every underworld informant got a visit from the Serious Crime Squad. The getaway cars used in each case had been stolen in the more affluent neighbourhoods of the south-city. The first gang ruled out of the investigation was The General's. The crimes simply did not fit his style.

Loughran and his team were all too aware that the police would now have them at the top of their 'most wanted' list. But they were exhilarated by their success and instead of keeping their heads down they increased their systematic plundering. With each robbery they grew more confident and appeared convinced that they were untouchable, too good for the police.

To prove the point, they struck again on 8 September, four days after their last 'job'. This time the target was the Bank of Ireland branch at Emily Square in the centre of Athy. In less than four minutes the blaggers had made off with £47,000 in cash. It was one of their largest hauls. Three days later, on 11 September, the bearded robbers vaulted the counter of Loughran's local Bank of Ireland branch in Coolock. This time they got just £3,000.

On 14 September the gang decided to change the game plan some-what and hit the Bank of Ireland branch in Dunmanway in County

Cork. They returned to Dublin £9,844 richer. A week later the gang terrified the customers in the Bank of Ireland branch in Gorey, County Wexford, where they made off with over £17,000. Their haul from the five robberies during the month was almost £100,000.

Back in Dublin, the Operation Gemini team were working around the clock, looking for a lead on the gang. With each new heist, they grew more determined to nab their adversaries. A large conference was held in Naas Garda station on 25 September, attended by officers from each of the divisions where robberies had taken place. Every piece of information and forensic evidence from the robberies was carefully examined and collated.

In the meantime, the Gemini squad kept up the pressure on the underworld. Conroy and his team knew that gang members, buoyed by their continued success, would drop their guard and begin displaying the signs of prosperity. The day after the Gorey robbery, they got the break they needed. An informant told the squad that Thomas Tynan and a sixth member of the gang, the criminal from Dolphin House, had been involved in the robbery spree which was now the subject of much eulogising in the underworld. Another source revealed that Brendan 'Wetty' Walsh was also involved with Tynan.

The Operation Gemini team mobilised the squad's surveillance unit to monitor the three suspects in a bid to identify the rest of the gang. The undercover operation was difficult. The gang members all employed counter-surveillance techniques to shake off any tails. Eventually, however, the discreet watch paid off. Loughran, Gardiner and Higgins were spotted regularly meeting with the criminals already targeted. The investigation team were happy that they had now identified the main suspects.

Further intelligence revealed that Loughran and Gardiner were the main planners of the robberies and organised the team's arsenal. The objective now was to apprehend the gang red-handed. The Operation Gemini team agreed that the most effective course of action was to nab the gang while in transit either to or from a robbery and in possession of firearms. But there were two inherent difficulties in achieving the squad's goal. Covert surveillance was extremely difficult, especially in the case of trained professionals like Gardiner and Loughran. The gang had also shown that they were prepared to shoot it out with the police rather than surrender.

In the meantime, the gang, unaware of how close the police were getting, continued their robberies unabated. On 3 October they struck again, at the Allied Irish Bank branch at Urlingford, County Kilkenny. The *modus operandi* was the same as in the other cases. On 12 October the gang were in Kilkenny, where they robbed £9,500. Four days later the target was the Bank of Ireland in Roscrea, County Tipperary, where the haul was £13,000 in cash. During the hold-up, one of the blaggers fired a number of shots. But this time the gang was not so lucky.

Austin Higgins and the sixth member of the gang were stopped as they made their way back to Dublin at a checkpoint near Edenderry, County Offaly. They were arrested under Section 30 of the Offences Against the State Act and brought to Portlaoise for questioning. Hickey dispatched two members of his squad to interview Higgins and his partner. Their brief was to glean as much intelligence as possible about the gang. During the interrogation Higgins began to talk and admitted his part in the robbery. There was also a piece of forensic evidence linking him with the robbery – a boot print on the bank counter he had vaulted before grabbing the money. The sixth gang member was released without charge because of lack of evidence. Higgins was charged with the robbery the next day and subsequently released on bail.

The charge now hanging over Higgins's head was his weak spot. He had never before faced such a serious accusation and the prospect of a long stretch behind bars. He agreed to turn informant. The problem about dealing with an informant is the reliability of the information he has to offer. 'Snouts' or 'touts' can sometimes use the situation to their own advantage. In the initial stages Higgins gave the Operation Gemini team an invaluable insight into the operation of the gang. He told the officers that Gardiner and Loughran would have no hesitation in blowing away any policemen who tried to apprehend them. The gang had a large cache of weapons stored in the Dublin mountains and in a number of locations south of Dublin.

The gang member revealed how the getaway cars were stolen. In each case the thieves burgled homes with high-powered cars parked outside, and stole the keys. The cars were subsequently fitted with false number plates and then parked. Hickey and the Operation Gemini squad immediately circulated stations throughout the greater Dublin area to report such burglaries and car thefts to the Serious Crime Squad. The net was closing on the gang.

On 20 October another major conference was held at the Carlow/Kildare divisional headquarters in Naas. Officers from Operation Gemini briefed their colleagues from the ten counties already targeted by Loughran's mob. The large assembly was informed of the identities of each of the suspect gang members and told that they were now being actively kept under secret surveillance. It was emphasised that the collection of forensic evidence following each heist was of paramount importance, especially if the gang were apprehended afterwards.

The gang never allowed the Gardaí to forget about them. That same day, Loughran, Gardiner, Walsh and Tynan hit the Allied Irish Bank branch in Ranelagh, Dublin, for some of Higgins's bail money. They took £4,622. The robbery showed why the gangs preferred country banks. In Dublin, where armed robberies were an almost everyday occurrence, banks did not hold large sums of money in the tills, whereas in the country the gang always got substantially more. The gang's total for October was £33,000. Two weeks later, on 3 November, the gang hit the Bank of Ireland in Bray, taking £11,693. Following the 'job' the Gemini team raided the homes of all the gang members, but nothing was found to connect them with any of the heists.

In the meantime, Conroy, Detective Inspector Hickey and Detective Inspector Ted Murphy, who was now also attached to Operation Gemini, requested the assistance of the Emergency Response Unit (ERU) in their preparations to take on the robbers, who were becoming more violent and aggressive. The ERU had been established the previous year and attached to the Special Detective Unit (SDU) which is responsible for anti-terrorism. The elite specialist unit replaced similar squads such as the Anti-Terrorist Unit (ATU) and the Special Task Force (STF). The previous units had been intended for tackling terrorist/subversive crime specifically but a review of Garda training recommended that the force needed a rapid response squad in support of other police units tackling heavily-armed gangs. The ERU was based on similar SWAT (Special Weapons and Tactics) units in America, Germany and Britain.

ERU personnel are handpicked after a rigorous induction course. Training is intensive, with fully qualified members of the unit under-going refresher courses every month. Members train with the Irish Army Ranger Wing (ARW), an elite commando unit which is the equivalent of the US Special Forces and the British SAS. In 1989 the ERU numbered thirty-two. Each member was equipped with a Smith and Wesson Model 59 semi-automatic pistol. They also had the Uzi submachine gun, Heckler and Koch automatic assault rifle and the Winchester police pump-action shotgun available to them. The ERU was put on immediate alert and made preparations for an inevitable showdown with the gang.

The ERU and the Operation Gemini team drew up an elaborate plan to intercept the gang. Firstly, the surveillance team, with the help of information supplied by Higgins and other intelligence sources, was tasked with locating and identifying some of the stolen cars which the gang had parked. The team obtained eavesdropping devices designed to be concealed in a car and capable of recording the conversations of the occupants. They also acquired a homing device which could be planted on one of the vehicles and monitored un-detected from an aircraft. The Air Corps made a Cessna spotter plane available for the job.

Working from the gang's previous record, the investigators compiled a list of 165 financial institutions within its operational radius in ten counties, including Dublin satellite towns. Each branch was given a specific code known only to those involved in Operation Gemini. The exact map reference of the town where each bank was located was also given a code-word so that even if the gang were scanning the Garda frequencies they would not know they were being tailed. Each officer involved in the operation familiarised himself with photographs of the six main suspects, each of whom was given a codeword and a number. Loughran was VIP 1, Tynan was VIP 2, and so on. Their personal vehicles were also coded for the same reason. The plan also identified every road leading from each town listed. The investigation team were then instructed to familiarise themselves fully with every road which could be used as an escape route. It was an awesome task.

On 14 November the investigation team learned that the gang planned to rob the bank at Mountrath, County Laois, the following day. An emergency conference was held, attended by the Operation Gemini team. All uniformed and detective units in the local division were put on alert. On the morning of 15 November the surveillance team confirmed that the gang had left Dublin around first light in a stolen red Mazda car with false number plates. But it was impossible for them to continue following the gang without being spotted. Loughran drove through the country at high speed along mostly back-roads.

During the morning, the ERU and Serious Crime Squad teams were deployed around Mountrath, waiting for the gang to turn up. At 2.58pm Loughran, Gardiner, Walsh, Tynan and Higgins did turn up, thirty-five miles east of Mountrath, at the Bank of Ireland at Tullow, County Carlow, and stole £3,000. The tip-off had come from Austin Higgins but there was no way of knowing whether he gave the team a false steer because he was on the job himself or had only been informed of the change of target on the way down the country. The game of cat-and-mouse would continue.

The next problem the investigation team encountered was convincing their own authorities to keep the investigation running. Allocation of scarce resources is a problem faced by every police force. The Serious Crime Squad, the surveillance unit and the ERU were now practically devoting all their energies to catching this gang. Senior brass in Garda HQ wanted results and so far, after a three-month-long intensive investigation, there were none. Chief Superintendent John Murphy, the overall commander of Operation Gemini, resisted high-level attempts to stand down the operation. He pleaded for more time. Everything was going in the right direction for his men. If they persevered and were patient they would get a result. Operation Gemini was given a reprieve.

Over the following weeks the gang remained quiet. The surveillance team planted the eavesdropping and homing devices on one of four cars which had been stolen and parked off-side. It was a hit-and-miss gamble as they did not have enough equipment to bug all of the gang's cars. Higgins, Gardiner, Walsh, Loughran and Tynan left their homes in the early hours of the morning of 8 December. As on the previous occasions, the raiders vanished into the darkened countryside. At 11.05am they reappeared in the Bank of Ireland branch at Castle Street, Enniscorthy, and robbed £21,700 in cash before escaping in a red Toyota Camry.

On 11 December the investigation team searched a portion of Killakee Woods at Rathfarnham in the Dublin foothills where they had been informed part of the gang's arsenal was buried. Again they drew a blank. Patience was wearing thin. That afternoon the Operation Gemini team pulled in Higgins, arresting him under Section 30 of the Offences Against the State Act. He was released without charge and went straight back to work.

Four days later, Loughran and the rest of the gang planned another heist. Higgins had indicated to his handlers in the investigation team that the 'job' was on, but he did not know exactly where. He would be told only on the morning of the robbery. Conroy and Hickey tried another tactic. This time they deployed their men in and around Killakee Wood, on the understanding that the gang would hide their weapons there following the robbery. By now the team were aware that the gang used the mountain roads as their route back to Dublin. In the meantime all Garda divisions in the south and Midlands were put on alert to expect a robbery. Details of the three stolen cars to be used were also given to units.

At 11.10am Tynan, Higgins, Walsh and Gardiner entered the front door of the Bank of Ireland in Liberty Square, Thurles, while Loughran sat behind the wheel of a Saab car outside. They made off with £17,620 in cash. As the gang were speeding away from the town, their path was blocked by a broken-down lorry. One of the hoods got out and attempted to fire a warning shot from an American M1 carbine assault rifle. The surveillance team in the mountains was informed and they waited and waited for their targets to turn up. The operation was aborted at 1am on the following freezing cold morning. The gang had never showed.

The two members of the investigation team who were dealing with Higgins arranged a subsequent meeting and inquired as to what happened. Instead of returning to Dublin after the Thurles 'job', Loughran drove to a wooded area near the village of Windgap in County Kilkenny. Loughran and Gardiner were dropped off with the guns and cash. They were collected later that night with the cash, having left the guns hidden in the wood. The following day, the Operation Gemini team searched the wooded area of Windgap. During the search they discovered a hideout but did not find any firearms.

Pressure was still mounting on the Operation Gemini team to stand down as Christmas approached. The Garda top brass were growing anxious at the amount of resources still being committed to the operation with no tangible results. Throughout the past two decades, organised crime had flourished, partly because the police did not have the manpower or money to run long-term, painstaking operations. The gang were notching up success after success while the police were waiting for the right time to move. The investigation team were given more time. The extraordinary game of patience continued.

Christmas Day and St Stephen's Day 1989 were appreciated by some of the Operation Gemini team. Banks don't open on those days. It was also a particularly good festive season for the blaggers, who celebrated a bountiful year at the various banks' expense. They had after all robbed over £300,000 in cash. But Loughran did not want his successful team getting too fat. He and Gardiner were out cruising through Tipperary, Kilkenny and Laois for their next target. On 26 December Loughran sent the word around that another 'job' was planned for the 28th. Again, all Higgins and the rest of the gang knew was that the target was to be a bank in a provincial town. By now, the Operation Gemini team no longer trusted the information that Higgins was passing to them. He was what is referred to in police parlance as a 'rogue informant'. They decided to rely on their own intelligence.

The 28th was the first day the banks were open after Christmas. Between shops and pubs lodging their festive takings the gang had a good chance of rich pickings. This time the gang would number seven in all, including the five members of the 'A' team.

The detectives attached to Operation Gemini were also back at work. They got the word on the 27th that a robbery was to be pulled the following day. The surveillance team had also been active over Christmas. Detective Superintendent Conroy called a conference of all the units involved in the case at the offices of the Serious Crime Squad. An urgent fax message was sent to all divisions warning that a robbery was likely and naming the gang members. Everyone on the investigation hoped that they would finally catch the gang who had eluded them for so many months. The team pulled out all the stops. A team of ERU and Serious Crime Squad officers were dispatched to the wooded area at Windgap where they conducted another search for the gang's arsenal. Again, this proved fruitless.

Before first light the following morning, the ERU and Serious Crime Squad took up positions in the wooded area near Windgap. The plan was to nab the gangsters as they retrieved their weapons. Back in Dublin, several teams of officers attached to Operation Gemini left to take up positions near banks in counties Wicklow, Wexford, Waterford and Kilkenny. The gang left Dublin early that morning in two cars, a black Peugeot and a white Celica, and headed for Kilkenny. Later that day part of the gang drove into Kilkenny but then aborted the heist. The Gemini team were informed afterwards that the raid had been cancelled simply because the two cars had failed to meet at a pre-arranged rendezvous. They were also told that

Loughran had spotted Garda activity in the vicinity of the targeted bank, but would still have gone ahead with the heist had the rest of the gang turned up. The police would have been 'dealt with'. The Operation Gemini team did not encounter the robbers. The gangsters took a break for the new year. The waiting game dragged on into a fifth month.

On 4 January 1990 the gang were on the move again. Two of them, Loughran and Gardiner, travelled to the country to case another potential target. The information was that the blaggers intended hitting a bank they had done previously. This time it was to be Athy. The surveillance team's work had paid off. The information came from a tape recording of a conversation which took place in one of the raider's stolen cars on the run to Athy. The sophisticated electronic device had been placed carefully under the car by the team. The homing device was never of any use because, due to cloud cover, the Air Corps Cessna had not been able to operate. During the trip Loughran and Gardiner could be heard discussing the routes in and out of the town of Athy where they had already made one of their biggest hauls, £47,000 in cash. Gardiner and Loughran discussed the operational details of doing the same bank again. If the alarm was raised they planned to hi-jack a lorry and pull it across the Dublin road to prevent police back-up getting into the town. And if the local Gardaí appeared the ex-Provos had a brutal contingency plan for them: 'We'll blow the fuckers away, take them out, shoot them.' At 2pm that same afternoon, local Garda Martin Harrington spotted the two men travelling out of Athy in one of the cars Operation Gemini had alerted all stations about.

That evening detectives from Harcourt Square drove to Athy to check out the town and local area. The following morning at 7 o'clock the Operation Gemini team gathered in the Serious Crime Squad offices with their colleagues in the ERU. A team of ERU and Serious Crime Squad detectives travelled to Athy while the surveillance squad attempted to keep tabs on the actual gang. The rest of the team involved in Operation Gemini was broken up and individual squads were dispatched to other likely provincial targets, just in case

Loughran and Gardiner changed their minds at the last minute. At any one time, the gang had a number of robberies planned and were capable of striking anywhere.

In Athy, Detective Inspector Hickey deployed the ERU in three buildings on Emily Square, including the Bank of Ireland. The Serious Crime Squad officers took up positions in an outer cordon around the town. Hickey and another team of officers based themselves in the local Garda station. But nothing happened. Later the team were informed that the gang could not leave Dublin due to trouble with one of their cars.

On the following Monday, 8 January, the same operation was again put in place around Athy and again the gang failed to turn up. Back in Dublin, however, Martin Cahill, the mentor to most of the Athy gang, was keeping the Gardaí busy. That same morning, he and his gang robbed the Allied Irish Bank in Ranelagh. Cahill was nearly caught while trying to run away after the heist and he shot an unarmed Garda, John Moore, in the chest and arm as he pursued him. The General got away, promising himself that he would never again go on a robbery. He admitted he was too fat and too old. His old pals should have followed his example and got out when the going was good.

In the early hours of the following morning, Loughran's gang stole a Mazda 626 for their next 'stroke', this time under the watch of the surveillance team. On the morning of Thursday, 11 January, they were again observed taking a high-powered BMW. The Operation Gemini team geared up for action yet again. The next morning, 12 January, the Athy gang left their homes before 6 o'clock. They picked up the stolen BMW and the Mazda 626 and went to work. They would use the BMW for the actual hold-up and the Mazda as a getaway car.

An hour later, the Operation Gemini team were gathered in Harcourt Square for a final briefing before departing to Athy. The intelligence report was that the gang had definitely left Dublin in the two stolen cars. To cover as many options as possible, teams were also sent to other provincial towns. Eleven members of the ERU were deployed in the local fire station in Athy and in a nearby yard at Leinster Street. Fifteen members of the Serious Crime Squad were in an outer cordon. Another detective sat in a car facing the bank to warn the rest of the team when the gang arrived.

At 12.20pm the gang drove into Emily Square in the stolen BMW and parked outside the front door of the Bank of Ireland. Loughran stayed behind the wheel while Gardiner, Higgins, Walsh and Tynan got out and walked quickly in single-file up to the bank door. They had long coats and their characteristic false beards and wigs. As they got to the door, they took out their guns. They pushed the porter, Noel Reddy, back into the bank. They began roaring at the customers and staff. 'Lie on the floor, stay down, this is a raid,' they shouted at the terrified customers, three of whom had children under the age of four with them. Three of the gangsters vaulted the counter and began rifling the tills as they had done four months earlier.

Just as their car had pulled up, the detective watching the bank, Sean Butler, calmly alerted the Operation Gemini team: 'The eagle has landed, the eagle has landed.' All hell broke loose. Tony Hickey and his team raced to a nearby car and roared off to the scene. On the way through the door one of the detectives exclaimed almost in disbelief: 'It's on, it's on.'

Detective Sergeant Nacie Rice and his team of five ERU men, who had been concealed in the yard on Leinster Street, also sprang into action. They raced down Leinster Street in two cars and into Emily Square. At the same time, Detective Sergeant Michael Shanahan and his team of four detectives sped from the fire station and turned immediately left into Emily Square. Rice and his team blocked the BMW from the rear while Shanahan and his team cut off the raiders' car at the front. Loughran began trying to shunt his way out from between the ERU cars by driving backwards and forwards.

The armed detectives fired a total of twenty shots at the wheels of the BMW in an attempt to immobilise it. Detective Sergeant Shanahan shouted at Loughran: 'Gardaí – stop, drop the gun, drop it.' Loughran lifted a pistol and pointed it at Detective Garda Comiskey, the driver of the ERU car blocking the BMW at the front. Shanahan, fearing for the safety of his colleague, took aim with his pistol and fired one shot. Simultaneously Detective Garda John O'Connor fired twice at Loughran with his pump-action shotgun. The driver's window of the stolen car shattered and the leader of the Athy gang slumped sideways in his seat. He had been hit in the neck and head. Shanahan reached into the car and turned off the engine. He recovered a gun from Loughran's lap.

Inside the bank, the rest of the gang heard the gunfire. Higgins and Walsh ran over to the window to see what was going on. They ran back to the others, shouting: 'We're set up, we're set up, the cops are everywhere.' Higgins began to panic: 'It's over, it's over, we're fucked ... I don't want to die anyway. They're shooting on the street, I don't want to die.' A third raider tried to get out through the back door of the bank. 'We can't fucking get out of here, we can't fucking get out.' Brendan Walsh shouted at Higgins: 'It's not over ... get a hostage, get a fucking hostage.' Higgins turned and grabbed bank official John Condron, holding his neck in an arm-lock. William Gardiner grabbed Thomas Shaw, a customer, and Walsh pulled the porter, Noel Reddy, off the ground. Tynan did not take a hostage but lurked among the huddled group of frightened robbers and terrified hostages.

The group shuffled to the front door of the bank building. Higgins, who was now very agitated, shouted out at the police: 'Get back or we'll shoot.' One of the ERU members shouted back: 'Leave down your guns and put your hands over your head and you won't be harmed.' Outside, in the confusion of the initial confrontation with Loughran, the keys had been left in one of the Garda cars used to hem in the BMW and the engine was still running. One of the car's rear doors nearest the bank was left open. The gang began shuffling towards the car in a bid to use it to escape.

The detectives, now taking cover in a semi-circle around the huddle of hostages and robbers, shouted at the gunmen that they were Gardaí and ordered them to lay down their guns. Higgins pointed his sawn-off shotgun in the direction of one of the ERU men. Then Higgins moved the gun to the back of John Condron's head and screamed: 'I'll blow his fucking head off if you don't move back.'

Detective Sergeant Nacie Rice was reloading his pistol in the doorway of the Leinster Arms Hotel, next to the bank, when the robbers emerged. He stepped out with his .38 pistol cradled in his hands. He could see Higgins's finger on the trigger of the weapon and knew that he was about to shoot his hostage. Rice warned the robber to drop his weapon. The other ERU men also screamed at the robbers to put down their weapons and surrender. Higgins didn't respond. Rice fired one shot, hitting Higgins in the right side of his forehead. The raider fell back on the pavement. Other detectives fired shots at the wheels of the police car to immobilise it.

At the same moment, Detective Patrick Comiskey and Robert Noonan ordered Tynan to drop his weapon. Just as Higgins was being hit Tynan turned and aimed a revolver at Comiskey and Noonan. As he was about to fire, Comiskey hit the former member of The General's gang three times. His partner also fired one shot at Tynan with his shotgun. When the shooting stopped, Tynan, Higgins and their hostage, John Condron, were lying on the pavement. All three were seriously injured. Condron had been hit in the back. Three of the detectives involved in the operation were injured. Two of them had suffered minor grazes and the third, Detective Sergeant John O'Mahony, had suffered a shotgun wound to the left leg. A pedestrian, Val Murphy, who was standing 100 yards down the pavement from the action, suffered a graze after being hit by a ricochet.

Walsh and Gardiner retreated into the bank with hostages Reddy and Shaw. Gardiner, who was carrying the M1 carbine rifle, was in a panic and began waving the weapon around. 'We're done for, we're done,' he shouted. The two robbers began arguing about what to do next. 'We can still do a deal,' said Walsh. He ordered one of the bank staff to call a priest and an ambulance. After a while they calmed down somewhat and allowed eight of the hostages to leave, including a pregnant woman, two children and Noel Reddy, who also had been injured in the elbow and the head. Gardiner and Walsh laid down their weapons and took off their disguises.

During the shooting, Detective Inspector Hickey made his way into the Leinster Arms Hotel from where he took command of the situation. Hickey negotiated on the phone with Walsh. He assured the raiders that they would not be harmed if they came out with their hands up. He also arranged to get them a priest. Father Patrick Mangan, the local curate, volunteered to go into the bank and bring Walsh and Gardiner out with him.

When they saw the priest, Gardiner started laughing and remarking that they were reliving the scene in the movie *Dog Day Afternoon*. He seemed to think that there would be batteries of TV cameras waiting outside. He fixed his hair. Walsh took a round from one of the guns they had discarded and handed it as a souvenir to the prettiest lady in the bank. They walked out into the winter sunlight on either side of the priest. The extraordinary cat-and-mouse game which began four months earlier had ended. The 'Athy Gang' had pulled their last 'job' together. No Irish town had ever experienced such an incredible scene.

Austin Higgins never regained consciousness and died some hours later in hospital. John Loughran, the leader of the gang who had resolved to shoot his way out if confronted, clinically died twice on the way to hospital but was revived each time. He would live, although he was partially crippled from his injuries. Tynan underwent emergency surgery and recovered and was later reunited with Walsh and Gardiner in Portlaoise prison. All three were charged and subsequently sentenced to twelve years each for their crimes. Due to his injuries, Loughran has never stood trial and he still lives in Dublin. John Condron, the bank official, never fully recovered from his injuries. His family and the staff of the Bank of Ireland later thanked the Gardaí for their work in taking on the gang that day.

In the aftermath of the Athy robbery, a Garda internal inquiry was ordered when it was discovered that the only firing done that day was by the ERU. All of the weapons recovered from the captured gang were cocked, loaded and ready to fire. When this fact emerged there were protests in the Dáil from the opposition benches. But within a few days the public overwhelmingly showed their support for the police action. It was later found that the Winchester pump-action shotgun was not suitable for confrontations in built-up areas. The pellets from the cartridges spread over a large area and caused most of the collateral injuries. A system of communication was also introduced for such situations whereby all the ERU team members would know exactly where gunfire is coming from.

In their public debut in Athy, the ERU had displayed great courage and zeal. Since 1990 they have been involved in scores of confrontations with armed criminals and terrorists, with a 100 percent success record. The investigation by the Serious Crime Squad, 'Operation Gemini', was a classic example of good, meticulous police work. It was a gruelling game of patience which finally paid off. As for gangland, Athy came to symbolise the end of an era when holding up banks was a pushover. Now the cops were fighting back. In the years since that afternoon, the number of armed robberies by well-organised gangs has dwindled. Jumping over bank counters is no longer fun.

The Psycho

To the casual observer, Peter Joseph Judge was an affable gentleman. He spoke with a calm, reassuring voice and had a warm smile which women found attractive. He was an unremarkable, average-looking man, who could have passed as a middle-class civil servant with a good taste in clothes. He helped old ladies across the road, was nice to animals and kids and was a devoted son to his widowed mother. But the facade disguised an individual who was the absolute opposite of what he appeared to be. Behind the cloak of respectability, lurked a chilling, cold-blooded monster. In gangland his name was synonymous with terror. He was called 'The Psycho'.

In the underworld no criminal was ever bestowed with a more fitting sobriquet. PJ Judge was a psychopath who used fear and violence to control a huge drug distribution network. He took pleasure in dispensing pain and death to those who crossed him or those who, in his paranoia, he thought had crossed him. Judge confirmed his blood-curdling reputation with one of the most horrific murders ever carried out in Ireland's gangland, earning himself the additional nickname 'The Executioner'. No single godfather has ever been so feared in the twilight zone of organised crime.

The Psycho even united the Gardaí and criminals. They all agreed that Judge was an extremely dangerous killer, who was afraid of neither cop nor robber. A retired detective who witnessed Judge's career for most of his life describes him in less sanguine language: 'I have known practically every major criminal in Dublin for over thirty years and I have never met one like Judge. There was a behavioural kink in the bastard. He was the worst, most evil fucker I ever came across. He commited two of the most brutal murders I have investigated and he even tried to murder Guards.' A criminal who once worked with Judge agreed with the worldly-wise policeman. 'He scared the shit out of everyone. There was something about that fucker that just wasn't right. He talked like butter wouldn't melt in his mouth but he could cut your heart out and smile into your face at the same time. Most criminals kill because it's just part of the business, but Judge loved it.'

But eventually it was the fear he brought to gangland which ended his life as brutally as he had lived it. In the underworld, fear fuels warfare. The politics of gangland dictate the way things will turn out. Kill the other guy before he gets a chance to kill you.

PJ Judge was born in Dublin on 24 July 1955. The youngest of a family of four – he had two sisters and a brother – he grew up in the family home at Ballygall Crescent in Finglas on the west side of the city. Judge went to school until he was twelve and dropped out to begin a life of crime. He was very close to his mother, Nellie, and his sisters but he did not get on particularly well with his father, Peter, who had a small truck delivery business. From the age of ten Judge was regularly getting in trouble with the local police. Those who grew up with him recall that he was a small, scruffy kid with a bad stammer. He always seemed to have to prove that he was just as tough as the other kids on the road.

Along with a few pals, he began robbing cars and breaking into shops and houses. He was a particularly skilled driver and became one of the city's first so-called 'joyriders', stealing cars and getting involved in chases with the Gardaí. The 1960s were, as already revealed in this book, the years which produced the generation responsible for the advent of organised crime in this country. Judge's first recorded convictions were in 1967, when he was twelve years old. They were for larceny, assault and burglary.

But while the rest of his contemporaries were still very much petty, street-corner thugs, Judge's propensity for serious violence began to emerge. In early 1969 he was friendly with a group of kids who lived in Sycamore Park, around the corner from his home in Finglas. His new friends convinced the small, fair-haired kid with the stammer that he should dye his hair a darker colour. He agreed and they did the honours. But when Judge went back to Ballygall Crescent his friends there began making fun of him and his new hair colour. They told him that the kids in Sycamore Park had made a fool of him.

The thirteen-year-old Judge was not impressed. He was angry and decided to do something about it. That evening he and one of his pals from Ballygall Crescent broke into a gunsmith's shop on Glasnevin Avenue, Finglas, and stole shotguns and ammunition. Around 4am the following morning Judge went to the home of the kids who had helped him dye his hair and fired a number of shots through the window as the family slept inside. Judge was later arrested and sentenced to two years in Daingean Industrial School for the attack on the property.

But his stint in detention did little to teach him the error of his ways. When he got out a short time later he went back to the same gun dealer's and stole more weapons. He later shot and seriously injured another teenager who had been picking on him. In November 1972 Judge was convicted and sentenced to six months for assault. The sentence was later overturned on appeal. PJ Judge, at the age of seventeen, had already earned himself a formidable reputation among his peers as a dangerous 'head case'.

The local Gardaí attached to Finglas station began taking a serious interest in Judge. 'From the first shooting incident we knew he was going to be a wrong one. He was a natural-born killer,' recalled one detective. Judge and his cronies got involved in progressively more serious crime, particularly armed robbery. The early 1970s saw the young generation of one-time petty thieves becoming professional 'blaggers' (armed robbers). Judge and four other Finglas lads began robbing pay rolls, post-offices, banks, anywhere there was a chance of handy cash.

They were also responsible for a series of so-called 'tie-up' jobs in north County Dublin. Tie-ups are aggravated burglaries where the victims are tied up at gunpoint while their premises or homes are ransacked. In one such robbery an elderly man died as a result of his terrifying experience at the hands of Judge and his men. Judge was a natural organiser and ran the gang like a business. They began hitting jewellers, warehouses and banks in the country.

Unlike the other gang members who spent their stolen cash on a good time, Judge invested his money from the various heists in buying guns. He also lodged the loot in various bank accounts under different names. He did not drink very much or take drugs. He ensured that the gang always had a pool of three or more cars parked around the city for use in the various armed robberies. His associate from that decade recalls: 'Judge was the man in charge and no-one messed with him, because they knew what he was capable of. But he was a good planner and there was good money in his robberies, although there were times he didn't pay everyone their fair share.'

Judge hated the Gardaí with the same passion as he loved crime and fast cars. From the time he was a teenager, he refused to speak while being questioned about crimes and never admitted to anything. In the mid-1970s, while driving a stolen car, he was chased by a uniformed Garda motorcyclist, Pat Mulhall, who was attached to Whitehall Station on the city's north side. Judge ambushed the policeman, ramming him with the stolen car. Then he tried to reverse over the Garda as he lay injured on the ground. A passerby rushed to Garda Mulhall's assistance and pulled him out of the way. The Psycho drove off.

Judge and his associates stole their high-powered getaway cars in the more affluent suburbs of south Dublin, which is something of a tradition among armed robbers in the city. One night during the late 1970s, Judge and a gang member were busy replenishing the gang's car-pool in the Donnybrook area. They had just got into a Jaguar car in the driveway of a large house they had hit. The Psycho was behind the wheel. Suddenly a uniformed cop emerged from the shadows and asked what the two hoods were up to. Judge, according to his associate, remained perfectly calm. He told the suspicious policeman in his soft-spoken voice that the car belonged to his brother-in-law who lived in the house at the end of the driveway.

The Garda asked for the keys and Judge handed them over. 'Come on up to the house with me and my brother-in-law will explain every-thing,' Judge suggested as he got out of the car. The cop looked at Judge and his partner, surveyed the darkened laneway and sensed danger. 'Tell you what, you and your brother-in-law can come into Donnybrook station in the morning and collect the keys and explain everything then,' the Garda said and walked briskly away. Judge and his associate left the area. Later his associate asked The Psycho what he had been playing at. 'The copper didn't have a radio and he was on his own. When I got him down that dark laneway, I was goin' to give him this in the back.' Judge grinned as he produced a pair of sharp scissors. The associate knew Judge wasn't joking.

On another occasion, Judge and the same criminal were driving through the city centre in a stolen Ford Granada car when they attracted the attentions of a Garda motorcyclist. As the car drove onto Parnell Square from O'Connell Street, the policeman pulled up alongside and told them to stop for a check. Judge tore off at high speed with the Garda in pursuit. He drove up around Parnell Square and down again onto O'Connell Street. He pulled off O'Connell Street and drove back onto Parnell Street at high speed through a series of side-streets.

The Garda motorbike, with blue lights flashing and siren wailing, kept up the pursuit. Judge was bringing him around in circles. He turned the Granada into a laneway off Parnell Square, followed by the motorbike. As he pulled into the lane, Judge braked to a sudden stop, putting the stolen car into reverse. The gearbox crunched and the car wheels screeched as he reversed at speed at the policeman, who had almost collided with the car when it suddenly stopped. He narrowly missed the cop who had driven onto a narrow kerb to avoid the car when he had rounded the corner. Judge sped off again, this time onto Dorset Street.

He drove down the busy street on the wrong side, forcing oncoming traffic to swerve out of the way. By now, squad cars were rushing from all over the north- and south-city. The associate recalled the chase: 'There were so many police cars after us that Dorset Street seemed to be lit up like a blue beacon. There was so much noise from the sirens that we had to turn up the radio. Judge stayed totally cool, concentrating on what he was doing. Behind a wheel he was an amazing driver.

'Judge was doing anything between eighty and ninety miles per hour and we were at the end of Dorset Street and through Drumcondra within what seemed like seconds. By then there were so many cop cars that they were getting in the way of each other. Then as we got near the Skylon Hotel going towards the airport they began pulling back because there was another bunch of them coming to meet us. Judge took a sudden left turn at the Skylon and then another one. We drove through a set of gates and through a college grounds and dumped the car. He was going so fast that the police couldn't keep up.

'We walked through the grounds of the college and back out onto the road. We sat in a chip shop and ate while the cops kept screaming up and down the road looking for us. I asked Judge why he had reversed at the copper. "To kill the cunt of course. It would be one less pig in the world," he told me, like he was talking about killing a fly. When the commotion died down outside, we went out and robbed another car and went home to Finglas. After that, I decided that he was a mad bastard and he was going to murder some copper just for the fun of it. I was a wild fucker at the time but I still had enough cop-on to go me own way.'

But Judge's career as an armed robber was not to last long. In 1979 during a hold-up with another hood at a post-office in Ballyfermot he shot and seriously injured the postmaster, Michael Delaney, in the leg. This time the Gardaí were hot on his heels and he was subsequently arrested and charged. While on bail for that offence Judge was caught again, robbing the Allied Irish Bank at Annesley Bridge in central Dublin. During the raid he was confronted by an unarmed Garda. Judge aimed his gun at the policeman and pulled the trigger. The gun jammed and The Psycho was nabbed again. In April 1980 Peter Joseph Judge was sentenced in the Special Criminal Court to ten years' imprisonment for the Ballyfermot robbery. On 25 October 1983, he was convicted of the Annesley Bridge hold-up and given another ten years. But the story of The Psycho was far from over.

When he was released in 1989, gangland had undergone a

dramatic change. Armed robbery was no longer the main source of sustenance for the organised crime gangs. During the following year, the dramatic capture of the Athy gang and the shooting dead of the armed robbers, Austin Higgins, William 'Blinky' Doyle and Thomas Wilson, had shown that the Gardaí now posed a serious health risk to people like Judge. Doyle and Wilson were shot dead during a dramatic car chase after a bank robbery, in the summer of 1990. During the 1980s drugs had become the stock-in-trade of the underworld. Most of the big armed robbers were now involved in distributing cannabis and heroin. In the first few years of the decade, heroin had gripped an entire generation of young working-class kids.

The prodigious profits being made by the gangsters changed the ethos of the underworld. Greed brought deceit and paranoia. Murder at the hands of a former friend or associate was now an occupational hazard for the average crook involved in the murky business of drugs. Gangland assassinations were a regular occurence. PJ Judge would have no difficulty adapting to the new scene.

Many of those involved in the drug business had known Judge. One of those was his neighbour, John McKeon, who controlled many of the cannabis rackets in the north and west of the city. The Psycho asked McKeon and others about the prospects of getting involved in the business. He still had cash hidden in 'off-side' bank accounts, which he now invested in drugs. At first he began selling large quantities of cannabis and the money came rolling in. Then he branched out into heroin, ecstasy and amphetamines.

Within two years of being released, Judge was on the way to becoming one of the biggest drug smugglers and suppliers in the underworld. He controlled 'patches' right across the south, west and north of the city, including the inner-city. He had extensive contacts with drug gangs in Limerick and Cork. From the time he got involved in the narcotic rackets, Judge was determined that he would not allow anyone to take advantage by ripping him off or not paying up in time. He let it be known that anyone who messed with him would be in for a severe beating or a bullet.

When The Psycho was released from jail, his stammer, which had caused him much embarrassment, was gone and he swapped his scruffy image for a more clean-cut appearance, wearing good clothes. He had also developed bisexual tendencies, according to his associates. He had a number of younger boyfriends who worked for him in his distribution business. He also had a string of girlfriends, some of whom were known prostitutes.

Judge would beat some of his male and female lovers quite severely for no apparent reason. On one occasion he gave a girlfriend such a beating that she ran into the Bridewell Garda station for protection. The police on duty did not need to be introduced to Judge who came bursting into the station demanding that the terrified woman leave with him. The police told him to get out or he would be charged. The girlfriend, however, was too scared to prefer charges and later moved out of town to avoid bumping into her psychotic ex-boyfriend.

Another girlfriend interviewed for this book recalled how he would take pleasure in hurting her. The young woman from a respectable middle-class background fell for Judge's charm. But it wasn't long before his dark side emerged. 'He would beat me and seemed to like it. Once he broke my fingers in a rage and refused to let me see a doctor. I had to sit there, sobbing and in pain, trying to bandage my flittered fingers together. PJ wouldn't let me get a doctor. He kept looking at me and laughing. On another occasion he left me for dead and I was forced to leave the country for over six months. I was like a down-and-out and wore disguises in case PJ or any of his friends found out where I was. I was so frightened of him – I was absolutely terrified. My father reported the assault to the Gardaí to get him off my back but he didn't seem a bit worried about them.'

But the Gardaí were beginning to take a serious interest in Judge as intelligence sources revealed that he had moved into drugs in a major way. On countless occasions the surveillance units attached to the Serious Crime and Drug Squads attempted to keep track of The Psycho's movements around the city. It was an extremely difficult task. Judge had trained himself in counter-surveillance techniques, which he also used to avoid being tailed by other criminals or anti-drug vigilantes. He was paranoid about an assassination attempt. He stayed at a variety of addresses around the city and used several cars.

Judge began making so much money he literally did not know where to put it. He used associates, who were too terrified to rip him off, to hold money under their names in various banks. He was regularly stopped and searched by the police who often found large sums of cash in his car. Judge also liked to bury his ill-gotten fortune. He always carried a change of clothes and a shovel in the boot of his car for the job.

On one occasion, when the Gardaí stopped him, they noticed a strong stench of manure from the car. Mud was on his boots and clothes and on the wheels of the car. In the boot they found a shovel, an iron bar, surgical gloves and a pair of rubber gloves. They recovered almost £16,000 in cash. When they questioned Judge about the money and muck, he didn't answer. The money was eventually returned to him because there was no legislation at the time allowing the authorities to hold it.

The Psycho was obsessive about anyone who ripped him off, made him feel in any way inadequate or look bad. Tragically, William 'Jock' Corbally managed to do all three. Corbally was four years older than Judge and came from around the corner, in Ballygall Parade. Jock had practically grown up with The Psycho and the two had been involved in crime together from when they were teenagers.

Corbally was very different from Judge. He was not violent or in any way dangerous. He was also a good-looking 'ladies man', a cheerful, cocky, Walter Mitty character who spent more time dreaming of pulling off the elusive 'big job' than actually doing anything about it. Between 1968 and 1993, when he was forty-two years old, Corbally accumulated a total of twenty-three convictions, the most serious of which was when he attempted to steal a truckload of beef. The same detective who earlier described Judge says of Corbally: 'He was a harmless lad, there was no badness in him. Whenever he did anything, he was caught. We [Gardaí] were always telling him to give up this crime lark, it simply didn't suit him.'

Some of Corbally's earlier larceny convictions were for crimes he committed with Judge. But friendship soon turned to resentment. When Judge was released from Daingean Industrial School in the late 1960s, Corbally was regarded by the other teenage crooks as the main man on the block. He beat Judge in a street fight and afterwards The Psycho threatened to burn his former pal out of his home by pouring petrol through the letterbox. He did not carry out the threat.

Around the time that Judge was released from prison in the late 1980s, Jock Corbally was jailed for two years for possession of cannabis with intent to supply. By the time Jock came out, Judge had replaced him as the main man in the street. Corbally began doing business with Judge, selling small quantities of cannabis for him in the Ballymun and Finglas areas. But the arrangement didn't last long. Judge accused Corbally of ripping him off to the tune of £1,000. He threatened to sort Jock out. On one occasion he broke up a car Jock was being driven in. Judge also let everyone know that it was now only a matter of time before Corbally was going to get what was coming to him.

In October 1990 Judge gave two of Corbally's sons £800 worth of hashish to sell for him. The two teenagers only managed to sell £200 worth and took the rest for themselves. The Psycho went to one of Corbally's brothers and warned of dire consequences if the money was not paid up. Jock was furious when he heard this. He didn't want his sons getting mixed up with Judge. He met Judge and promised to get the balance of the money back. Judge told Corbally he now wanted £1,500 instead of the £600 balance. It was interest on the drugs he originally gave the two kids. Corbally told Judge that it would not be possible to pay that kind of money. Judge smiled and walked away. In the meantime The Psycho continued to threaten the lives of Jock's two sons. In April 1991 the situation came to a head.

Jock and one of his sons, sixteen-year-old Graham, met Judge near Ballygall Crescent. Judge again threatened the Corballys, telling them he would spare them his wrath only if they voluntarily left the country. A row ensued during which Jock hit Judge with an iron bar across the head. The Psycho ran into his mother's house to get away from Corbally. He was later hospitalised and received thirty stitches to his head wound. Judge swore vengeance and deep down inside Jock Corbally knew what that meant. He had signed his own death warrant. There was no going back with Judge.

Six weeks later, Graham Corbally disappeared for two days and his father thought the worst. He reported his son missing to the police, who treated this particular missing persons case very seriously. They were aware of the conflict between Corbally and Judge. They were also aware of what The Psycho could do. A few days later, however, the emergency was called off when Graham turned up unharmed. In late 1992 Jock Corbally was given a reprieve from his problems with Judge, thanks to the team of detectives who arrested him behind the wheel of a truckload of stolen beef belonging to the Larry Goodman empire. The following March he was jailed for five years by the Dublin Circuit Criminal Court.

In the meantime, Judge built up a million-pound drug empire which he organised like a business. He became boss of a drug-dealing network which included a number of major dealers from Finglas, Ballymun, Ballyfermot, Crumlin, Clondalkin and the inner-city. One of them, a businessman from Ballyfermot, was given the job of organising so-called 'cash-counting centres'. These were houses where the money from The Psycho's network of drug-pushers was collected and counted. From there it was put through a myriad of bank accounts under false names both in Ireland and offshore. It was also laundered through a number of front companies, including a taxi firm. More of the money was literally buried by Judge while the rest was 're-invested' in the business by buying more drugs. The Ballyfermot man used his legitimate business as a front to hide the operation.

Another member of the team was an ex-INLA man from Crumlin in south Dublin. Originally from Belfast, he had served time with Judge for possession of firearms with intent to endanger life. He was now one of The Psycho's enforcers. Judge organised his network of dealers throughout the city like a military operation with strict rules. If they were drug abusers then they had to indulge their habit when they weren't working. There was a strict no-credit policy. Judge believed that allowing junkies to owe him would lead to others 'taking liberties'. If any of his pushers lost money or drugs, then Judge punished them by doubling the value of what was lost. If it wasn't paid then the errant pusher was severely beaten or even shot.

When a pusher was not working hard enough, he was dropped from Judge's 'golden circle'. The word would be put about and the pusher would be blacked by everyone in the business. It was not unusual for The Psycho to have his pushers out moving drugs around the city at three and four in the morning as he drove around checking up on them. He was guaranteed total loyalty and secrecy from his people for two reasons: they were absolutely terrified of the man and they made plenty of easy money.

The nearest the police came to catching Judge with his drugs was in August 1991 when he was spotted by detectives from Clondalkin station near the Grand Canal. When he saw the officers, Judge made a run for it, throwing a jacket into the canal which was later found to contain amphetamine tablets worth over £10,000. When the detectives caught up with The Psycho he fought to get away. On 28 August he was charged in the Dublin District Court and released on bail. A file on the case was sent to the Director of Public Prosecutions who decided there would be difficulties connecting Judge with the jacket containing the drugs. Meanwhile Judge continued his business.

Michael Godfrey was a small-time crook, much in the same vein as Jock Corbally. And like Corbally, whom he never met, he was unfortunate to get involved with The Psycho. Godfrey was born in Dublin in 1938, the youngest of seven children. When he was twenty-five years old he emigrated to England where he worked for an oil company. He returned to live in Dublin thirteen years later and worked in various jobs around the country before setting himself up as an insurance broker in 1985. Godfrey's business eventually foundered in 1990.

Throughout this time he got involved in a number of car insurance scams with Stephen 'Rossi' Walsh. Walsh was involved in the staging of accidents (see chapter 7, 'The Scam Man'). Godfrey's knowledge of the insurance business was a big help. He had succeeded in one fraudulent compensation claim for £40,000 and had others in the legal pipeline. Godfrey was also a bagman for a number of major criminals involved in drug rackets and armed robbery. After he was released from prison, Judge was introduced to Godfrey and the two got involved in a money counterfeiting scam. Godfrey had a contact in England who produced good quality Irish currency which Judge bought and passed off through his lackeys in Dublin. In June 1991 Godfrey was arrested at Heathrow Airport when he was found in possession of counterfeit Irish £20 notes. The following October he was convicted and jailed for thirty months on the charge. He was released on parole in 1992 but had to remain living in England as part of the conditions of his release.

The Psycho was a regular visitor to Godfrey before and after his release. They planned to set up a front company to import large quantities of cannabis, thus cutting out the middlemen and increasing Judge's share of the profits. In the summer of 1992 the Probation Service gave Godfrey permission to travel to Belgium. When he was there he met with Judge and a Dutch cannabis dealer who agreed a price for up to thirty kilos of the drug to be delivered when they had set up their Dublin front company. It was to be a pilot operation, and if it went well the company would place regular orders.

In February 1993 Godfrey returned to Ireland after completing his parole period. He got some money from Judge and rented a bedsit on the North Circular Road. Godfrey immediately set to work organising his new business venture for The Psycho. He rented a small industrial unit in Glasnevin, north Dublin, in conjunction with two other associates who had also agreed to act as front-men for the operation. In February Judge and Godfrey travelled to Amsterdam to see the shipment they'd ordered. Judge paid Godfrey £30,000 for the thirty kilos of hash. The stuff arrived on 12 March at the industrial unit in Glasnevin, in a large cardboard box purporting to be carrying thread.

When Judge inspected the shipment some days later, he refused to take the cannabis, because it was not the stuff he had sampled in Holland. The Psycho flew into a chilling temper and ordered Godfrey to get the money back. Instead Godfrey went about finding a buyer for the shipment and sold it over a week later to another drug dealer in the inner-city for almost double its price. Judge heard about it and flew into a rage. He told Godfrey he wanted all the cash from the transaction. But whether he got the cash or not, Judge had decided Godfrey's fate. He would have to pay the ultimate price for his perceived disloyalty.

The dope which Godfrey had sold was now being re-sold by a rival gang in the north inner-city. Judge went to one of his hideouts, dug up a .32 automatic revolver and went looking for the opposition. On the night of 31 March 1993, Judge shot the drug dealer in the leg in an attack at his home at St Joseph's Mansions in the inner-city. The man was hospitalised but refused to co-operate with detectives investigating the case. Judge was subsequently arrested for questioning about the shooting but refused to talk. He was again released without charge.

Three days later, Judge sent two associates to pick up Michael Godfrey at his home on the North Circular Road. At 11.30pm on 3 April, two armed and masked men took Godfrey from his flat and drove him away at speed in his own car. The small-time con-man was taken to Scribblestown Lane, a *cul-de-sac* situated in a sparsely-populated country area on the outer fringes of Finglas.

When the car arrived, Godfrey was taken into a field where Judge was waiting for him. The Psycho caught his victim by the throat and beat him. He hurled abuse at Godfrey who pleaded for mercy. Judge ordered one of his men to shoot him in the head with the .32 automatic pistol. Godfrey was shot in the side of the head and fell over. He was still alive and pleading for mercy. Judge grabbed the gun from his accomplice, cocked it and fired a shot at point-blank range into the back of Godfrey's head. The Psycho calmly walked away, got into his car and drove off. The following morning, Godfrey's body was discovered, lying in the field where he had been executed.

The detectives working on the case soon discovered that Judge was responsible but, because of the terror he instilled in everyone around him, no-one would dare give evidence in court against him. Judge was subsequently arrested and questioned. He refused to tell the police anything. There was insufficient evidence to substantiate a charge. In his warped mind Judge was beginning to think of himself as untouchable.

The brutal, cold-blooded murder of a small-time crook like Godfrey terrified a lot of people in the criminal underworld. From Judge's perspective it sent the right kind of message to everyone who worked with him. He would have no problem keeping people in line. The news of Godfrey's slaying passed around the landings in Mountjoy prison within a few days. Jock Corbally was probably glad he was inside.

Judge's name would feature in another gangland murder less than two years later, that of drug dealer David Weafer. Weafer, who was thirty-one years old at the time, had been threatened by The Psycho over the proceeds of a drug deal. Weafer had waited with a gun to shoot Judge outside his mother's house a week before his own assassination. Initially Judge was the prime suspect and he was arrested and questioned but eliminated from the investigation because he had an alibi. Detectives have never ruled out the possibility that he had helped to organise Weafer's murder. Whether he did or not, it helped to reinforce his formidable reputation.

By the time of the Godfrey murder, Judge had become a major supplier of heroin across the north side of the city. MST, or 'Naps' as they are known on the streets, are powerful painkilling tablets which are strictly controlled by law and prescribed to terminally-ill patients. On the streets, however, Naps are used as a heroin substitute, creating the same effect as the drug. In October 1993 an associate of Judge came to him with an interesting and potentially lucrative proposition. A doctor who was living in Dublin had informed Judge's associate that he was in serious financial trouble and was finding it difficult to pay his bills. It was a situation The Psycho could use to his advantage.

His associate went back to the medic and offered him a way of solving his money worries. He told the doctor that it would be worth his while if he could supply certain medicines in large quantities. The doctor said he could obtain the medicines in bulk by pretending to export them directly to a hospital in Africa. A short time later, Judge's associate went back to him with a large order for various drugs including ordinary painkillers, antibiotics, malaria tablets and 6,000 MSTs. The doctor placed the order with one of the large pharmacies in Dublin.

A week later, the doctor was invited by The Psycho's associate to lunch in a south-side restaurant. He was introduced to Judge, who asked the doctor how much the order for the medicines had come to. He said £11,000. Judge put his hand into his jacket and handed him a plastic bag. 'There's £12,000 in that to pay for the medicine. I'll call and collect them.' Judge and his associate left. The unsuspecting down-on-his-luck medical man had no idea of the trouble he was inviting upon himself.

Two days later, Judge's associate called and collected the drugs. He gave the doctor £12,000 in used notes for supplying the medicines. The two gangsters were only interested in the MST tablets. Judge and his associate sold them through their pushers to drug addicts around the city for an average of £20 each. The Psycho and his associate made almost £100,000 on the transaction. In January 1994 Judge called to the doctor's house and said he wanted a regular supply of MSTs. He ordered another 9,000 tablets, the total street value of which was £180,000.

In return for his assistance, Judge agreed to give the doctor an advance of £25,000 to set him up in a new clinic. In return he would pay the medic a profit of just fifty pence per tablet. The order for 9,000 tablets came to £18,000. Judge went to his house and handed over a plastic bag with the cash in used notes. Judge instructed the doctor to repack the MSTs in bundles of ten. He collected the tablets and gave the doctor the £25,000 advance he had agreed to.

A few months later, the doctor again found himself slipping into financial difficulties and offered to sell Judge more tablets. This time The Psycho wanted 18,000. The bill for the tablets was just over £21,000 which again was paid in a plastic bag and in cash. The doctor's payment for the deal was another £15,000. He paid Judge back £6,000 which was to bring his 'advance' down to £19,000.

In November 1994 Judge called his doctor looking for another prescription. This time he wanted 30,000 tablets, the street value of which was about £600,000. But because the doctor claimed the consignment was for export to an African hospital the order got bogged down in World Health Organisation regulations. Too many questions were being asked, as it was such a large consignment. The deal fell through. The doctor, still anxious to get his money, then contacted a friend in Britain who made arrangements for the large export order for the African hospital and its 'terminally-ill' patients. It was March before the order was actually secured. The bill for the tablets was £50,000, which Judge again gave the doctor in used notes in a very large shopping bag. The consignment of drugs was sent to Africa in late March. The doctor flew over to retrieve the order in Nigeria and fly them back to Dublin.

In Nigeria he re-packed the consignment. But as he tried to board a flight for London *en route* to Ireland, the local Customs seized the drugs. The consignment did not match up with the paperwork the medic was carrying. The doctor flew back to Dublin empty-handed. The Psycho was waiting to see him. Judge was furious and ordered the helpless medic to fly back to Nigeria and retrieve his drugs by whatever means possible and not to come back without them. The doctor flew back, but the African authorities refused to return the valuable consignment.

When the doctor returned to Ireland, Judge appeared more philosophical about the botched deal. He said he understood that it had gone wrong but reassured the worried doctor, telling him to forget about it. Instead the unpredictable Psycho suggested that they both go into the timber business together. The doctor-turned-businessman flew back to Nigeria and arranged a shipment of 'Iroko' timber for export to Ireland. Judge paid £20,000 for the shipment, which did not sell in Dublin. In October The Psycho rang the doctor out of the blue. He was in an angry mood again and ordered him to go back to Africa and get his tablets back. The doctor was on the next flight.

In Africa he was unable to get his hands on the 30,000 MSTs – they had long since vanished into the Nigerian bureaucracy. By now the doctor, like everyone else who had encountered Judge, was terrified of the man. Out of desperation he bought £2,000 worth of cocaine to bring back in a bid to make up for the lost tablets. When he arrived back Judge came to see him at his clinic. He flew into a rage, took out a pistol and told the doctor to leave the premises which he said he was now taking over himself. He also ordered the terrified medic to get whatever money he could and bring it back to him. The doctor cleared out his bank account and went back to The Psycho with £8,000. He was again ordered to leave his own clinic and this time Judge demanded the keys of his sports car, which he duly handed over. Judge told him to return in two weeks' time with a written document outlining in detail what he (the doctor) would be able to do for him (Judge).

The medic typed up his personal portfolio for Judge and handed it over to his associate. Judge phoned the doctor and said he could return to his clinic and resume his business. Then Judge called again, this time demanding the keys to his wife's car. By now the medic's life was upside-down. He was so terrified he had no idea what to do. A few days later The Psycho was again on the phone. This time he told the doctor that he should not go to work the next day because he had not paid his bill. The medic was so scared he did not go back to his workplace for a month. Judge was now taking sadistic pleasure in psychologically torturing his latest victim. In late December 1995 Judge informed the doctor that he would allow him to resume his business for a weekly payment of £500, which was payable every Saturday afternoon. The doctor agreed, although he found it almost impossible to come up with the money. By now his practice had dwindled and he was barely able to make ends meet. Over the next few months, whenever he fell behind in his payments the Psycho called to his premises and threatened to kill him. He told the medic that he would even take his house and move into it himself.

In April, Dublin gangland figure Johnny Reddan was shot dead in an inner-city bar as a result of a long-running feud. The next day Judge showed the doctor a copy of a daily newspaper, which had a feature about the previous fifteen unsolved gangland murders in Dublin. He fiddled with a pistol in his hand and snarled menacingly,

'I should have made a coffin from that wood and driven a stake through your heart and buried you in it.' Then he handed his doctor a penny and forced him to swallow it. 'Now by the time the penny drops you'll be able to tell me how you intend payin' me in full.' Judge got up and walked out. But events were about to distract the godfather.

The newspaper article about the fifteen gangland murders which Judge showed the petrified medic included the Godfrey execution. It did not, however, mention gangland murder number sixteen. In April 1996 William 'Jock' Corbally was still officially a missing person. Only the police and the patrons of the murky Dublin underworld were aware that he had been The Psycho's latest victim. The murder of Corbally is one of the most gruesome and depraved crimes ever perpetrated in gangland. What happened was this: In December 1994 Jock Corbally was released from prison and returned to Ballygall Parade to stay with his mother, Maureen. A gentle, God-fearing woman, Maureen Corbally prayed that her son was now going to go straight. But Jock was still on the look-out for that elusive 'stroke' which would set him up. He tried to stay clear of Judge, who was aware that he was back on the street. In the summer of 1995 Corbally was out walking with his third child, a five-year-old son from another relationship, when Judge drove past. The Psycho went berserk when he saw Corbally who, in the killer's sick mind, was beginning to epitomise all that was wrong with the world. Judge stopped his car and jumped out, got a hammer from the boot of the car and lunged at Jock in front of his terrified child. Corbally was well able to handle himself in a street brawl. He disarmed Judge and hit him a few defensive punches.

The Psycho stood snarling and spitting on the pavement. His cold blue eyes stared at Jock. 'You're a fuckin' dead man.' Judge suddenly composed himself, smirked and got back into his car and went home for tea with his mother. Jock Corbally had succeeded in humiliating the Psycho yet again. But he was terrified for his very life. He had to get out of town but couldn't until he had enough money. A lot of Jock's old criminal buddies were no longer into pulling 'strokes' with him. He had a habit of getting nicked every time he did something. There was also suspicion that he was a loose talker.

The only place to make money was in the drug business. Corbally began associating with a major heroin dealer and former armed robber from Clondalkin in west Dublin. Unknown to him, this man had only recently begun doing business with Judge. At twenty-five years of age he was already quite wealthy from his share of the heroin trade. The Clondalkin heroin dealer began using Jock as a courier to move drugs for him between Ireland and England.

In January Jock agreed to fly to Amsterdam to pick up a kilo of heroin for the Clondalkin dealer. Unknown to Corbally, Judge had also invested in the shipment. Depending on the original potency of the deal and how much it can be diluted down or 'cut' for re-distribution at street level, a kilo can be worth from £500,000 to £1,000,000. In return, the dealer was going to give Jock some of the 'gear' which he could sell for himself. Corbally hated heroin and what it had done to his two teenage sons and so many people he had grown up with. But he was desperate for cash and he accepted the job. In mid-January Jock arrived back in Ireland with the heroin and a dangerous plan. He tipped off a detective he knew that he had smuggled the heroin. He arranged for it to be recovered by the Gardaí near Sutton Dart station in north Dublin. Jock did not, however, tell the detective what quantity he had smuggled, just that it was a major haul. He took a quarter of the kilo of high-grade heroin, which he was going to quietly sell later and make enough money to leave town.

On 19 January Jock arranged to meet a known heroin addict near Sutton Dart station. He told him he was going to deliver a kilo of heroin to the Clondalkin dealer. A Garda unit which was passing the station spotted the pair and went over to talk to them. Jock and his companion promptly ran off, pursued by the cops. The heroin was recovered along the rail track. Jock and his companion got away. Later, a news report revealed how Gardaí had recovered a huge haul of heroin in Dublin. The haul consisted of 784 grams of high-grade heroin, worth over £500,000 on the street. Jock's latest hare-brained plan had failed.

This was the opportunity The Psycho had been waiting for. He would punish Jock for losing the heroin and accuse him of being a police informant. He told the Clondalkin dealer to do nothing about the missing heroin and play Jock along. When the time was right, Jock would get a good beating to teach him a lesson. The dealer accepted an explanation from Jock about what had happened. Judge's plan was finally coming together. On 28 February 1996 the Clondalkin dealer got a phone call from another of Judge's henchmen, Mark Dwyer. The twenty-one-year-old thug from Phibsboro was heavily involved in ecstasy and heroin dealing in the north-city and had been associated with The Psycho since he was a teenager. He had only recently introduced Judge to the Clondalkin dealer as someone who could supply him with bigger quantities of heroin. Dwyer told the Clondalkin dealer to set up a meeting with Corbally.

That afternoon Jock agreed to meet with the dealer in Chapelizod, near the Phoenix Park. The dealer told Corbally that he wanted him to help dig up some money for another big drug deal in Amsterdam. The dealer picked Jock up at a public phone box outside the Mullingar House pub. It was dark and particularly cold. The pair made small talk as Jock was driven the ten miles or so to his death. Dwyer had instructed the dealer to drive to a field just off the Baldonnel Road, a winding secondary road between the Naas motorway and the Air Corps base at Baldonnel.

When they arrived at the location, the dealer drove into the field. To Jock Corbally's horror, Judge's face suddenly emerged from the darkness and looked into the open passenger door of the car. He had a menacing grin. 'Jock, we want to have a word with you,' he said. Judge was joined by Dwyer and another unidentified henchman. Jock tried to beat them off but they dragged him from the car to the side of the field. They beat Corbally with iron bars as he screamed in agony, begging for mercy. But the more he screamed the more frenzied Judge became. 'Do you remember the time we fought before?' he screamed as he smashed Jock's body with an iron bar. Judge accused him of being an informant. 'Mountjoy is full of fellows because of you.'

Blood oozed from welts and cuts as Corbally tried desperately to fend off the flurry of blows and kicks. Judge was getting his revenge for the fact that Jock Corbally had been born and he was loving every horrific minute of it. He stopped to check if his victim was still alive. Judge didn't want Jock to die too quickly, which was why he did not execute him in the same way he had Michael Godfrey – with a bullet to the back of the head. When he heard Jock groan, he stabbed him a number of times around the body. Then he turned Jock around and smashed his pearly white teeth with an iron bar. A source who was in the field explained: 'Jock had always prided himself on his nice teeth. They were part of his good looks. Judge really enjoyed smashing them. It was a bonus for him.' Half-an-hour after Jock Corbally's ordeal began he ceased responding to the torture.

Judge, Dwyer and the other henchman lifted Jock and threw him into the boot of the doctor's sports car, which Judge had taken possession of a few months earlier. The Psycho ordered the Clondalkin drug dealer, who had not taken part in the violent orgy, to bring Dwyer back to Dublin. Judge and the other man drove off with Jock Corbally's body in the boot of the car. They drove at high speed to Straffan in County Kildare, where Judge regularly buried drugs, money and guns. Today he had dug another grave in anticipation of his meeting with Corbally. Jock's blood-soaked body was dumped into the grave and lime was thrown on top of it. It has been claimed that Judge cut his throat before the body was covered up. It will never be known whether Jock Corbally was dead or unconscious as he was dumped in his grave.

Later that evening, Mark Dwyer arrived at a friend's flat in north Dublin. His clothes and shoes were covered in blood. He told the people in the flat what had happened. He seemed to be in high spirits about the whole gruesome affair. Around 10.45pm Dwyer got a call from The Psycho. 'Is the baby asleep?' Dwyer asked. 'The baby has been tucked in and is sound asleep,' Judge is said to have replied.

News of Jock Corbally's murder soon began to leak out and sent a shiver through the underworld. In Garda headquarters a major investigation was launched to find the body. Deputy Commissioner

Noel Conroy, the former Detective Superintendent in charge of the Serious Crime Squad, had known and arrested Judge when he was a detective based in Finglas. He also knew Jock Corbally. He realised that Judge had to be stopped. It was decided that every effort would be made to finally put The Psycho out of business. A special investigation team was set up and units throughout the Dublin Metropolitan Area were put on alert to stop and search Judge whenever they spotted him. The heat was coming on hot and heavy.

Just over two months later, on 12 May, the *Sunday World* ran a special four-page feature on Judge and the murder of Jock Corbally. The newspaper revealed how he organised and controlled his drug empire. It also exposed his propensity for violence and his fearsome reputation in gangland. The story was accompanied by a number of pictures of The Psycho. The pictures had thin black stripes across his eyes. When he read the newspaper Judge went berserk and ordered a meeting of all his henchmen. Judge became even more paranoid and began an internal witch-hunt to find out who had been talking.

The following month, Veronica Guerin, the *Sunday Independent* crime journalist, was shot dead by another major drug gang. It was to spark the single biggest offensive seen against organised crime in almost three decades. New legislation was passed and the police were given the resources to put time into destroying the empires of people like Judge. Over the next few months Judge lost in the region of £100,000 in cash, which the Gardaí seized from him and his business partners. The money could now be taken under the new Proceeds of Crime Act.

Through the summer and into the autumn, the *Sunday World* continued a campaign against Judge, who began to find himself isolated in the underworld. The Jock Corbally murder had shown him up for what he was. It was also bad for business. When the Gardaí finished investigating the Guerin murder they planned to put all their resources into nailing Judge. The new Criminal Assets Bureau (CAB) began actively investigating Judge's wealth and hidden bank accounts in October. During that month a UTV documentary about crime in Dublin highlighted the Jock Corbally case. A source for the story was filmed as he explained what happened to Jock on the night of 28 February.

The voice of a Dublin actor was used to disguise the source's real voice and his face and body were shaded out of the picture to avoid identification. Judge was now so paranoid that he began to imagine he could identify the voice. In November he told one of his associates that he thought it was Mark Dwyer who had acted as the source for the *Sunday World* investigation and the UTV programme.

He also organised a team to abduct and murder this writer, who also took part in the UTV documentary. When it was pointed out to The Psycho that this was not a good idea in the light of the Guerin murder, he said he did not care. The police were tipped off about the plan and in turn placed a surveillance team around me to thwart Judge when he made his move. Surveillance was also mounted on his main associates. In the months after the Guerin murder gangland was thrown into a state of chaos. Criminals who were afraid of being associated with the gang responsible, broke life-long silences and told the cops what they wanted to know. The Provos began asking questions about major-league drug dealers, particularly Judge. Paranoia and fear pervaded the underworld. It became a very dangerous place.

On the evening of 7 December, Judge went for drinks to the Royal Oak pub in Finglas where he met a number of friends and a girlfriend. As he sat in the crowded bar talking and drinking shandy, another person sat watching him from a discreet distance. At 12.30am Judge left with his girlfriend and walked out into the carpark. He said good-night to the doormen and walked to a white Ford Fiesta car. Just as he was about to start the car, a figure emerged from the shadows and ran up to the driver's door. He fired two shots into the back of The Psycho's head. The underworld's most feared executioner slumped over the driver's seat, dead. A lot of people heaved a sigh of relief at the news.

Only a few individuals actually know who pulled the trigger on The Psycho. He had a lot of enemies and a lot of people were afraid of him. But there have been two main theories. The main one favoured by investigators is that it was the IRA who had decided to take out one of the city's top heroin godfathers. There had been a lot of concern in Judge's neighbourhood about what he had done to Corbally and also about the amount of heroin being sold to the local kids. Judge had shown that he couldn't care less about what anyone thought. And he was clearly as unafraid of the Provos as he was of other criminals or the police. Several major figures in the Republican movement across west and north Dublin were subsequently arrested and questioned about the murder, but no-one was charged and no serious evidence was gleaned. It was a professional hit.

The other theory is that Mark Dwyer, Judge's one-time partner in crime, either organised or actually did the killing himself. It is believed that Dwyer was terrified that Judge was going to kill him because he thought he had been the gang member talking to the Gardaí and the newspapers.

There is a third, equally likely possibility – that it was someone close to Judge, someone he trusted, who did the deed. The motive? To take over his money and his operation and probably avoid becoming the object of the Psycho's obsessive paranoia in the future. The truth will probably never be known.

On Wednesday, 11 December, Peter Joseph Judge was laid to rest in Glasnevin cemetery, next to his father. A lot of the city's major-league criminals were conspicuous by their absence. It wasn't wise to be seen mourning The Psycho. Three days later gangland was stunned by a second murder. Mark Dwyer, the young drug dealer who had helped Judge murder Jock Corbally, was himself abducted by armed and masked men in the early hours of Saturday, 14 December.

Dwyer was brutally tortured, beaten and stabbed with a baseball bat and a nail bar. It bore chilling similarities to the circumstances of Corbally's murder. After his ordeal Dwyer was brought to the same field at Scribblestown Lane where Michael Godfrey was murdered. He was put kneeling on the ground with his hands and legs tied. He was finished off with a shotgun blast to the back of the head. A murder trial would later be told that Dwyer died because £40,000 worth of ecstasy tablets he was transporting were stolen and he was the main suspect. One of Dwyer's associates, Scott Delaney, was subsequently convicted of taking part in the murder. A year later, the bloodbath continued when another gangland figure, Anthony 'Chester' Beattie, was shot dead in a Dublin pub for allegedly taking part in the murder of Dwyer.

At the time of writing, over two-and-a-half years after his disappearance, the body of William Jock Corbally is still missing. His grave has long since been overgrown and may never be found. Gardaí have conducted several intensive searches for the body in areas of Kildare where members of Judge's gang believe he was disposed of. Tragically for his family the secret of where his body lies probably died with The Psycho. His family, and particularly Jock's mother, say they will never mourn his death until his body has been found and he is given a Christian burial. The doctor whom The Psycho terrorised has rebuilt his life. He never got his car back. Judge had it burned out to prevent the police obtaining any forensic evidence from the murder. After May 1996 he left the medic alone.

Peter Joseph Judge will never be forgotten in gangland. Apart from a few relatives and close friends, he is not missed. Just before his murder he recorded a message on the voice-mail of his mobile phone, which still hovers around out there in cyberspace. On it Judge reminds the caller: 'Hello. I'm not here right now. Leave your number and I'll get back to you. Thank you.'

The Builder

In gangland there is a well-worn cliché: once a criminal always a criminal. For a gangster to go straight is an aspiration sneered at by both the villains themselves and the police who catch them. And the constant high rate of recidivism tends to justify the cynics. The commonly-held belief in the underworld is that the armed robber or drug dealer who has done time will eventually go back to being 'at it'. It's what was referred to in Tarantino's movie *Pulp Fiction* as 'the Life'. Once you are in you never get out. The tragic fate of former gangster Paddy Shanahan is proof of the theory.

The tall, burly robber-turned-builder was gunned down because he tried to break his links with gangland. He had retired from crime and had become a successful, legitimate business man until a disapproving Dublin godfather sent an assassin to give him the message – when he wouldn't play the game the gangster's way it was decided he would never play any game again.

Paddy Shanahan was considered something of a peculiarity in the underworld. He came from a respectable country family with no criminal background of any kind. He was well-educated and a good businessman. Born on 16 November 1946, he was one of three children and grew up in a modest gatehouse in the picturesque village of Kill in County Kildare, the heart of Ireland's horse-breeding country. His father Con worked as a groom in a nearby stud and the young Shanahan enjoyed a happy, trouble-free childhood, unlike most of his future partners in crime.

Shanahan was a model youngster who enjoyed the admiration of his peers. He was a bright, tough, physically well-built kid who liked sport. He was also a handsome young man who didn't smoke or drink in his formative years. He was enterprising and the first among his friends to own a car. Paddy was considered an excellent pupil who was destined for great things when he attended the Christian Brothers school in nearby Naas. He left post-primary school with a good leaving certificate and went on to study English and history in University College, Dublin. He dropped out of his course after one year and went to work in England for a short time. He returned in 1970 and began working for Burmah Oil as a sales representative. He left during the oil crisis in 1976, and in the same year he married Dublin woman, Miriam O'Dwyer.

Shanahan became an auctioneer and owned a tarmacadam business for a while. Then he began turning his hand to another business for which he had a natural aptitude – crime. Shanahan considered serious crime a glamorous occupation. The former Christian Brothers' star pupil actually made a conscious decision to become a criminal. He harboured romantic notions of holding up a bank at gunpoint and making off at high speed in a getaway car. But he just couldn't walk into an office and fill out an application. Joining such a rarefied breed was as difficult as getting started in any of the more exclusive professions in the legitimate world.

In the mid-1970s he began to associate with individuals on the periphery of organised crime in Dublin. Gradually he got to know Joey Skerrit, an armed robber from the south inner-city. Skerrit 'worked' with the Dunne brothers, Christy ('Bronco'), Shamie, Larry and Henry, who, at that time, were the most respected blaggers in gangland. When Shanahan won Skerrit's trust he was introduced to 'Bronco' and Henry. At first, the Dunnes were extremely suspicious of the enthusiastic, well-spoken 'culchie'. Dublin villains were close-knit and clannish and not well-disposed to outsiders. After all, most of the police who upset their business were from the country.

When the Dunnes took Shanahan on 'jobs', they were impressed by his ability. Henry Dunne would later recall how he and the rest of the gang were perplexed by the 'culchie': 'He loved crime; he was fascinated by the whole thing. He wasn't like the rest of us. We did it for a living, he did it for the sheer buzz. When we went on a stroke, it was like he was acting in a movie. He was a complete Walter Mitty character. He loved dressing up and handling guns. We often had to warn him that the shooters were only being used to frighten the people in the bank and to prevent any heroics. He was the type who seemed like he wanted to blow someone away. Fortunately he didn't get the chance.'

On one robbery Shanahan even scared the other gang members. They were holding a postmaster at gun point in his home and demanding that he open a night-safe holding the cash. When the terrified postmaster told the gang he could not open the safe Shanahan decided to push him a little further. He grabbed the man's child and held a gun to its head. 'We had to stop Paddy. No one wanted to hurt a little kid and we left the place. We didn't get any money but it showed how far Paddy was prepared to go to prove he had what it took to be a blagger. It was fuckin' scary and we didn't like him doing that,' recalls one of the robbers. Another criminal who worked with Shanahan had similar recollections of the 'culchie': 'He was capable of anything. Before doing a stroke he would be checking himself in the mirror to make sure he looked the part. He loved dressing up in different disguises, as a cop or a woman.'

Eventually, Henry Dunne introduced Shanahan to Martin Cahill. The General checked him out thoroughly before taking him into the gang. Shanahan's first robbery with Cahill was a raid on a cigarette wholesaler's warehouse in Johnstown, County Kildare. Shanahan, who now lived in the area, did the surveillance for the 'job'. The gang got away with over £100,000 worth of cigarettes. Shanahan later branched out and worked with other up-and-coming robbers. He and another criminal regularly robbed mailbags from the same Kildare train for a number of years without being caught. At the height of his 'blagging' career, Shanahan never came to the notice of the police in Ireland. But outside the country he wasn't quite as lucky.

Shanahan began travelling back to England and teaming up with London criminals for robberies. In 1980 he was caught by the police in Staffordshire after taking part in an antiques robbery with two East End villains, Alan Wilson and Nicholas Boyd. The three thieves called to the home of retired doctor Sam Firman, a well-known collector. Shanahan and his cronies posed as delivery men to get into the house. The seventy-two-year-old man was threatened with an iron bar, bound with sticky tape and left lying on the floor of his home during the raid. He suffered a heart attack and almost died. Shanahan administered first aid to keep him alive.

The gang stole antique clocks, watches, Japanese ivory figures, jade, gems and cash valued at £361,000. They smashed another £9,000 worth of valuables while ransacking the place. Following the heist, the police found a receipt book from which forensic examination uncovered the imprint of Shanahan's address in England. Within a week, he and his two henchmen were arrested and charged. On 29 May 1981, Shanahan was jailed for six years by Stafford Crown Court. He was thirty-five years old and described in court as an Irish estate agent. Alan Wilson received ten years and Nicholas Boyd seven years for their part in the crime. Shanahan was released after serving half of his sentence and returned to Ireland in 1984. The following year, his wife Miriam gave birth to a son, John, who would be the couple's only child. In the meantime Shanahan went back to working with the gangs.

In 1986 detectives keeping an eye on the General's gang began spotting an unknown man meeting with them on a regular basis. An intelligence report from Crumlin Garda station was passed to the Central Detective Unit. It read: 'A man named as Patrick Shanahan of Johnstown, Naas, County Kildare, is keeping company with our criminals as of late. We think it best to pay closer attention to this gentleman.' It was the first time Shanahan had come to the notice of the Gardaí.

At the time, Shanahan had good reason to be meeting with The General and his cronies. Before the Staffordshire robbery Paddy Shanahan had realised the value of antiques. Throughout Europe there was a huge black market, with plenty of willing customers prepared to pay for stolen heirlooms. Ireland's big country estate houses were full of millions of pounds worth of treasure which Shanahan would have little difficulty offloading through his under-world contacts in London. Upon his return from his prison sentence he began taking a keen interest in Sir Alfred Beit's splendid mansion,

Russborough House in County Wicklow, ten miles from Dublin.

The retired Westminster MP was a member of a wealthy South African diamond-mining family and had come to live in Ireland in 1952. Among the belongings which he brought to his new home was a priceless collection of art masterpieces, including works by Vermeer, Goya and Metsu. In 1974 Sir Alfred hit world headlines when an armed IRA gang stole nineteen of the paintings. Led by Dr Rose Dugdale, the daughter of an English millionaire, the Provos demanded a ransom of £500,000 as well as the transfer from English to Northern Ireland prisons of the Price sisters, who were serving jail terms for car bombings in London. Dugdale was caught eleven days later and the paintings recovered.

In 1985 Shanahan had discussed his plans to hit Russborough House with a London gang specialising in robberies of antiques. They were fully aware of Sir Alfred and his treasure. The patrician gentleman had featured in a number of television programmes in Britain, discussing his priceless collection and the failed Provo attempt to steal them in the name of the 'cause'. The London gangsters and Shanahan were particularly interested in the furniture, clocks and Ming porcelain, which were also featured on TV and for which there was a ready market.

Shanahan began 'casing' Russborough House. Then he made the mistake of discussing the potential of such a robbery with Martin Cahill, who was immediately interested in the idea of such a spectacular crime. Shanahan needed the General and his men to do the actual robbery. Then he and his English criminal cronies would take care of the rest of the job. But Cahill had other ideas. In May Shanahan went to London to get an underworld alarm expert to bypass the security system at Russborough House. The wily General pretended to go along with Shanahan's plan, but meanwhile went behind his back and organised his own heist.

On the night of 21 May 1986, Cahill and his gang walked into the Palladian-style mansion and made off with eleven of the most valuable works in the collection. It was the second biggest art robbery in history, but would bring nothing but bad luck to The General and his men. Shanahan was furious that he had been double-crossed and chided Cahill for taking the wrong stuff. He told The General that it would be extremely difficult to sell such world-renowned works of art. He was right. Nevertheless, Shanahan took part in two early attempts to sell the paintings through his contacts in London. But the paintings were literally too hot to handle. The police in several countries worked together to set a trap for the thieves and Shanahan decided it wasn't worth the risk.

After the Beit robbery, Shanahan began to lose his enthusiasm for participating in crime. In 1988 the Gardaí mounted a high-profile overt surveillance operation on the Cahill gang and Shanahan found himself the object of the Tango Squad's attentions. The surveillance team watched as The General regularly disappeared across the rear wall of Shanahan's home at Oak Apple Green in Rathgar, which he had bought in 1987. The former auctioneer did not like the attention Cahill was bringing on him and moved back into legitimate business. Over the following years he would sever his links with Cahill.

Shanahan became a property developer in Dublin and let it be known to the police that he was no longer involved in crime. In the meantime, however, he had begun associating with a number of crime figures on the north-side of the city who had a lot of money to launder. The criminals considered themselves a cut above the likes of Cahill and were interested in investing their ill-gotten gains. The building business was the perfect front. And posing as a respectable businessman, with no arrests or convictions recorded against him in the Republic, Shanahan became the ideal money launderer. He formed a loose cartel consisting of four major gangland figures who were involved in a variety of crimes including armed robbery, fraud and drugs.

Garda intelligence reported regular sightings of Shanahan meeting with the big north-side names. But, in the absence of proper money-laundering legislation, the police were powerless to do anything about this new business cartel. Shanahan had also obtained a number of legitimate mortgages and was involved in building projects around the city. In 1988 he refurbished an old apartment complex in south-west Dublin in conjunction with some of the members of the underworld cartel. The following year he bought eighty dilapidated tenement flats in Buckingham Street in the north inner-city. The property was paid for with a bank loan. Shanahan also built an additional block of twenty apartments on the site.

The development, which he named Buckingham Village, was an extremely successful venture. It was one of the first major investments in the depressed inner-city, before the construction boom began in the mid-1990s. The new apartments were rented mainly by recipients of Eastern Health Board rental support. Shanahan worked on the site fourteen hours a day and earned a reputation as an efficient builder, who turned out good work within his contract deadline. He was, however, considered to be somewhat hot-headed and argumentative. 'Paddy was a hot-tempered man and could be rough and ready, but he was a hard worker and ensured everyone he dealt with was paid fair and square. He was still a gentleman,' a builder recalled.

Shanahan bought up a number of other sites around the city and in County Kildare. Including the apartments he still owned in Buckingham Village, his property portfolio was valued at over £1.25 million in the early 1990s, about £5 million at 1998 prices. In 1993 Shanahan went into partnership with a respectable veterinary surgeon from the midlands, who had a number of property interests in Dublin and knew nothing of Shanahan's involvement in crime. He had obtained planning permission to build Drury Hall, a development of forty-three apartments and five retail units on Stephen's Street, in the heart of the business district of south-central Dublin. A construction company in which Shanahan had a large share, Side South Limited, constructed Drury Hall for £1.5 million and financial backing for the project was provided by a commercial bank. The development was another huge success and the apartments and shop units were sold off the plans.

The former oil salesman and armed robber-turned-builder stood to make in the region of £2 million profit from the project. He was making more money from hard work than he had from holding up banks and post-offices. In mid-1994 he began looking at other projects, including one a few yards from Drury Hall at the corner of Stephen's Street and George's Street. He planned to erect another sixty-five apartments and several shop units there and stood to make over £4 million from the venture. He was on the way to becoming a very wealthy man. But his connections with the underworld were coming back to haunt him.

In his business dealings Shanahan was a secretive man and did not confide in other people. His papers were stuffed into a yellow folder which he carried everywhere with him in his Pajero jeep. Not even his wife knew the full extent of his dealings. Sources interviewed for this book believe that Shanahan had more or less ceased his business dealings with the underworld cartel by the time he commenced the Buckingham Village development. Most of the individuals involved had made tidy profits. They also had the trappings of legitimacy behind which they could hide their ill-gotten gains. The arrangement over, they went their way and Shanahan went his. But one gangster had other ideas. He still had large amounts of cash he wanted to invest and he was greedy to match Shanahan's success. When the builder refused to work with him any longer, there was a blazing row. The gangster was angry. He was also jealous. Together, jealousy, anger and greed are a dangerous mixture of emotions. In gangland they are deadly.

On 18 August 1994, Shanahan's former partner in crime, Martin Cahill, was assassinated in Ranelagh, south Dublin, by an IRA hit-man. He had failed to sell off the Beit paintings. Instead, he had incurred the wrath of the Provos by trying to dispose of them through loyalist terrorists in Northern Ireland. The killing stunned the underworld.

In the weeks that followed the murder, Shanahan appeared to be extremely stressed. He confided to a friend that his former gangster partner had threatened to kill him. Those who worked with him on the Drury Hall site recalled that he was under cash-flow pressure to pay construction workers and suppliers. But in the beginning of September 1994 he began having serious panic attacks or seizures. He would collapse and be short of breath, as if suffering a heart attack.

On one Saturday afternoon in September he collapsed unconscious on the site and was given heart massage and mouth-to-mouth resuscitation to revive him. When he recovered, he would not allow anyone to call an ambulance, explaining that he had forgotten tablets he had been prescribed for a blocked artery in his neck. An autopsy would later show that he was in perfect health.

At home his wife Miriam also noticed how stressed Shanahan had become. She began receiving anonymous phone calls from a female claiming he was having an affair with another woman. Shanahan was distressed by the calls and warned his wife not to go out alone any more, especially at night. He also told Miriam that he wanted to be cremated if he died. He was deadly serious. The panic attacks continued. Paddy Shanahan was suffering his own personal hell at a time when he should have been enjoying his success. He was living in absolute fear for his own life and the safety of his family. But apart from one friend he confided in no-one. He did not even ask other criminal friends to help 'sort out' his problems.

On Friday, 14 October, Shanahan seemed more relaxed than in previous weeks. He paid the workers their wages and waited late for a delivery of concrete to the site. Most evenings after work he and his storeman, James Moran, went training in Sphere's Squash and Gym Club in Drimnagh. The two had been close friends since Moran began working for him in Buckingham Village. Shanahan had joined the club two years earlier and liked to keep fit, although he had slowed down somewhat in the previous few weeks since he began suffering the attacks. He was also receiving private karate lessons at the club which he never missed. The two friends arrived at the club shortly after 7pm. Shanahan parked his jeep in the carpark in front of the gym.

As he began walking towards the gym door, he asked Moran to check that he had locked the jeep properly. As Moran did so, a lone figure stepped out in front of Shanahan. He stood two feet away from the builder and fired a single shot from a pistol, hitting his victim in the face. Shanahan fell back onto the ground. The assassin turned and walked to the pedestrian exit. He fumbled with the latch of a gate before walking onto the nearby road. He kept his head down and jogged off, disappearing into the busy traffic and the darkening autumn evening. Two days later, on Sunday 16 October, Paddy Shanahan, former criminal, successful builder, died as the result of a massive internal head injury. He had been clinically 'brain dead' since the shooting.

In the hours following the shooting the Gardaí began yet another gangland murder investigation. Several individuals were arrested and questioned. A file requesting a prosecution in relation to the case was turned down by the Director of Public Prosecutions on the grounds that the evidence was not strong enough to sustain a conviction. According to Garda records, the Shanahan murder case is closed. The hitman has never been identified and the gangster suspected of ordering the murder is still prospering. In the end the continued existence of Paddy Shanahan would not have changed the gangster's fortunes. Like many gangland executions it was needless.

Four months later, in January 1995, there was a bizarre reminder of the Shanahan murder. The Pajero jeep he had been driving at the time of his murder was stolen and used by an armed north-side gang to rob over £3.5 million from the Brinks Allied cash holding depot in Clonshaugh, Dublin. Was it a symbolic tribute from the robbers to a former colleague who had gone straight, or was it just coincidence? It is just another of gangland's imponderables.

The Hitman and
The Penguin

Mickey Boyle was a one-man serious crime wave. His career in gangland spanned four decades and was more varied than those of most of the underworld's other luminaries. Boyle did it all. His *curriculum vitae* makes chilling reading. He progressed from being a burglar to being a professional armed robber. Then he added extortion and kidnapping to his achievements, before becoming a cold-blooded hitman for the mob. He was single-handedly responsible for a reign of terror and was both highly intelligent and totally callous. He was also rather unlucky in his activities and was caught several times. But no matter how often he was sent down he remained undeterred. In fact, his crimes grew more serious after each prison stretch.

Like Paddy Shanahan, Boyle came from a respectable, crime-free background and was well educated. Born in November 1946, he grew up in Bray, County Wicklow. The second eldest of six children – three boys and three girls – his father was a sergeant in the Irish Army and his mother a legal secretary. His home was at Scott Park, a modest terrace of ten houses with well-kept gardens, in the seaside town. One former neighbour recalls the family: 'His parents were decent, honest people who wanted to see their children doing well. His brothers and sisters all have good jobs and are decent like their mother and father.'

Boyle is remembered as a quiet, intelligent young man, a smart dresser with an athletic build. An accomplished sportsman, he played hurling and football for his county. Boyle studied for his Leaving Certificate at the Presentation College in the town, and was described as a hard-working, trouble-free student. 'Michael was a very talented young man who could turn his hand to anything. All of the family were very bright and he in particular had a brilliant mind,' the same neighbour gushed in admiration, appearing incredulous that he turned out to be an assassin instead of an academic. For when he left school Mickey Boyle quickly jettisoned his past.

He began hanging around with a number of local petty thieves. He worked as a builder's labourer and augmented his wages from the proceeds of burglaries. He liked to operate alone, and soon came to the attention of the police. He chalked up his first criminal conviction at the age of twenty, when he was given three months for burglary, larceny and escaping from custody. He was out again in a matter of weeks.

The year 1969 was a particularly hectic one for Boyle. He made what, in gangland terms, could be described as an impressive entrance into the 'business'. In February, he was jailed for fifteen months for seven cases of burglary and another seven for larceny and car theft. The following month, while serving this sentence, he got another six months for larceny and burglary. In May he was back in court again. This time he got a six-month sentence for burglary, larceny and escaping from custody. In October he was sent down for another four years for an armed robbery and possession of a firearm. Boyle had broken into the home of a widow in Shankill and held her up at gun-point.

When he was in Mountjoy for the Shankill robbery, Boyle married his girlfriend, Breda Moran from Dundrum. The couple would have two children. Boyle inveigled his way from the prison into Dundrum Mental Hospital, from which he then managed to escape. He was re-arrested and sent back to Mountjoy. In prison, Boyle's reputation as a young hot-headed desperado greatly impressed the older lags. He was befriended by some of Dublin's more notorious criminals and also by members of the quasi-Republican group, Saor Éire. The group, which had no political ideology, specialised in robbing banks for their own personal profit and a vague 'cause'. Saor Éire were responsible for the murder of Garda Dick Fallon during a heist in Dublin in 1970. He was the first Garda casualty in a crime war which was only beginning and would claim many lives over the next three decades. Boyle himself would be a formidable player.

He learned a lot from his new-found friends and admirers. After he was released in 1972, Boyle joined the British Army, but he deserted after a short stay in the ranks, going back to his wife and family in Bray. With his return came another crime wave. On 14 January 1973, Mickey Boyle was arrested and charged with fourteen burglaries. He was released on bail. Soon Boyle began to show he was not someone to be messed with. In September of that year he had a falling out with another local criminal, William Manley. A few days later, Manley was shot and injured by Boyle, who was armed with a rifle. Boyle was subsequently arrested but never charged due to insufficient evidence. Manley was too scared to give evidence against the gunman. Manley recovered from his injuries and he and Boyle made up their differences. Boyle admitted to him that he had been responsible for the shooting. However, the rapprochement did not last long.

On the nights of 22 and 23 February 1974, Boyle was out proving his hardman status again with the aid of his rifle. He fired shots into Manley's home. He also fired shots into the home of an acquaintance of his, James Davis, a married father of two children, who owned a garage in Bray. Manley and Davis both later identified Boyle as the shooter and he was arrested and charged with the offences the following day. On 8 March Boyle was again granted bail, despite vigorous opposition from the local Gardaí, who warned that he was fast becoming an extremely dangerous gangster. As his reputation for violence and intimidation grew, it became increasingly difficult for the Gardaí to prove cases against him, because witnesses were afraid to go to court. The lenient bail laws in Ireland would continue to frustrate the police in their dealings with gangland for over two decades. The laws are only being reformed in the final years of the twentieth century.

Mickey Boyle continued to pursue his career as an armed robber. At 12.53pm on Monday, 6 May 1974, Allied Irish Bank officials John Houston and William Doran were leaving the bank's sub-office in Enniskerry, County Wicklow. The two men were placing a briefcase containing £1,970 in used notes into the boot of Houston's car when a car screeched to a stop beside them. A masked man in a combat jacket and holding a pistol jumped out of the car. He pushed Doran from behind, knocking him to the ground, and ordered Houston to stand back. Boyle snatched the briefcase and two sacks of loose change, jumped back into the car and sped off. As he disappeared, the stunned bank employees heard a gunshot.

Boyle and his accomplice later dumped the car in a disused sandpit. The following day, Boyle went to collect the guns he had used in the robbery from a hiding-place at the base of Fassaroe Glen, a deep valley covered in furze, near a local dump. Hours earlier the Gardaí had recovered the gun and a number of jackets when they found the hide during a search of the area. They had also found the car used by the robbers in the sandpit two miles away. A detective who was on duty watching the glen spotted Boyle rummaging through the undergrowth. He approached him and asked who he was and what he was doing there. The bank robber calmly replied that he was 'Billy Manley from up the road'. He also told the detective that he regularly went shooting in the area. The real Manley had twice been the victim of Boyle's gun attacks. The police later positively identified the man they had approached as Mickey Boyle. He was their prime suspect for the robbery but, even with the recovered gun and other items, they didn't have enough evidence to charge him. He was arrested and questioned but denied all knowledge of the heist. The money was never recovered.

Meanwhile, Boyle's trial on the shooting incidents in February had been set for hearing in Wicklow Circuit Criminal Court on 4 July. But he had other plans. Shortly after the Enniskerry robbery Boyle approached William Manley and his wife Bridget on Main Street in Bray. He told Manley that if he gave evidence at the trial he would be shot. Manley and his wife reported the threats to the local police. Manley also wrote to the Department of Justice seeking police protection, because he was now terrified for himself and his family.

Detective Sergeant Hugh Hume was the man heading the various investigations into Boyle's activities. He had often expressed his frustration that the courts continued to grant Boyle bail despite the fact that he had clearly breached the conditions of his release several times. Armed with a statement from the Manleys, Hume immediately had Boyle's bail revoked and he was taken back into custody. Hume successfully objected to several subsequent attempts by Boyle to get bail in the Circuit Court, High Court and Supreme Court, on the grounds that vital witnesses would be intimidated and harmed if Boyle were free.

But the terror tactic was working. In May a bench warrant was issued for Manley's arrest when he failed to appear for the prosecution at Boyle's remand hearing in Bray District Court. In an affidavit to the High Court, Detective Sergeant Hume explained that Manley had disappeared out of fear. At the same time, two other witnesses vital to the State's case, James Davis and another man, were treated as hostile witnesses. In their initial statements to the Gardaí, the pair had clearly identified Boyle as the man responsible for the shooting incident at Davis's home. In court, they gave evidence contradicting these statements. Like Manley, they were terrified of the gunman.

In fact, it would emerge that Davis, out of fear of Boyle, had patched up his differences with the mad robber and they became 'friends' while Boyle was still awaiting trial for shooting into his house. Twenty-four-year-old Davis, who had known Boyle since he was a teenager, realised what he was capable of doing and obviously felt that the Gardaí and the courts were unable to protect him. He had given Boyle a lift on the morning of the Enniskerry robbery. The evening before the planned heist, Boyle's stolen getaway car had run out of petrol as he was casing the bank. Davis, initially unaware of what was going on, had got him a can of petrol and drove him to the stranded car. Boyle's accomplice, a criminal from Bray, was also given a lift in Davis's car. The two hoods had discussed their plans for the heist in front of the unwitting Davis. They were not afraid that Davis might talk. They knew he was too scared to open his mouth.

The result of Boyle's trial, which was adjourned to the Circuit Court on 11 November 1974, was a foregone conclusion. The charge of shooting at Davis's home was withdrawn by order of the judge on the grounds that there was insufficient evidence to sustain the charge. The judge also instructed the jury to find Boyle not guilty of the

Manley shooting charge. This case illustrated how slow the criminal justice system was in adjusting to the new phenomenon of organised crime. Mickey Boyle walked from the court a free man.

Unfortunately for the banks in the area, Boyle was also broke following his six-month remand in custody. After all, he had even had to borrow money from one of his own victims. On the morning of 28 November, Boyle stole a green Ford Cortina car from outside a house in the Deans Grange area of south County Dublin. He drove alone to Wicklow town with the intention of withdrawing some money with the aid of his handgun.

When he got to the town, he decided to abort the robbery because there were too many police on the streets. He drove along the back-roads to the sleepy country town of Rathdrum. At 10.40am Boyle marched into the town's only bank, the Bank of Ireland, shouting, 'This is a raid'. He was brandishing a revolver and his face was covered with a pair of nylon tights. He ordered the staff and customers to stand with their hands on the bank counter. He threw a carrier-bag to one of the tellers and told him to fill it. When the bag was full Boyle backed out the front door and warned that if anyone pressed the alarm bell he would come back and 'bullets would fly'. He ran outside, got into the car and drove north in the direction of Roundwood village. Between Roundwood and Newtownmountkennedy the stolen car, which had a faulty petrol gauge, ran out of fuel. Boyle abandoned the car and hiked across the Sugar Loaf mountain and back home to Bray. He had got over £4,000 in cash. By today's values it was a significant haul.

That afternoon he called to see James Davis at his garage and told him about what had happened in Rathdrum. Later that day Boyle returned to Davis's garage with copies of the *Evening Herald* and *Evening Press*, and read the reports of the robbery to Davis and his mechanic, George McGlashan. He handed them the newspapers and said how flattered he was that he had been described as much younger than his actual age, twenty-eight. Later that night, Boyle went drinking with McGlashan, Davis and a third man, Shay O'Reilly. He regaled all three with the story of how he had pulled off the robbery earlier that morning. He didn't even warn his boozing companions to keep their mouths shut. He reckoned they were too scared to spill the beans. It was a fatal miscalculation.

Back in the headquarters of the Central Detective Unit, which was then housed in Dublin Castle, a conference was held to discuss the continuing crime wave in the south County Dublin and north Wicklow area. Mickey Boyle had been their prime suspect for a long time. At the conference it was revealed how difficult it had been to make a case against Boyle because people were so scared of him. A team of detectives from the CDU and the Investigation Section of the Technical Bureau, based at St John's Road, were dispatched to Bray, Enniskerry and Rathdrum to assist the local units in their investigation. The team was under the command of Detective Sergeant John Courtney, who would later become the head of the Murder Squad.

The investigation team drew up a list of all of Boyle's known acquaintances. On 15 December the squad made their breakthrough. McGlashan, Davis and O'Reilly attended Greystones Garda station. All three gave the investigation team full statements, outlining what Boyle had told them at the various stages before and after the robbery in Rathdrum. The investigation team also succeeded in tracing some of the money stolen in the Rathdrum heist, which had been used by Boyle to pay for two cars.

On the morning of 16 December, Mickey Boyle was arrested under Section 30 of the Offences Against the State Act. When Detective Sergeant Courtney informed Boyle of the statements which had been made against him, he denied all knowledge of the crime. Then he said to the detectives: 'I'm fucked now. I'm not going to incriminate myself by making a statement. It's their word against mine. That finishes me with the family. If I go inside this time they'll be better off without me. I think the best chance I have is to keep my mouth shut. I have nothing to gain by helping and nothing to lose by not helping.'

Later that morning, Boyle was charged before a peace commissioner in Bray with robbing the Bank of Ireland in Rathdrum, possession of a firearm with intent to endanger life and having possession of a firearm without a firearms certificate. He was remanded to Mountjoy Prison.

Three days later, James Davis arranged an appointment to meet with Detective Garda Christy Godkin at Bray station. Davis told the detective that he was very anxious to make a statement regarding the earlier robbery in Enniskerry. He told the policeman that he was sorry he had not come forward earlier. Davis gave a full and frank statement about his involvement with Boyle. Davis, O'Reilly and McGlashan told the Gardaí that they were willing to give evidence against Boyle.

In April 1975 Mickey Boyle went on trial in the Central Criminal Court in Dublin. Always the desperado, he wasn't giving up without a fight – and it wasn't a legal one. On the second day of his trial in the Four Courts building in central Dublin, Boyle asked prison officers if he could go to the toilet. He was heavily guarded because of his earlier escapes and his reputation as a 'head case'. The officers dutifully stood outside a lavatory cubicle to allow the prisoner his dignity while relieving himself. Boyle, however, had only one kind of business on his mind. He reached into the cistern of the toilet and retrieved a pistol which had been carefully wrapped and left for him by one of his associates. Boyle flushed the toilet and walked out, waving the gun in the air and warning the shocked guards to back off. A number of accomplices were waiting for him around the building and the 'head case' vanished. He was recaptured two months later at a race meeting in Punchestown in County Kildare. Eventually, in July 1976, he was jailed for a total of ten years after pleading guilty to the two robbery charges. The Gardaí were happy to see what they thought was the end of their adversary. The crime wave abated considerably on his old stomping ground. But he would be back.

Boyle was released from prison in the middle of 1982, after serving six years of his stretch. He was thirty-six years old and about to briefly enter his third decade in serious crime. Although he hated life inside, Boyle was anything but reformed. This time the relentless hoodlum decided to apply his criminal mind to an even nastier and more terrifying activity than armed robbery – kidnapping.

In the late 1970s and early 1980s, Republican paramilitaries had been responsible for a spate of kidnappings around the country. In 1981 they abducted supermarket tycoon Ben Dunne from his Dublin home and held him for five days. He was released after a reported £750,000 had been paid in ransom. In another two cases, the daughters of two County Louth bank managers were kidnapped and released for ransoms in excess of £50,000. During his time in prison Boyle was closely associated with a number of paramilitary prisoners and became convinced that kidnapping was a much more lucrative crime. Within weeks of getting out Mickey Boyle was back in business. He formed a small gang and went straight back to work. He was closely connected with two well-known Provos, in Kingscourt and Virginia, County Cavan, and he was regularly observed travelling to meet them in the months following his departure from prison.

County Wicklow is a rich man's paradise – and a kidnapper's dream. Some of the country's wealthiest business people and professionals live in this breathtaking landscape of rolling hills and valleys. It is a beautiful place to live – if you can afford it. A short drive south of Dublin, it offers a tranquil world away from the hustle and bustle of the city. Magnificent mansions are dotted throughout the green carpet of lush forest. Mickey Boyle knew every forest, valley and back-road across north County Wicklow. He had spent a lot of his childhood trekking across the hills and the forests.

In the first six months of 1983 Boyle was responsible for at least six abductions where ransom demands were paid. None of them was reported to the police, because of the terror Boyle instilled in his victims. In one case a wealthy businessman who lived near Enniskerry, in the foothills of the Wicklow mountains, was forced to pay £25,000 in cash for the safe return of his wife. Earlier, an armed and masked man had entered his home and taken his wife hostage. The businessman was instructed to collect the cash from his bank and hand it over at a pre-arranged location somewhere in the Wicklow hills. Boyle's tactic was to demand a sum of money that he knew the victim could procure without causing suspicion in the bank.

Boyle told the man that his wife would be held in the woods and she would be shot dead if he called the cops. He left the house with the woman. The businessman rang his bank branch and told the manager to have the cash ready in used notes for his collection and not to ask any questions. On his way to collect the cash his car ran low on petrol. At a self-service station the businessman put £10 of fuel in his car, threw a £20 note on the forecourt and sped off. After the money was paid over, the businessman was informed that his wife was locked in the garage at their home. When the Gardaí were later informed of the incident, it didn't take long to pinpoint a suspect. At the time, Garda intelligence reports suggested that there had been other such abductions in the same area but that the victims had not come forward. Boyle was arrested under Section 30 of the Offences Against the State Act. He told the police nothing and two people, a leading barrister (now dead) and a known Provo, provided alibis for him. Boyle was released without charge.

William Somerville, a well-known solicitor, lived with his family at Dargle Hill, a large split-level house on a fifty-acre farm less than a mile from the picturesque village of Enniskerry. In the last weeks of July 1983, unknown to himself or his family, he was under surveillance by Boyle. On 9 August the gangster made his move. William Somerville and his wife Manon went for a short drive around 10pm, leaving their fourteen-year-old son James feeding his dogs in the yard at the house. As the Somervilles' car pulled out of the driveway Boyle, wearing a combat jacket and a stocking over his head and armed with a sawn-off shotgun, appeared out of the bushes. He ordered the teenager back inside. Boyle rummaged through the house and waited for the boy's parents to return home.

At 11pm the Somervilles walked in to find a masked man holding a gun to their son's head. Boyle told the horrified couple that he was taking their son hostage and demanded a ransom of £50,000 for his safe return. Manon Somerville pleaded with the gunman to take her instead. William Somerville suggested that he should be taken and his family left unharmed. Boyle told James Somerville to put on his coat and tied his hands. He took the kid outside but changed his mind and came back for the father.

Boyle and Somerville got into the solicitor's Range Rover. The solicitor was told to drive to the laneway on the St John of God's estate near Stillorgan in south County Dublin. When they were halfway up the lane of the estate Boyle ordered him to stop and get out. He tied Somerville to a tree. About twenty minutes later a car reversed up to where he was being held. A plastic bag was placed over Somerville's head and he was bundled into the back seat of the car. There was a second man in the car whom Boyle referred to as 'Harry'. 'Harry' was the owner of the car, Eugene Prunty, a thirty-two-year-old, unemployed fitter from Old Court in Bray. Boyle had picked Prunty because he had no criminal record and wasn't known to the police. The two had known each other since Boyle's release from prison.

The kidnappers drove to a forest near Kilpeddar, County Wicklow, and they tied Somerville to a tree with adhesive tape. They taped his knees, ankles and hands together, gagged him and left him there. At 2.15am Mrs Somerville called the Gardaí and arranged to meet them away from her home. Detective units from across south County Dublin and north Wicklow were alerted. Around 8am the following morning, Boyle left an apartment in Harold's Cross which he used for lying low and out of sight of the Gardaí. His girlfriend stayed in the apartment and he divided his time between her and his wife.

At 10.30am he met Prunty in Bray and they went to the Glenmalure pub. Boyle phoned the Somerville home. He told Mrs Somerville that her husband was in good health and, if she did as instructed, he would remain so. He told her the ransom was to be placed in two sacks at a location which would be given at a later time. The cash was to be in £10 and £5 notes. Unknown to the kidnapper, Gardaí were taping his conversation and a trace was being put on the call. The detectives keeping watch in the Somerville home instantly recognised Boyle's voice. Surveillance teams were ordered to locate him and keep him under observation from a discreet distance.

At 12 noon Boyle called again, this time from Lenihan's pub on Main Street in Bray. Mrs Somerville wanted assurances that her husband was safe. She told him that a business partner of her husband was arranging the collection of the ransom from the Northern Bank on College Green. It would be at least 4pm before the money was ready. Ten minutes before the noon phone call the team of surveillance officers spotted Mickey Boyle with Prunty, walking along the Main Street. When the two kidnappers left the pub, three undercover cops followed them. The pair were tailed to Wicklow town. They had lunch in the Grand Hotel, observed by a team of six detectives. They drove back to Bray, where Prunty went to the local Garda station – coincidentally the headquarters of the kidnap investigation – to present his licence and insurance documents. He had earlier been stopped at a routine Garda checkpoint and asked to present his documents.

Around 3.30pm William Somerville's business partner collected the money and brought it to Bray Garda station. Some of the cash was initialled so that it could be identified later. It was also photographed and the serial numbers noted. While the money was being collected Boyle rang the Somerville house again, earlier than agreed. He again reminded Mrs Somerville of what would happen to her husband if she didn't follow his instructions fully. As Boyle made the call, the surveillance team were watching him standing in the public phone box on Putland Road in the town.

At 4.10pm Boyle made his fourth call, this time from Lenihan's pub on Main Street in Bray. This time he spoke to Norman Brittain, Mrs Somerville's brother. Brittain told Boyle that the money was ready and asked for instructions on where to leave it. Boyle said he would call back at 5pm with the location. After making the call, Boyle and Prunty drove out of the town and the surveillance team lost sight of the two men. Shortly before 5pm Prunty was spotted again, walking back into Lenihan's pub. He left five minutes later and called the Somerville home from a public phone box on Main Street.

Prunty told Norman Brittain that the money was to be left in a burnt-out Rover car on Sandpit Lane, near Enniskerry. The car had been stolen by Boyle two weeks earlier at Merrion Square. Brittain requested that William Somerville be brought to the drop-off point, but Prunty replied that he was only relaying a message. Mrs

Somerville and her brother drove to Sandpit Lane and left the money as instructed, before returning home. Boyle observed the drop-off from a hide in the bushes nearby. When he saw that the coast was clear, he snatched the bags and disappeared again. The Gardaí had been informed of the location for the drop. At the same time as Boyle was making off with the loot, a team of heavily-armed police had surrounded another area. By the time the officers discovered they had gone to the wrong location, Boyle was well away.

A short time later, one of the surveillance teams circulating the Bray area spotted Prunty. At 6.20pm they moved in and arrested him. He was held at Bray Garda station. At 12.10am that night Boyle phoned the Somerville home and gave the family directions on how to locate William. Norman Brittain and a team of detectives found and released Somerville. He had been tied to the tree for almost twenty-four hours. On the same day Prunty was charged with demanding money with menaces from Norman Brittain. Meanwhile there was considerable embarrassment among the Garda top brass that Boyle had managed to get his hands on the kidnap ransom and escape. A manhunt was ordered across the country by Deputy Commissioner John Paul McMahon.

Detective Inspector Michael Canavan, who was based in Bray, was on holiday when the kidnapping took place. Canavan was one of the force's most experienced detectives, having been involved in the investigation of serious crime, terrorism and murder since the late 1960s. He was one of the youngest detectives ever appointed in the Dublin Metropolitan Area and had a formidable reputation as a tough and thorough investigator. He had recently been transferred to Bray from the Crime Investigation Section attached to Garda HQ. In that period he had made a point of acquainting himself with Mickey Boyle's activities. He had already ordered an investigation into the unreported abductions in the area. McMahon traced Canavan to where he was on holiday and asked him to return immediately.

During his earlier investigations, Canavan had become aware of the address of Boyle's girlfriend in Harold's Cross. On the morning of 12 October a team of detectives from the Serious Crime Squad, led by

Detective Inspector Gerry McCarrick, went to search the apartment. As they burst through the front door, Boyle jumped out the back. He was pursued by three police officers. Boyle, who was still a very athletic man, scaled several walls and managed to escape. In the meantime, Canavan ordered the arrest of Boyle's girlfriend. As a result of Canavan's enquiries, Boyle was arrested on 16 August, in Mulligan's pub on Poolbeg Street in Dublin, by Detective Sergeant Tom Scanlan and Detective Garda John McDermott from the Serious Crime Squad. Boyle was wearing a false wig and glasses at the time of his arrest.

Boyle was taken to Bray Garda station, but refused to make a statement. He had a rigid policy of never talking to the police or being seen to talk to the police. Canavan convinced Boyle that he had nothing to lose by giving up the ransom money. A few days later, Boyle agreed to tell Canavan where the money was. He drew a map pinpointing its location. When the police didn't find the money Boyle agreed to show them himself, but he would only travel to the spot in a Garda van with Canavan. In the corner of a field under straw they found the ransom money wrapped in Boyle's combat jacket.

On the evening of 18 August, Boyle was charged with the false imprisonment of William Somerville and also with demanding money with menaces. He was released on bail of £10,000. He appeared in court again on 9 September, and was further remanded to appear again on 21 October. But Mickey Boyle had other plans, of a less legal nature, for that particular day.

At 7 o'clock that morning, forty-six-year-old businessman Robert Manina and his wife Alma awoke to find an armed and masked man standing at the bottom of their bed in their home on Somerby Road in Greystones, County Wicklow. Mickey Boyle pointed a .45 revolver at the startled couple. A second man stood at the bedroom door, cradling a rifle in his arms. Boyle ordered the couple to shut up and lie face down on the pillows, covering themselves with the duvet. He demanded to know where their safe was. The couple replied that there was none. They listened as the gunmen rummaged through the house. After about ten minutes they were told to dress and herded downstairs. One of the two men grabbed Robert Manina by the back of the neck and began choking him. He let him go in the kitchen. The frightened couple tried to calm each other but were told, 'keep your fucking mouths shut.' Alma Manina was ordered to put on a coat and flat shoes and wear a scarf over her face. Boyle warned Robert Manina not to phone the police and told him that if he wanted to see his wife alive again he would have to pay a £60,000 ransom. The kidnappers left with his wife and drove off.

Boyle and his associate brought Alma Manina to an old, disused shed at the rear of a farmhouse garden in an area called Stylebawn in the rugged Rocky Valley, near Enniskerry. She was put sitting on an old mattress and locked into the shed which was used to store wood.

Meanwhile Robert Manina, who was distraught and in a panic, called a friend, Noel Geoghegan, to tell him what had happened. He wanted help in arranging payment of the ransom money. Coincidentally, Geoghegan lived next door to Chief Superintendent Michael Lynch, the officer in charge of the DMA Eastern Division and the man in overall control of the investigation into the Somerville kidnapping. He raised the alarm, and detective and uniformed units were told to watch out for one man – Mickey Boyle.

At 9.25am Detective Sergeant Basil Walsh and Detectives Michael Merrigan, Con O'Keefe and Gerry Ginty got a call to go to Stylebawn. They arrived at 9.35am and a local man told them of seeing two men acting suspiciously nearby. The four officers, with their weapons drawn, approached an area around a farmhouse. Behind the house Ginty and Merrigan spotted Mickey Boyle, standing beside the door of the concrete shed where he had just put his latest hostage.

Merrigan shouted at Boyle: 'Drop the gun, Michael.'

Boyle crouched down behind a stone wall and bushes. He darted across a garden and dived down between a wall and another shed.

He lifted the gun to aim at the pursuing cops. Detective Sergeant Walsh shouted: 'Armed Gardaí, drop the gun, Michael, and come out with your hands up.' Detective Ginty shouted at his colleagues to get down, as Boyle was about to fire. At the same time, Walsh fired two warning shots in the air. Boyle dropped his weapon and bolted, with Walsh after him. The kidnapper ran across a road and down along a rough, rugged valley. More shots were heard as Boyle struggled to shake off the cop. He ran through thick, thorny bushes. As he reached a roadway, Walsh jumped on him. He arrested Boyle, whose head and face were bleeding from the bushes. The other detectives found and released Alma Manina and brought her to Bray Garda station. It was 9.45am. Her ordeal had lasted less than three hours. Had things gone according to plan, Boyle could still have made it to court in Bray for his remand hearing.

As Boyle was being put in a squad car, he pleaded with the detectives: 'Shoot me, shoot me, I will get life for this anyway. I may as well be in now. There is nothing else left for me now. Come on, come on, do me a favour, shoot me now.' He was brought to an interview room in Bray station, where Detective Inspector Canavan was waiting to speak to him. Boyle was very shaken and shivering. He seemed depressed. Canavan asked Boyle for the name of the other masked gunman, who had escaped during the chase in the Rocky Valley. He told the DI: 'I was on my own, there was nobody with me. Ye have me for God's sake, what more do ye want? I will not incriminate anybody else.' Boyle added that he would not stand trial. Later he told Canavan: 'It's all over as far as I am concerned. I don't wish to talk about this thing any more, what is the point? I have let down everybody that meant something to me.' Boyle buried his head in his hands and refused to speak any more.

On the following afternoon, amid tight security, Boyle was formally arraigned in Bray District Court on four charges – false imprisonment, demanding money with menaces, possession of a firearm with intent to endanger life and using the same firearm to resist his arrest. This time Boyle, with his face covered in scratch marks, looked down at his feet. He did not seek bail. In July 1984 Boyle pleaded guilty to a total of six charges relating to the two kidnapping incidents. During his time on remand, Boyle suffered from depression and tried to kill himself. Sentencing Boyle to twelve years imprisonment, the judge described his crimes as 'detestable, appalling and horrid'. Boyle's partner in the Somerville kidnap, Eugene Prunty, subsequently went on trial in the Circuit Criminal Court, where he pleaded not guilty. During the trial, the prosecution played the recording of the call he made to the Somervilles, giving instructions as to where the ransom was to be left. Unfortunately for Prunty, he had a distinctive, high-pitched voice which was clearly distinguishable on the tape. He was convicted and sentenced to ten years in prison.

Mickey Boyle spent the rest of the 1980s behind bars. In the meantime, the underworld had become a much more sophisticated and brutal place. Drugs had become the stock-in-trade of most criminals, creating a new millionaire criminal elite. When he was eventually released in 1993, Boyle was almost forty-seven years old. Since he first got involved in crime he had served at least twenty years of his life behind bars, enough to have most gangsters considering retirement. But not Boyle. Within a short time the residents of north Wicklow were again being terrorised in their homes.

Extortion demands, armed robberies and kidnappings were inflicted on the area's wealthy citizens. Boyle saw nothing wrong with robbing the rich. Capitalism was a sin against the working classes. He was merely re-distributing wealth for their benefit. During the Summer of 1993, Boyle used the guise of leading a subversive group to organise a protection racket aimed at wealthy landlords and business people. In the early hours of 4 July, the stately home of the Earl and Countess of Meath near Bray was the target of an arson attack by Boyle. The fire destroyed the library, valuable furnishings, books and paintings. A few days after the attack the Earl of Meath, a popular figure in the local area, received letters from a 'group' demanding a large payment of cash to ensure the same thing did not happen again. In his letters Boyle stated that the group would attack British landlords throughout Ireland over the following months. Lord Meath immediately passed on the information to the Gardaí, who at first believed it was the work of a subversive group.

Letters demanding money were sent to a number of businessmen in the area. Again Boyle warned that the 'political' group would kidnap members of their families or attack their homes if the sums were not paid. One of the targets was high-profile millionaire financier Craig McKinney, who received letters threatening that he would be kidnapped unless he paid a large ransom. However, Boyle backed off when the extortion attempts were made public and Gardaí moved in to protect the targets.

In Garda HQ, intelligence sources and the experiences of the past quickly put Mickey Boyle's name high on the wanted list once more. The Garda National Surveillance Unit (NSU) tried to keep Boyle under constant watch in the hope of catching him in the act, but he proved an extremely difficult target. He used the forests and valleys and networks of mountain tracks to give his watchers the slip. Boyle had a warren of hides scattered throughout the area which were impossible to detect. One Garda recalled: '[Boyle] operated like some kind of Rambo and he was almost impossible to watch. He knew every rabbit-run in north Wicklow. He was hyperactive, always on the move and always planning crimes. In a lot of ways he was much more prolific than Martin Cahill.'

Garda intelligence suggested that within two years of his release Boyle was behind at least sixteen armed robberies and attempted abductions. In each case, the families of businessmen were held at gunpoint in their homes while money was paid not to harm them. In late 1994, Austin McNally, a former Superintendent in the Wicklow area, was appointed to the rank of Detective Superintendent attached to the Serious Crime Squad in Harcourt Terrace. McNally had had enough of Boyle's one-man crime wave and was determined to finally put him out of business. McNally and his squad were about to set in train an astonishing sequence of events, which would expose organised crime gangs in Britain and Ireland, as well as a multi-million pounds international drug-trafficking network, and send Mickey Boyle into gangland history.

On 22 February, following the hijacking of a lorry-load of vodka from a drink wholesaler's during the Christmas period, the Serious Crime Squad made their move. Boyle was arrested under Section 30 of the Offences Against the State Act. He was questioned about the spate of armed robberies and, in particular, an aggravated burglary (burglary where a firearm or other weapon is used) in Greystones, where a garage owner was tied up in his home and robbed. The squad reckoned they had enough evidence to sustain a charge for the hijacking, although they were subsequently proved wrong by the Director of Public Prosecutions, who decided that the case wasn't strong enough. Boyle's form was well known to the police over the previous three decades and they did not expect him to talk. But during his detention the Serious Crime Squad officers were stunned when Boyle agreed to co-operate. That night he brought Detective Inspector Tim Mulvey to a field on Lord Meath's estate. He showed him one of his hides, where he had stored a post office uniform, phone equipment and other paraphernalia used in his various 'strokes'.

Later that night, Detective Superintendent McNally, Detective Inspector Mulvey and Detective Sergeant John O'Mahony had a long conversation with Boyle in Dun Laoghaire Garda Station. As a result Boyle agreed to work as an informant for the Serious Crime Squad and was given the code-name 'Pius O'Callaghan'. The officers were delighted with their coup, but were still suspicious of Boyle. The vast majority of police intelligence comes from underworld informants, but detectives have to be extremely cautious. Informants, as in the case of Athy gang member Austin Higgins, can be selective about the intelligence they are passing on, and tend to use it to distract attention from criminal activities that they themselves are involved in.

The Serious Crime Squad reckoned that Boyle could help them nab an even bigger thorn in their side – George 'The Penguin' Mitchell. Since his release from prison, Boyle, who was now living with a girlfriend in Inchicore in west Dublin, had been a close associate of Mitchell's. Mitchell was one of the gangland figures who had done particularly well for himself in the new-look gangland of the 1990s. In 1984, when Boyle was sent down for the two abductions, George Mitchell, from Ballyfermot in north Dublin was just another armed robber.

Born in Ballyfermot in 1951, Mitchell grew up with the Cunninghams and the Cahills. He was a member of Martin Cahill's gang in the

1980s and was one of the hoods who took part in the theft of the Beit paintings in 1986. Another of his close associates was fellow Ballyfermot criminal John Gilligan, the former boss of the so-called factory gang which specialised in large-scale robberies from warehouses and factories around the country.

Mitchell was given his nickname by the *Sunday World* when he was first photographed and named by that newspaper in 1995. When he wasn't robbing warehouses or paintings, he worked as a lorry driver, delivering biscuits around the country. A major intelligence survey carried out into organised crime in the mid-1980s nominated The Penguin as an 'arch criminal' and one of the top ten gang bosses in Dublin.

In 1988 Mitchell and another hood were jailed for five years for the armed robbery of over £100,000 worth of cattle drench. His pal Gilligan, who organised the robbery, joined him a few years later when he was sent down for another factory robbery. When he was released from prison in 1991, Mitchell set himself up in the drug-trafficking business and quickly became one of the country's top suppliers of cannabis and ecstasy.

Mitchell is reputed to be worth in the region of £10 million as a result of his 'business', and he has extensive links with organised crime gangs in Britain, Holland and Colombia. He had introduced Gilligan to the business. At the end of 1998 Gilligan, who himself controlled a multi-million-pound drug empire, is fighting attempts by the Irish police to have him extradited back to face charges of drug trafficking and ordering the murder of *Sunday Independent* journalist Veronica Guerin in 1996. He has openly admitted that he is the prime suspect for organising the murder.

Mickey Boyle had his first meeting with his Garda contacts on 3 March 1995 in Jury's Hotel in Ballsbridge, south Dublin. Detective Inspector Mulvey and Detective Sergeant O'Mahony attended the meeting. Boyle gave the two officers general information about Mitchell and his associates. He told them that The Penguin had been planning a major bank robbery, but had aborted the idea when the £3 million robbery from the Brinks Allied Cash Centre made headline news, on 24 January that year. Only one piece of information passed on by Boyle that evening was to be of any major significance. Boyle gave them the name of The Penguin's main business partner in England, a London East End gangster called Peter Daly. Boyle told the SCS men that Daly was having major problems at the time with another East End crime family called the Brindles, but he didn't elaborate any further.

The next meeting between the two detectives and Boyle took place on 13 March. He informed the officers that Mitchell had just returned from Spain, where he and Daly had negotiated a big cigarette deal. The consignment was to be smuggled into Ireland via the port of Rotterdam in the Netherlands. Again the information was of no real value.

In the meantime, however, Boyle continued his other activities. On the night of 2 May 1995, Boyle and three other armed raiders arrived at the home of businessman David Cahill in an area known as The Meetings in Avoca, County Wicklow. Boyle and his gang had raided the Cahill home in the previous September, armed with a machinegun, rifle and sawn-off shotgun. That time Boyle got away with £7,000 in cash after terrorising the Cahills. On this occasion, however, David Cahill was prepared for an attack.

As Boyle and his cohorts approached the house they made a lot of noise. All four men were dressed in military combat clothing, balaclavas and gloves. David Cahill heard them and rushed his wife Evan and their two children, a thirteen-year-old boy and a ten-year-old girl, into a specially-secured bedroom in the house. In the bedroom, Evan Cahill pressed a panic alarm and also phoned the Gardaí in Wicklow station. After the previous attack, David Cahill had fortified his house with extra security devices, including special doors on each room which were not easily broken down. Boyle and his team smashed their way through a rear door of the house, but had difficulty getting to where the owner was. They kept shouting 'Cahill, come out.'

David Cahill reached for a shotgun and loaded it. He fired a shot over the head of a raider who was standing outside a side window. The gang fired a number of shots back. David Cahill instantly recognised Boyle's voice from the previous raid. In the commotion, Boyle had cut his hand and his leg getting through the window. It would later emerge that the businessman could have killed him had he not decided to shoot over Boyle's head.

Boyle, armed with a machinegun, ordered Cahill to put his hands up and stand against the wall. The two were alone in the house. The other raiders kept screaming 'Come out, Cahill!' because they couldn't get through a specially-fortified door into the room. The businessman struck Boyle hard across the jaw, knocking him to the ground. Then a voice on the raider's walkie-talkie informed him that the Gardaí were at the front gate of the house. Boyle told the businessman that he would be shot dead if the Gardaí came in. The two uniformed cops arrived at the front door. Boyle and the other gangsters ran away from the back of the house and across a field to two waiting cars. The Cahill family, badly shaken but uninjured, were placed under armed guard.

Two days later, Detective Inspector Tim Mulvey got a call from Boyle at his office in Harcourt Square with some dramatic news. Boyle informed the detective that he and four other well-known Dublin criminals had been summoned to a meeting by George Mitchell. Boyle, needless to say, did not mention the attempted robbery at the Cahill home. The Mitchell meeting took place in the home of another gangster. George Mitchell discussed the ongoing problems his business associate, Peter Daly, was having with the Brindle family in London. He had been asked to help the Dalys 'sort out' the ongoing feud.

The two organised crime gangs had been at war in what was one of London gangland's bloodiest feuds since the days of the Richardsons and the Krays. The war had broken out in August 1990, when two associates of the Brindles walked into the Queen Elizabeth pub in Walworth in the East End and threatened Peter Daly's brother, John, the pub owner. The Brindles are related through marriage to once-notorious gangland enforcer-turned-celebrity, 'Mad' Frankie Fraser. When Peter Daly arrived in the pub a gun was placed in his mouth.

The following month there was a return match. Ahmet 'Turkish

Abbi' Abdullah was a member of a feared south London crime family called the Arifs. The Arifs, who were involved in armed robbery and drug smuggling, were associates of the Dalys and sworn enemies of the Brindles. The head of the Arif family, Dogan Arif, had been jailed for his part in an £8.5 million cocaine smuggling operation. Thirty-year-old Abdullah, who was on release from prison after serving time for manslaughter and under investigation for drug racketeering, walked into a drinking club where Stephen Dalligan, a Brindle henchman, was enjoying himself. He shot Dalligan seven times but the victim survived the attack.

'Turkish Abbi' was next to be whacked. In March 1991, two gunmen walked into a south London betting shop and blasted him several times at point-blank range. He was not as lucky as Dalligan. Twenty-seven-year-old market trader Tony Brindle and his brother Patrick, the thirty-year-old manager of a cab firm, were charged with the murder. While they were on bail, their younger brother David went into Daly's pub, the Queen Elizabeth, and began throwing his weight around. He was badly beaten by another underworld enforcer, James Moody, a former member of the Kray gang and an associate of Peter Daly. Moody had escaped from prison along with Provo prisoner Gerard Tuite twelve years earlier, and was still on the run. David Brindle later threatened to have John Daly and Moody murdered.

A few weeks later, in August 1991, David Brindle was killed in The Bell pub in Walworth, south-east London, when two hitmen burst in and sprayed the place with machinegun fire. One of the killers shouted: 'This one is for Abbi'. An innocent drinker, a grandfather, was also killed in the attack, and five others were injured. In May 1992 the trial of the Brindle brothers made British legal history. Jury and witnesses were screened from the public gallery and the dock where the brothers sat during the trial. The jurors were also given armed police protection for the duration of the trial. One witness who managed to make it to the stand told the judge that he could not give his evidence because he feared for his life. The Brindles were acquitted.

In June 1993 a gunman walked into the Royal Hotel pub in

Hackney and ordered a pint of lager. He took a long gulp from the pint, wiped his lips and coolly turned to fifty-two-year-old James Moody and shot him four times in the head. In August 1994 another contract killer shot dead two innocent men in a devastating blunder. One of the victims, a fifty-eight-year-old father of four, was mistaken for Peter Daly. His drinking partner bore an uncanny resemblance to one of Daly's henchmen. It was against this background of unprecedented blood-letting, which had turned London's gangland into a tinderbox, that George Mitchell had been asked for help.

On 5 May 1995, Boyle travelled to Salthill in Galway to meet the men from the Serious Crime Squad. He outlined Mitchell's plan. He and the other criminals who had attended Mitchell's meeting were to travel together and carry out three murders in the one night. The targets were George and Patrick Brindle and at least one of their closest associates. Surveillance had already been carried out by Daly's hoods and it was reckoned that Tony Brindle was too secure for a hit. Boyle also gave the detectives the name of the gangland armourer being used for the assassination plot – David Roads, a fifty-two-year-old south Londoner and associate of Peter Daly. Boyle admitted that he had already been over to London to take part in the surveillance operation. He even described in detail the location of a safe house where guns and other hardware were stored for the operation. Mulvey and O'Mahony told Boyle to distance himself from the operation and that they would inform the English police. Boyle was astonished that the two cops were concerned about the London hits. 'But it's not on your patch, why would you be concerned?' he asked incredulously.

In the early hours of the morning of his trip to Galway, Boyle had been busy with other criminal matters. He liked to keep himself busy. A drug dealer in Bray received a letter, containing a photograph of an armed man with a balaclava and a note informing him that he would receive a phone call the following morning. The drug dealer called the police, who in turn put a trace on his line. While Boyle was away informing the Serious Crime Squad of The Penguin's plans for the Brindles, two of his associates made a number of phone calls to the drug dealer's home, threatening him and demanding protection money.

Four hours after his meeting in Galway, undercover surveillance officers spotted Boyle with his two associates. One of them was an ex-RUC officer from Fermanagh who was wanted on warrant for extradition to England, where he was to face charges relating to the importation of fifteen kilos of heroin. The other man was a twenty-eight-year-old criminal from Bray. The team observed the trio making calls from a number of public phone kiosks around Bray. All the calls were made to the drug dealer. The following morning, Detective Superintendent McNally gave the order to arrest Boyle and his pals. During his detention, Boyle told the detectives that if they released him he would take them to London and show them the location of the flat being used to store the weapons for the proposed hits. They declined the offer.

Boyle was later released while a file on the intimidation case was being compiled with a view to charging him and his cohorts. On 9 May McNally called his colleagues in the South-East Regional Crime Squad (SERCS) and passed on Boyle's information. They decided that Boyle was a rogue informant, who was passing on information in the hope of distracting the Serious Crime Squad from his own activities. But the information which came back from the SERCS showed that there was substance to Boyle's claims about the proposed Brindle hit. Meanwhile, Boyle's extraordinary crime spree continued. This time, working alone, Boyle hit the home of Joseph and Patricia Kenneally, Kilquade House at Newtownmountkennedy in County Wicklow. Shortly after 4am on 22 May, Boyle broke into the house and woke the Kenneallys up in their bedroom. He pointed a rifle at the couple and ordered them to take him to their study where they had a safe. He took over £2,000 in cash and another £2,500 worth of jewellery. Two weeks later, he hit the owners of a pub near Bray and took off with £2,000 in cash, after again holding up the owners with a rifle.

Boyle's final meeting with the police was on 20 July. By now, apart from the string of armed robberies, he was a suspect in the gangland murder of Fran Preston, who had been shot dead in June. A lone gunman on a bicycle had blasted Preston outside his home in Baldoyle, north Dublin. Preston had fallen foul of a close associate of George Mitchell. Mitchell was also arrested at the time under Section 30 of the Offences Against the State Act and questioned about the hit. During this last meeting the hitman had another rather extraordinary offer for the detectives. Boyle wanted £20,000 from the police, to set up what he described as an advice centre for criminals. He said that he would be in a position to glean a lot of valuable information from criminals across the city as a result. By now the two detectives seriously doubted Boyle's reliability and, indeed, his grasp on reality. They told him they weren't interested. Boyle's rampage was headed for disaster.

A major surveillance operation, code-named 'Partake', had been organised by the police on both sides of the Irish Sea. The objective was to foil the Brindle assassination bid, and also to arrest Boyle and the other members of the killer gang. Throughout the rest of the summer Boyle was observed making several trips to London. Operating from a safe house organised by David Roads, he was watched as he, in turn, watched various members of the Brindle family. Boyle was meticulous in his surveillance methods and compiled detailed intelligence on the movements of his targets. His movements even led the police to a holiday home belonging to one of the Brindle brothers which they had not been aware of before. The police also managed to identify the second safe house, at Chaffinch Close in south London, where Roads had stored the firearms and other equipment. The surveillance operation went on for more than eight weeks.

By the end of August, the plans by the London-Dublin crime organisation had changed. It was now decided to hit Tony Brindle. The idea of a co-ordinated series of dramatic executions was dropped for logistical reasons. Over the next few weeks, the surveillance teams watched Boyle watching Tony Brindle's home at Christopher Close, a small square of terraced houses in Rotherhithe. The SERCS, backed up by Scotland Yard's specialist firearms squad, SO 19, moved into the area to prepare for the showdown. The locals knew something was afoot when a British Gas van took up almost permanent residence in the cul-de-sac – all the houses in the area were fully electric. A furniture van also pulled in and stayed. Again, no furniture was loaded or unloaded.

Boyle also used a van to watch Brindle's house. He was very patient. One day, after waiting several hours, Boyle was video-taped by the surveillance teams running to a café for a quick sandwich. In the few minutes he was away, Brindle walked out of his house, got into his BMW car and drove off. When Boyle returned to discover he had missed his target the police video-taped the expression of frustration on his face. But soon the underworld stalker would have his opportunity to pounce.

Around 7.30am on 20 September 1995, Boyle, wearing a false wig, took up his position outside Brindle's home. He parked his stolen van ten yards from Brindle's car. He removed the van's wing mirror, opened the driver's window and hid behind a makeshift curtain behind the driver's seat. He had given himself a field of fire to the driver's side of Brindle's car, enabling him to hit his target as he got into the car without having to leave the van. Boyle was equipped with a 9 millimetre Browning automatic pistol and an even more powerful magnum revolver as a back-up.

At 10.42am Brindle emerged from his house and walked to his parked car. The teams of officers from the SO 19 squad braced themselves for action. The police had planned to take on Boyle when he got out of the van. They hadn't calculated on him staying inside. As Brindle reached his car Boyle fired three shots, hitting the London gangster twice. One round hit him in the left elbow and the lower left side of his chest and the other got him in both thighs. Brindle turned and began staggering back to the safety of his house. Boyle jumped from the van and chased his target to finish him off. He lifted his pistol to take aim. At that moment two marksmen, who had been concealed in the British Gas van nearby, sprang into action. Using high-powered Heckler and Koch rifles, they fired a total of fourteen shots at Boyle. The hitman was hit five times – in the elbow, chest, shoulder, left heel and ear. He crumpled to the ground as armed officers raced up to cover him. The drama had been captured on police video. In a follow-up operation, David Roads was arrested and guns, explosives and a large quantity of ammunition recovered.

Boyle was in a critical condition and was removed to hospital by air ambulance. In the hour after the incident he had to be resuscitated twice and was semi-conscious for a number of weeks. He was in hospital under armed guard for over two months. When he recovered, he was charged with attempted murder and two counts of possession of firearms with intent to endanger life. Brindle also made a full recovery and discharged himself from hospital a week after the incident. He refused to co-operate with the investigation, claiming that the police had been hoping that he would be killed when the initial shots were fired. In the East End the family say he is considering suing the police for not warning him about the hit.

Boyle's trial in the Old Bailey began in January 1997, and lasted three months. Armed police officers ringed the courtroom while marksmen, attached to the same unit which had shot Boyle, kept watch from the surrounding rooftops. As in Tony Brindle's trial for the Abbi Abdullah case, the jurors were placed under round-the-clock protection. Boyle, true to form, put up an extraordinary defence, which he hoped would win the jurors' sympathy and a 'not guilty' verdict. But he did more to terrify the jurors than actually ingratiate them to him. He claimed in court that he had been an intelligence officer for the IRA and had also been a member of the INLA. He said he believed in the aims of the IRA, but hinted that he left the organisation because he preferred methods which were 'less dangerous to the public'. In reality Boyle had never been in the IRA.

Boyle also told how he had worked as an informant for the Serious Crime Squad in Dublin. He said he had hoped that the police would intervene and prevent the shooting. He claimed that he had been 'allowed' to shoot Brindle before the police opened fire on him. He had been aiming for a 'non-fatal' part of Brindle's body and had merely wanted to knee-cap him. Boyle also put the boot into his old friend George Mitchell.

He claimed that he had carried out the Brindle attack because he had been coerced into doing so by The Penguin. He insisted that his gang boss would have killed his girlfriend's young daughter had he not carried out his orders. 'Mitchell told me that if I sorted out the Brindles that he would be able to re-establish himself in London and that we would all be better off,' said Boyle. 'I was only there because of the pressure I was under. If I wanted to kill Brindle I would have chosen a pump-action shotgun because it would have been impossible to miss from that distance,' the hitman told the jury, who were shown the video of the incident. Boyle wanted to paint a picture of a desperate man caught between the police on one hand and Mitchell on the other.

The three Garda officers who were called to give evidence denied that they considered Boyle 'expendable'. Commander Roy Clark, who had co-ordinated the operation, said that Brindle had not been informed of the murder plot because it would have resulted in an escalation of violence. 'Given the bloody background to this feud, if Brindle had been informed, it would be a signal for a preemptive strike by his side,' the police commander revealed.

On Monday 24 March, the jury found Mickey Boyle guilty of all three charges. His sidekick, David Roads, was jailed for ten years for possession of explosives and firearms. He had been acquitted of the attempted murder charge. Boyle stood impassively in the dock as Judge Sir Lawrence Verney gave him three life sentences. 'Of all the classes of killer, the contract killer must be regarded as the worst. You are a man who is prepared to offer his services to take the life of someone totally unknown and to do so. The background to this is a feud which has lasted many years and cost eight lives. It is something of a miracle a ninth life was not lost as a result of your conduct,' he told the one-man crime wave. The foiled Brindle hit sent shock waves through gangland in London and Dublin.

Since then George Mitchell has had plenty of problems. Peter Daly, his London underworld connection, has fled to live in Spain. Mitchell began living in Holland following the botched hit, to avoid the attentions of the English and Irish police. He decided to make his residence permanent following the murder of journalist Veronica

Guerin. The Criminal Assets Bureau, set up in the wake of the murder to identify and seize the ill-gotten-gains of major league criminals, put Mitchell at the top of their target list. So far they have demanded payment of over £100,000, which they claim is the proceeds of his drug operation. The rest of Mitchell's wealth, which is estimated at several million pounds, had been moved out of Ireland before the CAB got to it.

Mitchell has been under investigation by drug enforcement agencies throughout Europe. In 1996 the Irish police named him in connection with a plot to ship over three tons of high-quality cocaine from Colombia into Europe through Ireland, on a vessel called *The Tia*. The street value of the shipment was estimated at up to £250 million. Mitchell was also named as the 'dangerous criminal' behind an attempt to establish an ecstasy factory in Dublin in the summer of 1995, at the same time as plans were being made to deal with the Brindles. The factory, which was found by the National Drug Unit before it had actually gone into production, had been capable of churning out millions of pounds worth of the drug. Three men have since been convicted.

Mitchell continued to stay one step ahead of the law until February 1998, when he was caught red-handed stealing over £500,000 worth of computer parts from a truck which had been driven from Ireland. 'Operation Wedgewood' had been set up by the Gardaí to smash a multi-million-pound trade in stolen computer parts from Irish factories. Mitchell was organising the racket from his safe haven in the Netherlands. Following an undercover operation involving forces in Ireland, England, Belgium and the Netherlands, the untouchable gang boss was arrested near Schipol airport in Amsterdam, behind the wheel of a forklift offloading the goods. In September 1998 George Mitchell was jailed by a Dutch court for almost three years. The court, in its verdict, said it believed that The Penguin was the mastermind behind an international crime syndicate. When he is released, the police in Dublin will also want to talk to him.

His old friend Mickey Boyle will not be by his side. In the Old

Bailey in 1997, Judge Verney recommended that Boyle serve at least fifteen years of his sentence. He will be sixty-six years old when he is eligible for release. Mickey Boyle's extraordinary criminal career will have cost him over his half his life behind bars.

The Scam Man

In the early hours of Saturday 12 September 1992, a massive explosion demolished a north-city Dublin pub. Within minutes, Gardaí, ambulances and fire units rushed to the scene at Ballybough Road where, a few hours earlier, Collins's public house had stood. Firemen extinguishing pockets of fire in the ruins heard a voice coming from the middle of the smoking rubble. The firemen turned off their motors and hoses to find the exact location of the man's voice. 'In here ... get me out,' the man called again. The firemen uncovered the injured man from the centre of what had been the main front bar. He had somehow survived the devastating explosion. The figure cast an eerie shadow as he emerged from the devastation, blood and dust caked on his face. His clothes had been burned off, he had a gash to his forehead, his hair was singed and there were burns on his face, hands and arms.

But, despite his condition, the unrecognisable survivor walked to a waiting ambulance. Later in the emergency room of the Mater Hospital, as nurses cleaned away his mask of blood, soot and dust, the onlooking Gardaí could scarcely believe their eyes. For sitting there before them was one Stephen 'Rossi' Walsh, one of Dublin's best-known and most elusive gangsters. The once slippery godfather, who had been the target of scores of serious crime investigations over twenty years, had just handed himself to his hated enemies on a plate. The capture of Rossi Walsh is probably one of the most extraordinary of its kind in gangland.

The careers of many of the underworld's major players are like constant cat-and-mouse games between them and the law. A gangster's main occupational hazards, apart from the consequences of crossing a competitor, are the police and prison. And very often the stature of a villain is decided by two things: how ruthless he is at achieving power and how clever he is at avoiding capture. Rossi Walsh had been ruthless and clever.

On the other side of the coin, a criminal can get caught for a variety of other reasons. He can become a victim of his own success and start believing he is invincible, inevitably leading to carelessness and long-term, rent-free accommodation provided by the Department of Justice. He can also come a cropper by being outfoxed by the work of much cleverer police. Or he can be unlucky or just plain stupid. In the end Walsh thought he was untouchable, but his luck had run out.

Stephen 'Rossi' Walsh, alias Stephen Byrne, was one of Dublin's most feared criminal godfathers. He was involved in armed crime, violence, extortion, intimidation and compensation fraud. One detective who had dealings with Walsh since the early 1970s recalled: 'Rossi was a psychopath and he loved the power that carrying a gun brought him. Every thug on his patch was absolutely terrified of him because of his violent nature. A lot of policemen were also scared of him. Rossi was one of the most dangerous criminals ever to have come out of that end of town.'

Born in 1949, Walsh was reared by his grandmother in Pearse House, a grim complex of south-inner-city corporation flats. His father left home when he was a child. He used two names, Walsh and Byrne. Walsh was his father's name and Byrne his mother's. It was from Pearse House that Walsh established his 'patch', which stretched from the Garda 'B' district of Pearse Street across to the 'E' district, which covers Ringsend and Irishtown near dockland. As with a lot of his contemporaries, petty crime was a way of life. In 1965, at the age of sixteen, the up-and-coming godfather received his first conviction in the Dublin district court, for stealing a bicycle. For his first criminal act he was given probation and told not to do it again. Two years later Walsh was back in the same court and convicted on a larceny charge. He was again given probation. Over the next ten years Rossi Walsh's encounters with the law were of a relatively minor nature.

Walsh was a talented soccer player and was invited on a number of occasions for trials by top English clubs, including Arsenal. A nifty inside forward, his former teammates say he was nicknamed 'Rossi' after the famous Italian centre forward Paolo Rossi, who scored six goals in the 1982 World Cup which Italy won. Ironically, the real Rossi was suspended from playing as a result of corruption. The English clubs turned down the Pearse Street hood, although he played League of Ireland football for Shelbourne Rovers and later Liffey Wanderers for several years. Soccer pundits say that he could have played for Ireland had he put his mind to it. Former armed robber Dave Brogan, who once did 'jobs' with Walsh and knew him at the time of the soccer trials, said: 'He never made it into professional football because he was so aggressive and arrogant. The Brits wouldn't put up with that kind of shite.'

Off the field, however, Walsh pursued a more lucrative career as an armed robber. He did jobs with practically every blagger from both sides of the River Liffey. In the mid 1970s he was arrested and charged with two armed robberies. The first was a hold-up in a pub in Chapelizod in west Dublin. During the Holy Hour – a now defunct aspect of Dublin pub life which obliged pubs to close between two and three o'clock every afternoon – Walsh and another criminal robbed the takings, around £2,000, at gunpoint. Detectives caught him after finding his fingerprints on the glass he had been drinking from while waiting to make his move. In July 1977 he pleaded guilty and got a two-year suspended prison sentence.

But this close shave did not deter the soccer player. In the same year he was back in the Circuit Criminal Court on another armed robbery charge. This time he had held up the post office in Ringsend, east Dublin. During the raid Walsh terrified postmistress Patricia Shaughnessy, held a gun to her head and tied her up. He got away with £4,000. When the local detective unit arrested him in Irishtown, Walsh openly boasted to them about how he had done the job. The detectives took down everything he said and used it in court as verbal evidence. During the trial Rossi denied that he had opened his mouth to the police, and the case was aborted when the jury failed to reach agreement on a verdict.

Before his second trial began in April 1978, Walsh had it transferred from the Circuit Criminal Court to the Central Criminal Court. Switching trials from one court to the other was then the legal right of a defendant. Mostly it was used as a delaying tactic by criminals, which eventually forced the legislature to change the law during the 1980s. All criminal cases are now conducted in the Circuit Criminal Court, with the exception of rape and murder trials which are held in the Central Criminal Court. Walsh was found guilty and got eight years. But his luck held and, much to the amazement and anger of the police, the sentence was suspended. No-one was as furious as the victim herself. After the trial, Patricia Shaughnessy wrote letters of complaint to the Minister for Justice, the Chief Justice, the President of the High Court and even the President of Ireland. But Rossi remained a free man.

The robbery cases established his reputation in the underworld as a serious criminal, who could play the system and appear to get away with it. From then on he became a major player in gangland. Over the next fourteen years or so Garda intelligence pinpointed Walsh as the prime suspect for several serious crimes, and detectives investigating armed robberies, murder and other crimes arrested Walsh over twenty times under Section 30 of the Offences Against the State Act. But each time there was insufficient evidence to sustain a case and they never managed to convict him.

Walsh was a cunning gangster who played his cards close to his chest. He took part in scores of armed robberies, often operating alone. When British Home Stores first opened in O'Connell Street in Dublin, Walsh, using a handgun, was their first robber. He got away with over £50,000 in cash. He also took part in a major heist from a security van in Henry Street, during which several shots were fired at Gardaí. Later three members of the gang were caught in Phibsboro. Walsh managed to escape and walked home to Ringsend. It was lucky for the cops that they didn't find him. Walsh was carrying two firearms and five grenades, which he later told an associate he would have used if confronted. Walsh loved firearms, and built up a large arsenal, which he buried in various places around his patch.

One of his most successful rackets was the organised theft of containers of goods from the docks, where a number of his associates worked. In the early 1980s he organised the theft of three container loads of video recorders, worth millions of pounds. Using bogus documentation, his men simply drove in with trucks fitted with false plates, backed up to the containers and drove away. On another occasion the gang stole two containers of Bacardi. Three County Monaghan criminals with paramilitary links were subsequently arrested by the RUC with some of the stolen drink. The information they gleaned led directly back to Walsh but, again, there wasn't enough evidence to charge him. Another time, Rossi and his bandits robbed three containers of Mars bars. He had believed the containers to be full of new televisions. The kids in Rossi's neighbourhood ate a lot of Mars bars that year.

Following his three armed robbery trials in the late 1970s, Walsh took a keen interest in the law. He set himself up as a barrack-room lawyer, advising criminals on how best to utilise the system to beat the rap. Rossi would read books of evidence in cases involving his fellow rogues, charging them between a few hundred and £1,000 for his services. He also advised members of the IRA. He was a regular patron of the criminal and civil courts. He could be seen strutting through the corridors of the Four Courts in his shiny tracksuit and runners, with a carrier-bag stuffed with legal books across his shoulder. Walsh thoroughly enjoyed arguing points of law with defence barristers, whom he regarded as snobs.

Walsh also ran what police described as a 'Fagin's school' for up-and-coming criminals, from the converted attic of his luxury four-bedroom home in Sandymount. He had bought the house in the early 1980s for £70,000 in cash, despite the fact that he was officially unemployed and in receipt of social welfare money. The only record of Walsh ever being involved in anything legal was a cab company he owned for a short time. Walsh built up an extensive library of legal books in his attic. He advised other hoods about their legal rights, the attitude they should adopt while in custody and how to arrange good alibis which would convince a jury of a criminal's innocence. In particular, he stressed to other hoods the importance of keeping their mouths shut while in custody. It had been 'verbals' which had convinced the jury of his guilt in the Ringsend post office trial. Rossi knew a lot of the angles but some policemen reckon that he wasn't such a genius. 'Fellows who took Rossi's advice in how they approached their trials often ended up getting longer sentences as a result,' recalled a detective.

In 1987, the Government set up the Garda Complaints Authority, to investigate allegations of misconduct by members of the force. Rossi Walsh now had a new tool for fighting the system. He advised gangsters who had been caught and charged with an offence to immediately make a complaint to the Board against the arresting officers. It was statutorily bound to conduct an investigation into each and every allegation made. While an investigation was ongoing a trial could not take place. And the more complaints there were, the longer it took to investigate them and the longer the period of time before any case came to court. At one stage, as a result of Walsh's advice, the system practically seized up, leading to a public outcry from the association representing middle-ranking police officers. Walsh's antics even took centre stage at one of the annual conferences of the Association of Garda Sergeants and Inspectors. Delegates complained bitterly that the Petrocelli of Pearse Street was successfully disrupting the criminal justice system. In fact, at the height of the complaints blizzard, Walsh boasted to his cronies that there were more cops under investigation than criminals.

In his local area of Pearse Street, he nurtured an image of a Robin Hood-like figure. This was his regular stomping-ground, even though he had moved out in the early 1970s after marrying Monica O'Reilly. If one of his old neighbours had a problem, then Rossi dealt with it. The locals called Walsh instead of the police. He and his team of heavies, which included two martial arts experts, enforced their own brand of rough justice in the flats complexes. If anyone stepped out of line, he or she was severely beaten. Walsh had no qualms about beating up women. Throughout his patch he ran an extensive protection racket, extorting cash from pub and restaurant owners. One pub which refused to pay up mysteriously burned down twice in the space of five years. Walsh instilled terror in everyone who crossed him, whether criminals or not. The local Gardaí regularly received reports that he had threatened people with firearms, but out of fear none of them would make a complaint. In Ringsend he got into a row in a pub with a local docker who had had enough of his bullying tactics. Walsh won the fight after sticking a gun down his opponent's throat in front of at least twenty witnesses. He had no worries about anyone going to the police. They were too scared.

In 1984 Walsh was arrested and questioned about the murder of Jackie Kelly, a local barman. A lone gunman had walked into Grace's Pub on Townsend Street in the inner-city and shot Kelly at point-blank range. Walsh was later released without charge. Some time after the incident, the soccer player was again arrested and charged, this time with beating up both Kelly's mother and sister. He sought judicial reviews and used various other ploys which delayed the case for almost eight years, after which it was dropped.

In Pearse House he organised and sponsored soccer tournaments for the kids. They looked up to him as the local godfather and they wanted to be like him. As some of the kids grew up, he coached them on more than soccer. Off the field he helped guide them in their criminal careers as well. The people of the area argue that Rossi was a neccessary evil. His fearsome reputation for violence and disapproval of drug abuse ensured that dealers steered clear of the flats. To bolster his image as a local hero, he would regularly splash out and bring the elderly residents on day trips. On one occasion he brought a group to a rugby international in Landsdowne Road. After the match they were brought for a meal and drinks to Jury's hotel, where the unemployed villain picked up the tab. He once called to the local school to introduce a celebrity to the kids, someone famous they had all seen on television. That man was Martin Cahill, The General.

Cahill was one of Walsh's closest underworld associates. Garda intelligence reports from the early 1980s identified Rossi Walsh as a member of The General's gang. He was one of a dozen criminal associates who took part in the multi-million-pound Beit art robbery in

1986. In late 1987 Garda surveillance watched a meeting between Walsh and a Dutch criminal, Kees Van Scoaik. The General had sent Rossi to discuss a possible deal to sell the paintings.

Van Scoaik handed over £10,000 in cash to Walsh for the stolen Francesco Guardi painting, 'View of Grand Canal, Venice'. Unknown to Walsh, at the time Van Scoaik was working for the Dutch and Irish police in an international sting operation, intent on snaring The General and his gang and recovering the paintings. The elaborate operation ended in failure in Killakee Woods in the Dublin mountains, in September 1987. Cahill slipped away with the paintings right under the noses of the Gardaí.

After this incident, Walsh went his own way. In the same year he discovered a lucrative new scam. He organised staged 'accidents' throughout the city and then made fraudulent compensation claims through the courts against the public utilities and insurance companies. Over a three-year period, the Irish insurance industry estimated that Walsh was behind dozens of staged accidents, where compensation and legal costs of between one and two million pounds were paid out. He used a core group of twenty-three individuals, all of whom were friends or former soccer teammates. He exposed a system which was wide open to abuse.

The compensation deluge was an indirect result of a devastating gas explosion which had killed two people in a block of private apartments at Raglan House in Ballsbridge, on New Year's Day 1987. A major investigation of the system found that the gas supply system was rotting and leaking. Over the next few years, in an extensive refurbishment of the system, hundreds of city streets and sidewalks were dug up.

To Rossi, the holes were gold mines. He found suitable holes for his associates to fall into. Others drove into them. There were so many holes that he could take his pick. The most popular 'injury' was whiplash. An accident involving a car could result in as many as four claims, for up to £30,000 each. It was a spectacular scam. Soon the compensation claims were flooding into the courts. Sometimes, if Walsh liked a particular location, he used it over and over again.

Members of the group took turns, alternating between playing the roles of the injured and the witnesses.

One member of the accident-prone group was David Glass, a dodgy garage owner from Tullycaughey, near Castleblayney in County Monaghan. Glass, despite being a Protestant, was closely associated with members of the INLA and the IRA along the border. He also had extensive contacts with the criminal underworld. He provided logistical support for the 'injuries' scam by supplying stolen and re-plated cars. Walsh met Glass through their mutual associates in the two paramilitary organisations. One of Glass's associates was renegade INLA killer Dessie O'Hare, who kidnapped Dublin dentist John O'Grady in November 1987.

Glass specialised in the theft and disposal of cars. The elaborate operation was concealed in an underground garage near his premises in County Monaghan. In 1987 the place was raided by the Gardaí and several stolen cars were found buried in Glass's yard. One of the cars had been used by Dessie O'Hare in an armed robbery in Arva, County Cavan, in December 1986. Glass was charged with running the racket and he appointed Walsh as his legal adviser before and during his trial.

But, before his case came up, the two hoods worked on getting a nest egg to compensate the Monaghan crook for the loss of his business. During the Summer of 1987 Glass had three collisions in three months, at City Quay, Holles Street and the Naas Road. Among those 'injured' in the accidents were seven associates of Walsh and their relatives. One of the injured, a friend of Walsh's, had featured in at least five similar cases. Later that year, Glass was convicted in the Circuit Criminal Court of running the stolen car racket, and received a hefty jail sentence of twelve years. During the trial Walsh was ordered out of the court by the judge, because of his constant interruptions of Glass's legal team.

Four years later in the High Court, Mr Justice Richard Johnston dismissed an injury claim by David Glass for the accident at City Quay, after hearing evidence that Walsh, who had no standing in the case, had stopped an insurance company official speaking to one of the plaintiffs named in the compensation proceedings. Detectives also gave evidence of how Walsh had acted as an informal legal adviser for Glass. The Judge said he was satisfied that Walsh had been involved in the Glass compensation scam and asked the DPP to investigate possible criminal conspiracy and fraud in the case.

Walsh's antics led to a major overhaul of how insurance companies and public utilities dealt with compensation cases. Companies began spending more money investigating the background to individual claims. A Claims Task Force and a data base was established to analyse each claimant and to identify whether the individual concerned had made any previous claims. Apart from repeat litigants, the task force also kept details of solicitors, doctors and witnesses who featured in dodgy cases. In one of Walsh's scams, the investigators were lucky to locate an eyewitness to an accident which occurred in November 1991 on Temple Road in Dartry, south Dublin. The female eyewitness was walking down Temple Road around 9.30pm at night when she noticed a red Isuzu jeep driving up and down. The middle-aged driver seemed to be talking on a mobile telephone or radio. The driver was Rossi Walsh. A few days earlier a large hole had been dug up by Bord Gáis at the side of the road. It was large enough to fit a car.

The eyewitness then noticed an orange Fiat car driving down the road with two men in it. The jeep came back up the road and passed the car. The two vehicles drove up and down six times and then stopped while the occupants of the car and the jeep spoke to each other. Walsh then drove down to Richmond Hill and picked up another man. The Fiat drove up to the top of Temple Road to the road works. The occupants got out and removed barrels and red and white tape which were being used to barricade the hole. The passenger got out and moved three of the barrels, putting them on the footpath. Then Walsh, in the jeep, came back up the road and parked opposite the road works. The Fiat parked just beyond the road works.

Walsh made a phone call and told his friends that their accident was waiting to happen. A few moments later a white car came around the corner from the top of Temple Road. It drove very slowly, straight into the Bord Gáis hole. The eyewitness later told investigators that the car was driving so slowly and carefully that there was no bang or crash. She recalled:'I think he did it on purpose, because he did it so slowly. It didn't look like it was an accident at all.'

Of the five people in the car that night, three sued for compensation, seeking a minimum of £15,000 each in the High Court. Bord Gáis, in its defence, claimed that the case was fraudulent. The solicitor who was acting for the plaintiffs in the case withdrew from representing them. One of the people 'injured' in the accident had played Leinster League football with Rossi Walsh. The case was dropped.

Rossi's constant presence in the courts as a legal adviser, and his association with so many compensation cases, soon came to the attention of the judiciary. In February 1993, three people from Ringsend and Irishtown brought a case to the Circuit Court, claiming compensation of up to £30,000 each for an accident involving another Bord Gáis hole in the road. A married couple from Irishtown said that they were the occupants of a car driven by a friend of theirs from Ringsend when it crashed into the hole on Sandwith Street in June 1990. The driver claimed that there were no cones, tapes or other markings around the hole at the time to warn him of the danger. But an investigator for the gas company claimed that the car had been 'driven very slowly, very deliberately, into the hole.'

Judge Frank Martin was having none of it. The previous July he had thrown out another compensation case against Dublin Corporation in which one of these claimants was a witness. At that time, the Judge had described the case as 'another Rossi Walsh production, fraudulent from start to finish'. In this case, the three claimants admitted to being friends of Walsh. Judge Martin directed that the Fraud Squad be called in to investigate, and said he was perturbed at the number of bogus claims coming before him. Behind many of them, he said, was 'the malign name of Rossi Walsh'. The Judge announced angrily: 'We've had him [Walsh] in here a few times where he was running fraudulent claims for people. He runs a dial-a-witness service.' As a result of the judge's comments, Walsh was named for the first time in the Irish media. Rossi Walsh's days as a compensation fraudster had come to an end.

By early 1993, Walsh had other pressing problems on his mind. In the previous September he had been found in the smouldering rubble of Collins's Pub in Ballybough. That was the night that Rossi's luck ran out. His motive for causing the explosion is still shrouded in mystery. On the night of 11 September, Walsh had been drinking in the Widow Scallan's pub on Pearse Street. He left the pub around 2.30 the next morning. He gave a number of friends lifts to their homes and then drove his car to Ballybough Avenue where he met two accomplices, one of whom was a thirty-year-old convicted armed robber from Pearse Street. He parked his car, a Volkswagen Golf with a big sticker in the back window which read, 'Yes, I am a filthy rich bitch.'

Collins's pub was at Ballybough Avenue at the corner of King's Avenue. It had a mainly working-class clientele and was owned by brothers James and Christy Collins, relations of world boxing champion Steve Collins. They had bought the premises two years earlier. Around 3am, Walsh and his armed robber friend lifted the security shutter over a side door and managed to enter the pub.

He and his accomplice had two twenty-five-litre containers filled with a petrol and diesel mixture. They also brought three gas cylinders and an electric fire into the pub. Inside the ground floor of the pub Walsh and his associate spread the petrol and diesel mix. The liquid, having vaporised through the pub, was to be ignited by the electric fire after the two hoods had made their exit. The cylinders would also explode, destroying the building. Unfortunately for Walsh, the vapours were prematurely ignited, perhaps by a spark from another electric appliance. The blast ripped through the building, throwing Walsh into the middle of the bar and covering him in burning rubble. His partner also suffered burns, but managed to get to the door. Within seconds of the blast, locals spotted a man staggering towards a waiting car. He discarded a burning anorak as he did so. The car sped off as squad cars were speeding to Ballybough Avenue to investigate the explosion. The criminal went missing for over two months. Detectives searching for him received information that associates had been observed buying medical dressing and lotion for treating burns on a daily basis.

On his way to hospital, Walsh gave his name to an accompanying Garda as Tony Jones from Pearse House. He said that he had been the only person in the pub when it exploded. Then he changed his mind and said that there were three or four more in the bar at the time of the blast. But while he was being treated for his injuries in the emergency room of the Mater Hospital, Garda Brendan O'Somachain recognised Rossi Walsh. He had known him for several years.

Walsh remained in hospital for a month and made a full recovery. During that time, he had several visits from the two men heading the investigation, Detective Superintendent Jim Murphy and Detective Inspector Mick Duggan. The two experienced policemen had known Rossi's form for a long time. The only explanation he offered for his presence in the rubble was that he had been walking past the bar when the explosion occurred and was sucked in with the blast. But a thorough forensic investigation found that, if Walsh had been walking by the front of the pub, he would have been blown into the front showroom of Annesley Motors across the road. A large security shutter, which was pulled down and locked across the front main entrance and window of the pub, had landed in the forecourt of the garage.

The investigation team also found the two containers Rossi had used, within a few feet of where he was found by the firemen. The forensic sleuths discovered traces of the vaporised fuel in Walsh's burned tracksuit, consistent with his having handled the petrol. On 16 November, Rossi was arrested and brought in for questioning to Store Street station. He refused to answer any questions, protesting that his detention was illegal. He was later released without charge.

On 28 July, Detective Inspector Duggan arrested Walsh and brought him before the Special Criminal Court, where he was arraigned on five charges of unlawful trespass, criminal damage, arson, and attempted fraud. The investigation team requested that Walsh be tried in the non-jury court because of his links with a number of subversives for whom he had acted as a legal adviser. He also had links with loyalist paramilitaries. In August, Detective Inspector Duggan objected to a High Court application by Walsh for bail. He told Mr Justice Fergus Flood that he had known Walsh for a long time. 'He is engaged in criminal activity in the city and influences people by way of intimidation. I believe he will do this if released,' he said. The detective also revealed that a potential witness in the case said he was more afraid of Walsh than he was of going to prison. The court, however, granted the gangster bail.

Rossi Walsh's trial was almost as remarkable as the manner in which he was finally caught. It started on 19 October and lasted for three weeks. Walsh denied all the charges. On the fourth day of the trial he sacked his legal team, barristers Michael Feehan and Luigi Rea and solicitor Tim McEniry, and took over his own defence. Prior to discharging his counsel, Walsh had constantly interrupted them while they cross-examined witnesses, frantically passing them hastily-scribbled notes. One interruption followed another. At one stage the barristers were spending more time turning around to listen to Walsh than actually facing the witnesses. Dressed in a tracksuit, Walsh grilled the detectives who had investigated him and were trying to secure his conviction. He accused them of tampering with evidence and questioned their professionalism. One of his assistants in the case, an associate who also wore a tracksuit, acted as his note-taker for the rest of the trial.

Each morning Walsh arrived in court with a large bag stuffed with legal books. Under cross-examination by Rossi, James and Christy Collins admitted that they had also been arrested and questioned about the pub explosion. Christy Collins said that he had been threatened a month before the explosion that the pub 'would be left like a carpark'. He claimed that he did not know who made the threats. Walsh also had several run-ins with the judges, accusing them of being biased and improperly constituted. On one occasion he accused Judge Buchanan of falling asleep. 'It's an outrageous situation to say that a member of the court should lapse into a lack of concentration. I am calling on the court to have a retrial,' he demanded. After a short adjournment, Judge Morris, whose patience was obviously wearing thin, refused Walsh's application and assured him that his fellow judge had not been asleep.

In his closing remarks, Walsh declared that he couldn't remember the events of 12 September 1992. 'I have absolutely no recollection due to the incident about it. That's basically it.' He asked the court for a 'not guilty' verdict, claiming that the State had not proved its case against him. On 9 November, however, the Special Criminal Court found the evidence against Rossi overwhelming. He was found guilty as charged.

Before sentence was passed, Judge Frederick Morris told him: 'You, either acting alone or with others, deliberately assembled the paraphernalia of destruction in the licensed premises, with the clear intention of destroying it without regard for the owners or members of the public. This type of conduct cannot be tolerated in a civilised society.' On the charge of arson, Rossi Walsh was sentenced to fifteen years in prison, and he got ten years each for causing criminal damage and for trespassing with intent to cause criminal damage.

As soon as the sentence was passed, Walsh was on his feet again. He applied to Judge Morris in his capacity as a High Court judge for a *habeas corpus* order under Article 40 of the Constitution. Judge Morris had had enough of Rossi and curtly replied 'No'. Walsh was handcuffed and brought under armed escort to Portlaoise maximum-security prison.

Rossi's bad luck did not stop when he went inside. Three weeks into his sentence, he was beaten by a few of his former partners in crime. It was later claimed that Rossi had tried to take over the landing which held several members of The General's gang and the Athy mob. They were also doing long terms and had no intention of allowing Rossi to have his way. He was then transferred to Limerick high-security prison, where he got a severe beating from another member of a hardened Dublin gang. Walsh was hospitalised and had to receive physiotherapy for injuries to his back, arm and neck.

Since he was jailed, Walsh has clogged the legal system in Dublin with dozens of appeals and High Court applications. He is suing the State for the beating he got in Limerick. This time, however, his injuries are genuine. He made a lengthy submission on several points of law relating to his conviction to the Court of Criminal Appeal. These were rejected. Walsh then appealed the decision to the Supreme Court. Another district judge described as 'frivolous and time-wasting' an appeal against convictions he received for road traffic offences. Shortly before his trial, Walsh had been banned from driving for three years and jailed for six months, for riding a high-powered motorbike without insurance or a licence and refusing to give an alcohol breath test.

In April 1994 Walsh was back in the Dublin district court to face five charges, of beating up three women and two teenage girls. In May 1993 his twelve-year-old daughter had had a row with two other teenagers. Walsh thought that the two girls had assaulted his daughter. He punched one of them, a fifteen-year-old, in the jaw and slapped the other, a thirteen-year-old, across the face. He also threatened to smash their heads with a hammer. Later that evening, Walsh's wife Monica and another daughter attacked two other teenagers near their home.

That night, while he was out drinking with his wife in the Irishtown House pub, he got into a row with three women about his earlier encounter with the two young girls. Walsh punched one of the women four times in the face, breaking her nose and leaving her with two black eyes. When the second woman in the company tried to intervene, Walsh punched her in the face, breaking her nose and leaving a gash which required several stitches. He then turned and punched the third woman, a fifty-one-year-old, in the chest. The case was brought to court while Rossi was in jail. Judge Michael Connellan imposed a total of two years for the string of assaults, which he ordered Rossi must serve at the end of his fifteen-year stretch for the pub explosion. 'You beat up young, defenceless women and children and this cannot be allowed,' the Judge told Walsh. His wife and daughter were also convicted of assault. Monica Walsh was bound to the peace and her twenty-two-year-old daughter Sandra was given a two-year suspended sentence.

But Rossi Walsh refused to allow the Irish judiciary to forget about him. His cell is equipped with a fax machine and a word processor, from which he processes appeals and submissions on a whole range of matters for the High Court and Supreme Court on behalf of other prisoners. In 1995 he even applied to the Supreme Court to be granted permission to represent other prisoners in court in Dublin. The spectacle of tracksuited Rossi Walsh being escorted from Limerick every day to represent his 'clients' in the Dublin criminal courts was an idea which the judges found too much to contemplate. The application was refused.

Rossi Walsh, the scam man, will not be eligible for release until the year 2005. Detectives who had battled with him for many years still smile when the circumstances of his capture are mentioned. But one officer, who knew him for over twenty years, reckons that prison may have saved his life. 'If Rossi had kept going the way he was, stepping on a lot of people's toes, then there's a good chance he would have been shot. He probably doesn't appreciate it, but prison may have saved his neck.'

The Boxer

The repercussions from two major events in 1979 and 1980, which took place many hundreds of miles away, were to influence major changes in gangland, with dire consequences for the rest of Irish society. The first was the Iranian revolution in 1979, when Islamic fundamentalists overthrew the Shah and his ruling class. The other was the outbreak of war in Afghanistan a year later. Both incidents resulted in a sudden flood of high-quality, cheap heroin on the world market. The Shah's fleeing supporters and the Afghan rebels off-loaded countless tons of the drug to finance their disparate causes. Organised crime enthusiastically cashed in on the glut and ensured the flood reached the streets of every European city, establishing a permanent, insatiable demand for one of the 20th century's greatest evils.

In Ireland the Dunnes were the first of the criminal fraternity to discover heroin through their drug contacts in England. They foisted 'gear' on a generation of kids and adults who had no idea of what they were letting themselves in for. In 1980 heroin struck Dublin's south inner-city neighbourhoods like a tornado. The golden brown powder had a stranglehold on the depressed, run-down ghettos of the south-side in a matter of weeks. The spiralling addiction rate created a voracious demand for heroin and a market which the Dunnes alone could not satisfy. Other criminals soon began filling the demand.

In 1981 heroin hit the streets of the north inner-city with the same dazzling speed as it had south of the river. Street pushers gave out free introductory deals to children as young as twelve in order to get them hooked. The heroin epidemic brought devastation and despair. It caused a tidal wave of crime, disease and death, creating a human wasteland strewn with the debris of broken lives. By the summer of

1981 heroin addicts were shooting up on the streets and in the flat complexes of the north-side, which was to suffer most from the drug explosion. That same year, in the midst of this mayhem, Thomas Martin Mullen celebrated his tenth birthday. It would not be long before he too would cash in on the misery around him.

Born on 13 October 1971, Thomas Mullen witnessed at first hand the human horror caused by heroin in his neighbourhood. The youngest of three brothers, he lived in Dominick Street flats in the north inner-city. The dilapidated complex was ravaged by heroin abuse. Successive governments and local authorities had allowed the already bleak neighbourhoods to decay into run-down, no-hope ghettos, an ideal breeding ground for the spread of heroin addiction.

With the economy in full recession, these areas suffered the highest rates of unemployment. There was also a chronic shortage of educational and training facilities. The drop-out rate from school was the highest in the country. The numbers entering third-level education were the lowest. The Mullens, like their neighbours, were living on the breadline. Thomas Mullen hung around street corners with his mates, watching the pushers selling to the growing army of addicts. There had been a crime explosion of muggings, handbag snatches, burglaries and robberies in the area as strung-out junkies tried to get money to buy 'gear'. On the odd occasion that Mullen bothered to go to school, it was not unusual for him to have to step across the zonked-out addicts as they lay around the stairwell of his block. But Thomas Mullen was one of the lucky ones.

From around the age of ten he was a member of a local boxing club where he proved himself to be a talented fighter. In fact, boxing was one of the only sports to keep the kids off the streets and away from drugs. While many of his neighbours and friends were succumbing to heroin, Mullen was steering clear of drugs and becoming a boxing champion. By his mid-teens he was representing Ireland as a light-middleweight champion at tournaments around the world. He dropped out of school at the age of fourteen but remained unemployed. Like most of the other kids he grew up with, he dabbled in petty crime, joyriding and stealing from cars. When he was nine years old he received his first conviction, for larceny and receiving. By the time he was seventeen he had another three convictions for theft and road traffic offences. But in the prevailing climate his record was unimpressive.

By 1990 Mullen, who was now nineteen, had become a local hero as a result of his success in the ring, and had started coaching local youngsters in a boxing club at Buckingham Street. He was the star attraction at an exhibition fight during a local community festival which he helped to organise. Mullen, who would become known on the streets as 'The Boxer', was the very picture of youthful health, fitness and clean living. He was tall and well-built, with tightly-cropped blond hair. The neighbourhood kids looked up to him and the local people regarded him as a good example. He was the very personification of how good life could be if the kids stayed away from drugs. He became a symbol of hope in an otherwise depressed world. But behind the facade of respectability Mullen harboured dark aspirations.

He was attracted by the potential wealth to be made selling heroin. Despite witnessing the devastation it caused, he made a conscious decision to become a dealer himself and contribute to the misery which blighted his neighbourhood. Greed overshadowed any moral dilemmas his business posed. Mullen and an associate, another inner-city boxer of the same age, were introduced to a supplier in Liverpool through another Dublin drug dealer. They both invested money in small quantities of heroin which they smuggled into Dublin with the help of a number of local junkies who were paid for their efforts with free heroin. Mullen and his partner had little difficulty in turning the consignments into profit. The profit was re-invested. Gangland had a new breed of ruthless drug dealer.

Mullen and his partner fully exploited their ties to the neighbour-hood in order to establish their business base. With deep roots in the local community, they had the perfect cover for their nefarious trade. Most of their customers were neighbours and kids he had grown up with. The Boxer had learned from the mistakes of the dealers who had dominated the market throughout the 1980s. He and his partner began discreetly filling the gap left by the big barons who had been jailed. Mullen had seen the anger generated by the drug epidemic in the mid-1980s and the rise of people-power in the shape of the Inner City Organisation Network (ICON). As a teenager Mullen had even participated in anti-drug marches in his community.

The ICON had succeeded in pushing the dealers out of the worst-affected areas. Their tactic was to march on the homes of known pushers and remain there until the pushers were forced to leave the neighbourhood. The ICON also placed 'checkpoints' around estates to keep the dealers and their addicts out. On the southside the IRA had given their support to the movement, which had helped convince the heroin suppliers it was in the interests of their health to leave. The angry people staged mass protests outside the Dáil and finally focused the minds of the Government on alleviating the socio-economic misery of the city's neglected ghettos.

But by the time Mullen began dealing, the ICON across the city was largely defunct. Heroin abuse was as bad as ever. The people had grown weary of their war of attrition with the endless army of pushers and addicts, who had gradually returned to ply their evil trade. AIDS, transmitted through shared needles, had also spread like wildfire through the heroin-abusing population. Whole families had quite literally been wiped out by the new 20th-century plague. Mullen and his associate kept a low profile and were not flamboyant like their predecessors. Mullen rarely handled the drugs himself, a fact which would create major problems for the police in the future. The Boxer organised a sophisticated network of loyal dealers and couriers, who kept their mouths shut because they were terrified of him and his associates.

Among those loyal employees were some of the kids he had been entrusted to train as boxers. One local source interviewed for this book angrily recalled Mullen's use of the kids in his business: 'The lads looked up to him and were happy to move stuff around for him. Out of loyalty and fear they told no-one what was going on. Here was this bastard everyone considered a clean-cut hero exploiting these innocent kids. Some of them became addicts themselves and he often paid them with free smack. He didn't touch the stuff himself and he didn't seem to give a fuck about the damage he was doing. He was an evil bastard who was motivated solely by greed.'

But Mullen and his partner weren't the only sporting icons to be corrupted by the lure of drug money. Another local lad who had excelled at sport was now also dabbling in heroin distribution and becoming a wealthy young man. Like Mullen, he did not abuse hard drugs himself.

The Boxer organised his business from a run-down flat in the Lourdes House complex off Sean MacDermot Street. He had moved in there to live with his girlfriend and childhood sweetheart, Allison O'Brien, a local girl he had been going out with since leaving school. The couple had two sons, one born in 1987 and the second in 1991. The money began to roll in as Mullen's operation expanded. With the steady flow of cash he no longer concealed his wealth. He began to buy expensive, high-performance cars, designer clothes and costly jewellery. Despite being unemployed, Mullen never bothered to claim social welfare. At first he gave locals the impression that he derived his money from armed robbery and claimed he was a member of The Monk's gang. Traditionally in working-class areas of Dublin, so-called Ordinary Decent Criminals are accepted. The perception of the blagger is that he is not harming his own people and is getting on the best way he can.

As business flourished, Mullen and his partner eventually went their separate ways. Mullen continued to control the heroin trade while his partner moved into cocaine and ecstasy distribution. Mullen carried on dealing with a Liverpool-based crime family who could provide large quantities of heroin. The streets of the inner-city were flooded with heroin and there was an upsurge of drug addiction, particularly among young teenagers. By early 1992 suspicion began to fall on Mullen. But the community was divided about The Boxer, who continued to coach teenagers in the boxing club. A lot of people refused to believe that he was a drug dealer.

By now he no longer wanted to rear his family in the drug-infested environment to which he had contributed so generously. He didn't want his children growing up amid such desolation. He wanted to secure a good future for them. In April of that year Mullen paid £16,500 in cash for an old cottage in the more salubrious neighbourhood of Clonliffe Avenue, a safe distance from his inner-city patch. He completely gutted and rebuilt the house. The twenty-one-year-old unemployed drug dealer lavishly refurbished the place, spending an additional estimated £40,000 in cash for every possible luxury, including an expensive security system.

The month before he bought the house, Mullen had opened a deposit account with a building society. Every few days he lodged large sums, ranging from £1,000 up to £7,000. He also made regular large withdrawals of cash. Between 1992 and 1996 he lodged a total of over £150,000 in this one account. Mullen was extremely shrewd with his money and could account for every dishonest penny he made. In September 1993 he opened an investment account with the building society, with a down payment of £20,000 in cash. Between September 1993 and December 1994, a period of fifteen months, the wealthy drug baron lodged a total of £200,000 to the account. When he eventually closed the account in July 1996 it had made him a profit of £63,000.

He also lodged large sums of cash in the names of relatives and in banks in England. He splashed out on long lavish, holidays in the Mediterranean, St Lucia and Jamaica for his extended family. He also indulged his love for boxing, and never missed a big fight anywhere in the world. He and his pals flew around the world to major title fights, including a trip to Hong Kong to watch another former inner-city boxer, Steve Collins, defend his world title. Mullen flew everywhere first-class and stayed in the best hotels.

One man who had long been suspicious of Thomas Mullen was local independent TD, Tony Gregory. Gregory probably knew more about the devastating effects of drug abuse on the downtrodden city ghettos than any other public representative ever elected in Ireland. He was born and reared in the north inner-city and lived in Ballybough. When he left university he threw himself into working for the local community. In 1979 he was elected to the city council and three years later he won a seat as an independent socialist TD.

Gregory was one of the first community activists to urge local people not to tolerate the heroin scourge. Since that time he has been an implacable enemy of the dealers and, together with a group of community workers, constantly monitors the source and movement of drugs in the inner-city.

In late 1991 and early 1992 Gregory, aware of the fresh flow of heroin to the streets, began compiling intelligence on the new drug dealers. Through his sources in the community Gregory soon identified Mullen as one of the main suppliers. Another big dealer was the local sporting hero, who was still making a name for himself. At first Gregory had difficulty convincing the community that Mullen was a dealer.

He recalled: 'He was well-liked in the area and people simply did not want to believe that Mullen was selling heroin to their kids. It was hard to contemplate such an act of betrayal on his own people.' Gregory began the job of trying to rebuild the anti-drugs movement in the area with the help of people like community activist Mick Raftery and Sinn Féin councillor Christy Burke, both of whom were seasoned campaigners. In the boxing club, Gregory's intervention led to internal tension between those who believed that Mullen was a drug dealer and those who didn't. Eventually however, after he had moved out of the area, the majority were convinced that their local TD was right. Mullen left the club before he was kicked out in late 1992.

Gregory also brought his information to the attention of the Garda North-Central Divisional Drug Squad, based in Store Street Station. At the time it was under the control of Detective Sergeant Mick Finn, a dedicated cop who had been instrumental in putting several of the big local suppliers behind bars in the 1980s. Finn now turned his attention to Thomas Mullen. His team began keeping tabs on the former boxing star and passed on their information to the Drug Squad attached to the Central Detective Unit (CDU) in Harcourt Square. Mullen's was one of scores of names of street-dealers the Gardaí had collected. No-one, not even Tony Gregory, had yet realised just how big The Boxer had become. Unperturbed by the growing local concern at his activities, Mullen continued to build his empire. He was becoming a swaggering, cocky gangster. The Boxer considered himself too careful to be caught.

In 1993 Mullen was introduced to twenty-four-year-old Deanna Bird while she was visiting a friend in Dublin. Bird, from Liverpool, knew a number of Mullen's drug contacts in the city. He asked Bird was she interested in a 'bit of business', working for him as a drug courier. She agreed and Mullen arranged to contact her in England through a mutual friend the next time he had a shipment to transport.

In September she got a phone-call at her mother's home in Liverpool. It was Mullen. He told her he was on his way over from London and he wanted to meet her. Accompanied by a friend, Bird met Mullen in Lime Street railway station around midnight. He gave her a parcel which was tightly wrapped with brown tape. Mullen told her to take the parcel on the ferry from Holyhead to Dun Laoghaire. He said the boat was safer because the Customs never searched the person, just their bags. He gave her money for expenses and a telephone number to call.

Bird and her friend took the morning sailing from Holyhead. She concealed the heroin down the back of her jeans. When Bird arrived in Dublin she got a taxi to a city-centre pub where she met Mullen. He drove her to the Forte Crest Hotel at Dublin airport. On the way she handed him the package and he paid her £1,000 in cash for her efforts. That night she stayed in the hotel and the next morning flew back to Liverpool. The heroin she had smuggled in, when cut for street sales, was worth £250,000.

In January 1994 Bird received another call from Mullen. He said he had more work for her. Two days later, on Friday the 28th, he called again and instructed her to take the train to London where he arranged to meet her in Watford station. When Bird arrived Mullen was waiting on the platform. She walked with him to a car he had parked outside the station. He opened the boot and showed her a shopping-bag containing two brown-paper parcels, each one similar in size to the packet she had delivered in September. They contained a total of 460 grams of forty-seven-percent pure heroin.

At the time Mullen paid his Liverpool suppliers around £25,000 for the haul. In Dublin the price of heroin had risen sharply due to increased demand, and the street value of the consignment was almost £500,000, of which Mullen stood to take almost £200,000 in profit. Deanna Bird took the train back to Liverpool. The following afternoon she took the ferry from Holyhead to Dun Laoghaire in the company of a male companion. She rang Mullen from Wales and he instructed her to meet him in the Forte Crest Hotel at Dublin Airport as before.

Unfortunately for Bird, the Drug Squad were waiting for her at the ferry terminal in Dun Laoghaire. Detective Sergeant Noirín O'Sullivan and her team had received information that Bird was bringing in a quantity of heroin. At the time they didn't know where or to whom the drugs were to be delivered. O'Sullivan was one of the force's most experienced narcotics officers, having spent practically all of her career catching drug dealers. She had been a member of the famous 'Mockeys', the seven-member squad of young officers who had worked undercover, posing as drug addicts, in the early 1980s. During a two-year period between 1982 and 1984 the Mockeys, all of whom were native Dubliners, had been hugely successful and became something of a legend in the inner-city. The squad was a totally new departure in the force and had evolved mainly because of the officer's own initiative.

Deanna Bird got off the ferry and the undercover team watched as she was joined by her male friend. The detectives thought he was her minder. They tailed the taxi the twenty miles or so across the city to Dublin Airport. At this stage O'Sullivan was worried that they might 'lose control' of the situation, which in police parlance means losing the target. They still had no idea where the stuff was to be delivered. Just as the taxi was stopping at the hotel entrance, Detective Sergeant O'Sullivan ordered her team to intercept the courier.

Realising what was happening, Mullen promptly left the hotel. As happens in many major police investigations, the Drug Squad had stumbled across a major breakthrough. They were surprised by the quantity Bird was carrying. It was one of the largest heroin hauls in several years. And when they interviewed Deanna Bird they realised it was destined for The Boxer. For the first time the Gardaí discovered how big Thomas Mullen had become. Before this he was considered to be just another average drug dealer. Now he was one of Dublin's biggest suppliers of heroin. They had evidence which put him in the big league of multi-kilo international drug traffickers.

Deanna Bird later made a full statement outlining her involvement with Mullen. The Drug Squad searched Mullen's house at Clonliffe Avenue, where they found £2,000 sterling, the sum Mullen had agreed to pay Bird. They also seized a mobile phone registered in his name. It matched the number he had given Bird to call him. O'Sullivan's squad believed they had enough to sustain a conspiracy charge against him and forwarded a file to the Director of Public Prosecutions. The DPP decided, however, that the case was not strong enough for a successful prosecution. Mullen later applied to the courts to have the confiscated money returned. The application was refused and the money granted to the State. Deanna Bird was charged and released on bail.

A major conference was called in the Drug Squad's headquarters at Harcourt Square. Detective Inspector Malachy Mulligan launched an operation to put Mullen out of business. It was appropriately code-named 'Operation Knockout'. The investigation team began compiling intelligence on Mullen and profiling his associates. A surveillance team was put together to keep tabs on the main targets. The objective of Operation Knockout was to identify and locate The Boxer's distribution centre and catch him and his lieutenants in possession.

The arrest of Bird led to a serious disagreement between Mullen and his suppliers in Liverpool, who threatened to come to Dublin and beat him up. The threat was never carried out. In the meantime The Boxer teamed up with another major dealer, a thirty-one-year-old convicted armed robber from Artane. The dealer, like Mullen, was an extremely clever gangster who controlled a complex distribution network without coming into direct contact with the stuff himself. He was also feared as a violent thug. The Artane dealer had been doing business with a London-based Turkish syndicate. He introduced them to Mullen during a trip to England. The Turks, who smuggled the heroin from their home country, could provide eighty-percent pure heroin, twice the strength of the stuff coming from Liverpool. The average street deal in Dublin contained twenty-five-percent pure heroin. Dealing in Turkish 'gear' meant that Mullen could dramatically increase his profit margins.

With business booming he needed a distributor he could trust. In March he offered his cousin, Thomas Brannigan, work as a heroin delivery man. A builder's labourer from Dorset Street, Brannigan accepted the offer. The twenty-eight-year-old father of one was perfect for the job. He wasn't a drug abuser himself and, with no criminal record, was unknown to the Gardaí. Mullen told Brannigan it would be a 'handy job'. Mullen rented a flat at St Patrick's Road in Drumcondra under a false name for his cousin to use as a safe house for storing and preparing the drug for street deals. He showed Brannigan how to cut and weigh the heroin and provided a number of motorbikes, registered in various names, for his 'rounds'.

The Boxer had learned to be more careful after Deanna Bird's arrest. He devised a system whereby he could stand even further apart from the drug racket. When a shipment was smuggled into the country Brannigan would be told to drive to a certain location in his car and wait with his window down. Another courier on a bicycle would ride by and throw a package of heroin, normally one or two kilos in quantity, into the car before disappearing again. Brannigan would then stash the heroin in the flat. Each morning Mullen would ring him with a list of orders for the day. He used codes for the different quantities to be prepared. A 'ticket' was an ounce and a 'package' a kilo.

Later, when he had the deliveries prepared, Brannigan would meet Mullen in the Daniel O'Connell pub on Aston Quay in the city centre. Mullen would give him a list of names and addresses where the 'gear' was to be delivered. Brannigan would make three or more delivery runs around the city every night. He was paid £50 for each delivery. Brannigan never collected the money. Another member of the gang collected the cash. The Boxer operated a strict rule of not giving credit to customers: no money, no heroin.

Meanwhile the Drug Squad in Harcourt Square were continuing their investigations into The Boxer's operation. Intelligence led them to Brannigan, and he was placed under surveillance in October 1994. After several weeks the operation paid off. On the evening of 15 November, Detective Sergeant O'Sullivan and her squad got information that the Artane dealer who had provided the introduction to the Turkish suppliers was expecting a delivery from Mullen. The pair operated a barter system between them to augment each other's supplies. Brannigan travelled to Finglas village where he handed over the high-quality uncut heroin to Alan Costello, a courier recruited by the Artane dealer. Costello had run into debt and had agreed to work as a courier as a pay-off. Detective Sergeant O'Sullivan decided to swoop on Costello as he rode off on his bicycle with the bag of heroin thrown across the handlebars. When he was surrounded the courier threw his bike at the armed detectives, who promptly arrested him. The seized haul was seventy-six-percent pure heroin.

Following the arrest the surveillance remained on Brannigan. The squad were hopeful of catching him and Mullen together with the heroin. They still didn't know where the 'gear' was being stashed. Meanwhile, Brannigan was being blamed for setting Costello up, because he had just delivered the heroin when the Gardaí swooped. Mullen sent someone up to Mountjoy Prison to warn Costello about making allegations. The Artane dealer was also worried and he had Costello shot in the leg while he was out on bail as a warning not to give names to the Drug Squad. The luckless courier was too terrified to make an official complaint about the incident to the Gardaí. He subsequently pleaded guilty and was jailed for ten years. In court, Detective Sergeant O'Sullivan said that Costello had good grounds to fear naming the godfather he had been working for.

A few days after Costello's arrest, Drug Squad officers John Fitzpatrick and Tom Madden stopped Thomas Brannigan for a drug search as he was driving through Fairview. The detectives suspected that he was in the process of moving a shipment of heroin. A thorough search proved negative. The following day Brannigan told Mullen that he wanted to get out because he was scared at how close the cops were getting. The Boxer asked him to hang on for another while, that everything would be OK. But everything would not be OK.

A week later the Drug Squad swooped again. This time they had followed Brannigan to the flat on St Patrick's Road and caught him with almost 700 grams of heroin. The maximum street value at the time was estimated at over £500,000. During an interview with detectives, Brannigan admitted to handling over five kilos of heroin for Thomas Mullen and explained how he had got involved in the operation. But the detectives believed that he had handled much larger quantities. When he was asked how he would describe his cousin, Brannigan replied: 'He is a real tight cunt, he never touches the stuff himself.' But again there was insufficient evidence to sustain charges against Mullen. Brannigan said he was too scared to testify against his cousin for fear that he would be shot.

In the meantime the Boxer continued to enjoy the fruits of his labours. His efforts to keep a safe distance from his product had paid off. He had survived two attempts by the Drug Squad to nab him. In September 1994 he began house-hunting again. The twenty-three-year-old drug dealer fancied a new development of four-bedroom homes at St David's in Artane. The homes were priced at £85,000 each. Mullen placed a £1,000 cash deposit on one of the houses in the name of a relative. At the same time he opened a new building society account in the same relative's name with a cash deposit of £1,000. Over the next twelve weeks a total of £104,000 was lodged to the account. Two cheque withdrawals were used to pay for the house in December 1994. The relative in whose name the house had been bought made a legal agreement, signing the property over to Thomas Mullen.

In January 1995 Mullen paid an interior design company over £25,000 in cash to lavishly decorate his new home. He spent another £25,000 on furnishings and an elaborate security system which included closed-circuit cameras. The house had expensive wooden floors, mirrored wardrobes and brass light fittings.

The following month Deanna Bird was jailed for seven years for her role in bringing in Mullen's heroin. Shortly after being sentenced she was granted temporary release to give birth to twins. The following December Judge Michael Moriarty suspended the rest of her sentence on compassionate grounds. Detective Inspector Malachy Mulligan told the Dublin Circuit Criminal Court that the courier had made a remarkable statement of admission. She had been exploited by others and had got involved through naiveté.

In March Mullen found another willing employee to do his dirty work. Martin Gannon had grown up with Mullen in Dominick Street. Again, Gannon was perfect for the operation. The thirty-one-year-old married man was a carpenter; he had no criminal record, nor was he a drug abuser. Like Mullen he was motivated solely by greed and suffered no moral qualms about what he was doing. He agreed to replace Thomas Brannigan, who vouched for him. Mullen showed Gannon how to cut and re-package heroin for street deals.

Gannon built up a large number of customers for Mullen's heroin and within a short time was himself earning an average of £1,000 per week. But the Drug Squad team targeting Mullen soon heard about Gannon's operation through the grapevine and observed him meeting with The Boxer. They gave him their undivided attention from a discreet distance for several weeks.

On 24 August 1995, members of the Operation Knockout team stopped Gannon as he was driving in the Summerhill Parade area of the north inner-city. He had just collected 300 grams of heroin from Mullen and was on his way to his flat to re-pack it into street deals. Detective Garda Dave McInerney found the 'gear' when he searched Gannon.

A subsequent search of his flat in Dominick Street uncovered a weighing-scales, notebooks detailing his drug operations, plastic bags for holding deals and over £9,000 in cash. When questioned by detectives Gannon admitted to earning £1,000 per week during his relatively short career as a drug baron. In a statement he confessed: 'It was well worth doing. I don't do the stuff myself, I tried it once but didn't like it. The whole game was to make money. I suppose it is easy money. I am sorry about all this. I can't tell you who I'm doing the gear for because I would be killed.' Thomas Mullen had again narrowly escaped a serious charge.

Back in the inner-city, Mullen's heroin was causing a new addiction crisis on the streets and the local community could endure no more. There was no longer any doubt among the residents about The Boxer's involvement in drugs. He had become Public Enemy Number One and the media began taking an interest in the under-world's newest millionaire. He was referred to in stories as The Boxer or Ringmaster but because of libel restrictions was not named.

In July 1995 Tony Gregory, the man who a few years earlier had raised the alarm about Mullen, described the conditions his constituents had to endure as a result of the heroin epidemic. In an article he wrote for the *Evening Herald,* under the heading, 'The sick, unfeeling scum who prey on our lovely children', the campaigning politician described to the wider public how Mullen enjoyed a lavish lifestyle out of the misery he was helping to create.

Gregory wrote: 'He is a local who would have grown up with the families whose children he is now destroying with heroin. Even children who went through his boxing club have become heroin addicts and are now pitiful HIV-positive junkies. Only sick, unfeeling scum could watch this happen to lovely young children. The houses and the new cars were paid for by the misery and suffering of their addict victims.

'They don't seem to care that all this money came from the hand-bags of pensioners or other innocents attacked by crazed, desperate addicts often armed with infected blood-filled syringes. The Ringmaster and those close to him flaunt their wealth while their victims die slow painful deaths.'

Gregory went on to attack the inability of the various Government agencies, especially the Departments of Justice and Health, to deal with the spiralling problem. He also questioned why the Revenue Commissioners had not investigated how people like Mullen, who was unemployed and not claiming social welfare, could afford such a lavish lifestyle. In the north inner-city the anti-drug movement re-organised and eventually took part in a citywide initiative. They targeted The Boxer.

Despite the growing pressure from his former neighbours and the police, Mullen conducted business as usual. He believed himself untouchable and too clever to be caught. In London his main connection in the Turkish community was a middle-aged butcher called Turhan Mustafa who worked from a shop in Tottenham. Mustafa was the front man for the Turks and organised Mullen's orders. As part of the deal he also organised couriers to deliver the stuff to Ireland, thus reducing the risks for The Boxer.

In December 1995 Mustafa introduced Mullen to Katherine Brooks as a new courier for his heroin. Thirty-year-old Brooks was to become a pathetic, helpless figure in the plot. She came from a good home and had gone to boarding school. After leaving school at the age of sixteen she began working as a hotel receptionist. She went out with a drug addict who introduced her to heroin. Brooks became hopelessly addicted to the drug and eventually turned to prostitution to feed her habit.

In early 1995 Turhan Mustafa had hired her for sex. He had convinced Brooks to stop working as a prostitute and started a relationship with her. The Turk paid for her apartment, clothes and food. He also gave her free heroin and gradually increased the quantities. Over several months she became totally dependent on Mustafa and his heroin, progressing from smoking to injecting the drug to get a hit. On the street her habit would have cost £200 per day. Brooks had effectively become Mustafa's prisoner. He began putting pressure on her to repay him for all the free heroin. He regularly beat her, and threatened to stop giving her 'gear' or to kill her.

Her payback, he told her, was to work as a courier for Mullen. When she refused Mustafa threatened her with a kitchen knife. In January 1996 Mustafa sent Brooks on a dry run to Dublin, to familiarise her with the route. She took the ferry from Holyhead to Dun Laoghaire. When she arrived in Ireland she saw only a few

Customs officers and wasn't searched. The following day she returned to London and reported to Mustafa.

A few weeks later she received a package from Mullen. In it Brooks found a car key and a note with a registration number and the make of a car. A few weeks later Mustafa phoned and told her that she was going to Ireland for Mullen. That afternoon the Turkish heroin trafficker arrived in Brooks's flat and wrapped up a consignment of heroin in gift wrapping. He instructed his courier to take the package to Dun Laoghaire on the ferry. In the carpark near the terminal building the car described in Mullen's note would be parked. She was to open the car and put the heroin package in the glove compartment.

Brooks took a flight to Dublin instead of the ferry and got a taxi across the city to Dun Laoghaire where she found the car and did as instructed. She then went to the Port View Hotel. Mullen had pre-booked a room for her under the name Kathy Jenkins. Some time later a man, accompanied by a woman and child, called to the hotel. He went to her room and handed her a shopping-bag full of money. 'This is from Thomas,' he said as he handed it over. The following day Brooks flew back to London.

A few weeks later Katherine Brooks was again dispatched with a consignment of heroin to Dun Laoghaire. The same car as before had been left in the carpark. This time she went to a different hotel and waited for the money to arrive. After an hour Thomas Mullen called to her room and handed her a carrier-bag stuffed with used notes. She returned to London. She made another trip a short time later with a similar quantity.

Back in Ireland things were getting hot for The Boxer. In February a list of names of known drug dealers was issued anonymously to a newspaper. It was dubiously claimed that it was an IRA hit list. One of the men on the list, Gerry Lee, was shot dead a few weeks later in his home in Malahide. Lee, a thirty-year-old married man with children, had been a former armed robber who had also made the switch to dealing in drugs. His speciality was ecstasy. It later transpired that Lee had been shot for different reasons entirely and his murder had had nothing to do with the hit list. But The Boxer was now a scared man.

In April 1996 Tony Gregory took the momentous step of using Dáil privilege to name Mullen and the Artane drug dealer during a session of the Public Accounts Committee. Gregory asked representatives of the Revenue Commissioners why they were not investigating the financial affairs of these two drug barons. The following week *Sunday Independent* journalist Veronica Guerin named Mullen for the first time in a newspaper article. She managed to talk to Mullen for a short time, during which he claimed he had gained his wealth as a result of an inheritance. He also claimed it came from savings he had made while working as a roofer in England over several years.

Within a matter of days The Boxer, together with his girlfriend and children, left Ireland in a hurry and went to Spain for a two-month holiday. He rented two villas in the Costa del Sol for £1,000 per week each. In the meantime he attempted to run his drug business from the sunshine.

For several months the Drug Squad in Dublin had been sharing intelligence with Scotland Yard about Mullen's operation. Scotland Yard had been running an operation, code-named 'Aldemere', in a bid to catch the Turkish syndicate. On 12 June Katherine Brooks was arrested by the Area 3 Drug Squad while on route to London City Airport. Officers found a kilo of heroin on her and in a search of her flat they discovered another three kilos hidden in the loft. Mustafa was arrested and charged.

In the follow-up investigation it became clear that the shipment of heroin had been destined for The Boxer's operation in Dublin. On 26 June, Veronica Guerin was assassinated by a hit-man working on the orders of a major Dublin crime boss. The godfather who organised the murder had set a chain of events in train which would turn gangland upside-down. The murder led to a raft of tough new legislation and the most comprehensive criminal investigation ever undertaken in the Irish Republic. For the first time since the evolution of organised crime the State was finally taking on the gangs who, as a result of two decades of poor Garda management and Government indifference, considered themselves above the law and untouchable.

One of the most significant developments was the establishment of the powerful Criminal Assets Bureau (CAB). This squad is made up of specially-trained detectives, as well as Customs, Revenue and social welfare officials. It also has its own team of accountants and senior legal advisors, and has wide-ranging powers to identify and seize assets belonging to individuals suspected of being involved in crime. The CAB has the authority, under international anti-drug legislation, to investigate and trace criminals' bank accounts throughout Europe. It would become one of the most effective crime-fighting weapons ever introduced in Europe. One of the most astonishing revelations as a result of the CAB's enquiries was the amount of money being made by the drug gangs. The gang who murdered Veronica Guerin had alone made over £25 million from selling cannabis in less than two years.

Within a few short months Ireland had become a very uncomfortable place for the Boxer and his like. Mullen decided to move his operating base to London. He rented a luxury home in Finchley, north London, paying £7,000 in cash as an initial deposit. At the same time he frantically began cleaning out his accounts in Dublin before the Criminal Assets Bureau could get near them.

In July he closed his investment account, withdrawing a total of £263,000 in cash. The following October he sold the house at Clonliffe Avenue for £60,000. The Boxer decided that the house in Artane could not be seized, because it was still in the name of a relative. It is also widely believed that at a meeting in Amsterdam with his partner from Artane and George Mitchell, The Penguin, The Boxer entrusted them with £3.5 million to hide away from the prying eyes of the authorities.

Also in July, Mullen's half brother, Sean Paul Mullen, was caught by the Operation Knockout team, picking up a consignment of firearms, including two hand-guns and ammunition. He was subsequently jailed for two years. In the same month Thomas Brannigan pleaded guilty to his role in his cousin's business. In court the following October, Detective Sergeant John Fitzpatrick described Brannigan as an 'essential cog and a trusted lieutenant in a tightly-knit drugs operation'. Fitzpatrick said that at the time the seizure was one of the biggest in Dublin. The detective told the Circuit Criminal Court: 'His cousin, who is known as The Boxer, was number one and he [Brannigan] was number two in this operation.' Judge Kieran O'Connor told Brannigan: 'That puts you in a special position and I am going to give you special treatment.' Brannigan was jailed for six years.

In the months following the Guerin murder several major crime figures fled Dublin. Over at least two months the flow of drugs into the country slowed to a trickle as the gangsters tried to regroup and take stock of what was happening at home. Among those to flee was Mullen's partner from Artane. Over the following months the Drug Squad, which had been renamed the Garda National Drug Unit, and the North-Central Divisional Drug Unit arrested and charged over a dozen of The Boxer's former associates. Millions of pounds worth of heroin were also seized.

But, despite the increasing pressure, Mullen continued to send heroin into Dublin. On several occasions he slipped in and out of the country to monitor his business. He was too greedy to know when to give it up. Every time he entered the country Mullen was watched closely by Garda surveillance teams. During one visit a team of anti-drug vigilantes had planned to assassinate The Boxer in north Dublin. But as they prepared for the gun attack they spotted the undercover cops and aborted the operation.

At the same time the community organisations launched an aggressive campaign against drug dealers throughout the greater Dublin area. The anger spilled out onto the streets, and riots broke out between local people and police when the locals tried to attack the house of one of Mullen's street pushers. The organisation put up posters throughout the city with the banner headline: 'Enemies of the community wanted for drugs murder'. The posters carried pictures of four people.

On 12 December 1996 over 1,000 angry people took part in a march on Mullen's empty house in Artane. Chanting, 'Pusher out, pusher out,' the protesters left a white coffin on the front doorstep to signify the scale of human devastation his business had brought to their lives. They also carried a banner which read: 'Mothers have cried as their children die from the drugs The Boxer sold them.' Events were beginning to catch up on The Boxer. His time was running out.

Katherine Brooks had been in an appalling state of addiction when she was remanded to Holloway Prison. She went into the prison's detoxification unit, where she spent four agonising weeks being weaned off the drug. As her mind cleared she began to realise how she had been used and misled. Mustafa, who was also on remand on drug trafficking charges, had promised that he would tell the truth about her involvement in the operation.

The day before the march on Mullen's home, Katherine Brooks talked to detectives attached to Operation Aldermere. With a clear mind she gave the officers a detailed, fourteen-page statement about her involvement with Mustafa and Mullen. She pleaded guilty to her role in the operation and agreed to give evidence in court against both men. She was sentenced to three years' imprisonment. Faced with this prospect Mustafa also pleaded guilty and was also jailed. Detectives put out an alert to forces throughout Britain that they wanted Thomas Martin Mullen, alias The Boxer, arrested.

In early 1997, 'Operation Spiderweb' was launched by Scotland Yard's Robbery Squad to catch a team of armed robbers in North London. The detectives believed their targets were storing their money in the Hampstead safe depository in Finchley. On 10 March the detectives spotted Thomas Mullen leaving the depository with a woman. They suspected that he was one of the armed robbers. On 14 March The Boxer was back. As he was leaving the building carrying a hold-all the cops swooped. When they searched the bag they found £105,000 in cash. Mullen had another £1,000 in his pocket.

A search of his safety deposit box uncovered another £100,000 in cash. Within a few hours the Robbery Squad had contacted the Area 3 Drugs Squad. Mullen was arrested and charged at Stratford Magistrates Court with conspiracy to smuggle heroin into Ireland between December 1995 and June 1996. A few weeks later the

Criminal Assets Bureau in Dublin obtained a High Court order preventing Mullen's representatives selling the house in Artane. The sale of the house was brought to the attention of the CAB after eagle-eyed Tony Gregory and his workers spotted a 'for sale' notice for the house in a local estate agent's. The Boxer's career as a big-league drug dealer was coming to an end. He was twenty-six years old.

Back in Ireland Mullen's courier, Martin Gannon, pleaded guilty to unlawful possession of heroin for the purpose of sale or supply. He again refused to name The Boxer for fear for his life. In his summing--up, Judge Cyril Kelly remarked: 'The evidence before this court is that this was a big operation. Clearly it was approached in a cold, clinical manner on a business footing, solely for financial profit and the accused was making a lot of money.' The Judge also noted that Gannon was a skilled man with no previous record and no addiction. He was involved in drugs purely out of greed. He sentenced Mullen's lieutenant to nine years in prison without leave to appeal. Gannon subsequently sought in the Court of Criminal Appeal to have the sentence reduced. The court refused, suggesting instead that it was tempted to increase the jail term to a much heftier twenty years.

Mullen went on trial at Snaresbrook Crown Court in September 1997. During a lengthy trial The Boxer told an astonishing tissue of lies. He claimed that he was the victim of a conspiracy between the IRA and the Gardaí. Denying any involvement in drugs, he implied that he was involved in a series of high-profile multi-million pound robberies in Ireland and said the IRA were trying to extort a million pounds from him. He also claimed that Tony Gregory was a front-man for the Provos. Katherine Brooks gave evidence of her involvement with Mullen and identified him to the court. But at the end of the trial the jury failed to agree on a verdict. Mullen smiled.

In January 1988 he was again tried in front of a new jury and again made the same outlandish claims. On 15 January it took the jury less than four hours to unanimously find Mullen guilty as charged. Passing sentence, Judge Timothy King told Mullen: 'You have been convicted in my view upon compelling evidence, indeed some might consider it overwhelming evidence. Those who traffic in class A drugs are the purveyors of misery, degradation and all too frequently death.'

The Judge said of Katherine Brooks: 'One only needs to see a person like Brooks to see just what devastation can be brought on the life of an individual who is addicted to a drug like heroin.' Detective Sergeant Dave Osborne, who arrested Mullen, Brooks and Mustafa, told the judge that The Boxer was the 'foremost drug trafficker in Dublin in the supply of heroin.' Thomas Martin Mullen was sentenced to eighteen years in jail. The Boxer, standing in the dock handcuffed to a prison officer, flinched when he heard the sentence. He was ashen-faced as he was led away. That night there were celebrations in the north inner-city at the news.

In the months since his incarceration British police have begun a major investigation to locate the rest of Mullen's ill-gotten fortune. If he does not tell them where it is then he could face another ten years in prison on top of the sentence he is already serving. The Boxer will be at least forty years old when he is released from prison.

Today in Dublin there are an estimated 15,000 heroin addicts. And despite the successes of the police and the local communities in taking on the dealers, the problem is as bad as ever. For every Boxer there are another five willing to take his place. As long as there is demand there will be supply and the appalling misery will continue.

THE MONK

The cocky youngster with the jet black hair stood on the street corner, his piercing blue eyes scanning the passing cars for his next victim. He and his mates could break the passenger window of a woman's car and be away with her handbag before she had time to blink.

It was the late 1970s and RTÉ Radio's Leo Enright was doing a story about a notorious gang of young tearaways called the Bugsy Malones. The kid was delighted to tell the nation about his fledgling criminal career:

'I can't give up robbin'. If I see money in a car I'm takin' it. I just can't leave it there. If I see a handbag on a seat I'll smash the window and be away before anyone knows what's goin' on. I don't go near people walking along the street ... they don't have any money on them. They're not worth robbin'.' The sixteen-year-old was relishing the opportunity to shock. When asked what he would like to be when he grew up, he giggled and smugly predicted: 'I'd like to be serving behind the bank ... just filling up the bags and jumping over the counter.'

On 12 June 1998, a smartly-dressed businessman was caught in photographer Padraig O'Reilly's camera lens, leaving a gleaming downtown Dublin office block with his accountant. Two senior detectives attached to the Gardaí's powerful gang-busting squad, the Criminal Assets Bureau, were also in the frame. Minutes earlier, the Revenue Commissioners had agreed to adjourn the businessman's appeal against a £385,000 tax bill, which the CAB detectives said he owed the State as a result of one of his well-organised hold-ups. Teams of armed detectives, parked off-side in unmarked cars, closely scrutinised the respectable-looking thirty-five-year-old as he drove off with his financial adviser. Gerry Hutch had come a long way since he bragged about robbing cars on an inner-city street corner. The wild young Bugsy Malone had become a shrewd gangland celebrity called The Monk. Today, however, he was saying nothing and his accountant was doing all the talking.

Apart from The General, Gerry Hutch is one of Ireland's best-known criminal masterminds. This quiet-spoken family man is part of a dying breed in the underworld – a so-called ordinary decent criminal, or ODC, who has deliberately shunned the burgeoning drug trade. He has nurtured the image of an ethical crime boss who prefers the more traditional method of making a dodgy living – extracting large sums of money from banks. It was in 1995 that the elusive Monk first blasted his way into the headlines. He became the country's most talked about gangster overnight, when he was linked by Garda intelligence and the media to a spectacular £2.8 million heist. He was also suspected of planning another, equally dramatic robbery eight years earlier, when a team of gangsters took £1.5 million from a security van. Unlike the kid on the radio, the adult Monk would have preferred if someone else was enjoying the spotlight.

Gerry Hutch is a very unlikely gangland figure and lives up to his rather remarkable nickname. He keeps to himself, rarely drinks alcohol and never touches drugs. He is neither flamboyant nor boisterous. He doesn't throw his weight around and carefully avoids aggravation. Policemen who have been on Hutch's case admit harbouring a grudging admiration for him. He is what they describe as a 'clean player'. In the old neighbourhood where he grew up, he is admired and respected by many of the locals.

Hutch was born in 1963 in Summerhill, in the heart of Dublin's run-down north inner-city. Traditionally, in this neglected part of town, there was very little apart from thieving to engage the energies of a young tearaway. For Hutch, appearing in court was often a way of getting a day off from school. He eventually dropped out of education altogether. Hutch's first conviction was at the age of eight, when he appeared in the Children's Court on a charge of larceny. He and his friends hung out in a gang which terrorised the city centre in the late 1970s. They were called the Bugsy Malones after the famous children's gangster spoof of the same name. The bad guys in the

Hollywood blockbuster were armed with Thompson machineguns which fired cream cakes.

As they grew up, the Bugsys found that they preferred live ammunition to cream cakes. Their crime spree was so extensive that it attracted the attentions of the national media, and the young tearaways relished their newfound notoriety. As teenagers, they would rob enough funds to go on holiday in Spain, from where they sent cheeky postcards to the judges and policemen with whom they were acquainted at home. In 1996, in the only newspaper interview he ever gave, Hutch readily admitted his criminal origins: 'We were kids then, doing jump overs [jumping over bank counters to steal cash], shoplifting, robberies, burglaries. Anything that was going, we did it. That was normal for any inner-city kid then.'

During the next twelve years, Gerry Hutch notched up over twenty convictions, for burglary, larceny, car theft, 'joy riding' and malicious damage. He was jailed eleven times and served his sentences in St Patrick's Institution for young offenders and in Mountjoy. While inside he educated himself. 'I taught myself to read and write, firstly by reading comics and then books,' he explained. Hutch's last recorded conviction was in December 1983, when he got two years for malicious damage. He was released in May 1985. The Monk was twenty-two years old.

When he came out of prison, Hutch joined a close-knit team of young criminals with whom he had grown up on the streets of the inner-city. At one stage, he and his pals worked for Eamon Kelly, a former member of the Official IRA and a professional armed robber, who also came from the inner-city. Kelly once featured high up in the list of the city's violent thugs. Eventually, the young Monk and his mates went their own way. In 1993 Kelly was jailed for fifteen years for importing cocaine. Hutch and his cronies were soon making names for themselves in gangland as formidable blaggers, pulling well-organised robberies. In an interview at the time, Martin Cahill referred to the growing notoriety of a northside gang leader and his gang and the prospect of a power struggle. The General said that if it ever came to a confrontation between him and this gang leader, one of them would have to die. In the end, Gerry Hutch has outlived The General and many other gangsters.

In underworld history very few gangs get to pull off multi-million-pound cash robberies. As Ireland nears the end of the millennium, there have been three such heists, worth an estimated total of over £8 million. As a measure of the success of The Monk and his cronies, various members of the gang have been named by Garda intelligence and the media as suspects in all three. The Monk himself has been linked to two.

On the afternoon of 26 January 1987, a Securicor van, with three crew on board, left the main Securicor depot at Herberton Road in Rialto, to commence 'Run Number Two'. Over the next three hours they collected cash from bank branches across the north side of the city. At 5.20pm they made their fifteenth stop, at the Bank of Ireland at Marino Mart in Fairview on the Clontarf Road, where they collected £125,000. It was their last call on the run. They had collected a little under £1.5 million, which was to be transported to Securicor's main cash holding centre. It was 5.30pm as the front seat observer, Brian Holden, was getting back into the van outside the bank. As he did so, a red BMW pulled up behind and three armed and masked men jumped out.

One of the raiders pointed a handgun into Holden's face. 'Get out or I'll blow your fucking head off,' he shouted. A second raider, armed with a rifle, joined the first, and they both pulled Holden from the van and threw him to the ground. The security officer was kicked and warned to stay down or have his head 'blown off'. At the same time, a third raider appeared at the opposite door and pointed a gun at the head of the driver, Thomas Kennedy. He was ordered to hand over the keys and get out.

One of the raiders jumped in behind the wheel of the van. A second one got into the passenger seat of the BMW while the third got into the passenger's side of the van. As the van drove off, he hung out of the door, still pointing the weapon at the security men. As the van sped off up the Malahide Road in the direction of Coolock, the raider in the passenger seat pointed his weapon at the third security officer,

Simon Foley, who was in the vault in the back of the van where the money was stored. The van stopped and one of the raiders unlocked the vault door and pulled Foley out. The van sped off again. One of the raiders driving behind the van in the BMW pointed a rifle at the startled security man, who dived for cover across a garden wall.

The gang drove the van a short distance into the grounds of Coláiste Mhuire, off Griffith Avenue. They stopped on waste ground behind the college complex, near St Vincent's GAA club, and offloaded the loot. The robbers abandoned the car and the van and took off in a second car. At 5.50pm Gardaí located the abandoned vehicles. The raiders had vanished with the money.

Later that night they went to a safe house to count the day's takings. They had expected to get between £25,000 and £100,000 at most. It took them the whole night to count the money, and when they had finished the robbers were practically speechless. The stack of money sitting in the middle of the floor came to an astonishing £1,357,106. They had left another £78,000 in cash and £8,500 in cheques behind in the van, because they had no space for all the money bags. It was the biggest cash robbery in the history of organised crime in Ireland at the time. The young robbers had pulled off what most big league gangsters could only dream of.

The robbery investigation was based at Raheny Garda station and headed by Detective Chief Superintendent John Murphy and Detective Superintendent Noel Conroy of the Central Detective Unit. Once the gang had managed to make their escape the trail had gone cold. Follow-up searches had also proved negative. The only way of tracing them would be when they tried to launder the cash. Murphy and his investigation team did not have long to wait.

The gang leader set about disposing of the money. The plan was to lodge it in a number of banks and building societies across the border in Newry. The operation would take around two weeks to complete. He approached two men to move the cash. Francis Joseph Sheridan and Lonan Patrick Hickey were perfect for the job, as they weren't known to the police and had no criminal records. Thirty-one-year-old Sheridan was a timber salesman who lived with his wife and three children in Swords, County Dublin. An ex-soldier, he had been introduced to the gang leader by a middle-aged businessman who has been involved on the periphery of organised crime for several years. Hickey was the same age as Sheridan and lived at Church Avenue in Drumcondra. He was well-educated and fluent in French and Spanish. When he was seventeen, Hickey had worked as a translator for a Mexican TV company. He moved to live in the USA and got involved in the carpet business as a salesman, a job which he continued in Ireland and then England. He ran his own carpet business in Dublin for a time, until it went bust, after which he started working for a finance company. In 1984 he broke his back in a car crash and was mildly disabled. Shortly after that he became unemployed, and found himself in serious financial difficulties.

Four days after the robbery, on 30 January, Francis Sheridan met the gang leader, and was asked to hold some of the cash. Sheridan would be given instructions over the next two weeks to deliver quantities of the cash to Lonan Hickey. Sheridan was paid £2,000 for his trouble. That night in Swords, County Dublin, Sheridan was handed two large bags. They contained over £320,000 from the robbery. Sheridan stored the bags in his home. On 4 February Sheridan received a phone call, and was told to take £30,000 from the stolen haul and deliver it to Hickey in Drumcondra.

Following the handover of the cash, Hickey was instructed to drive to Newry, County Down, in a hired car. He went to a bank in Newry and attempted to obtain a sterling bank draft payable to a local building society. The bank advised Hickey to go directly to the building society himself and open an account there. The building society would not accept the £30,000 in Irish money. He changed it into sterling and opened the account in the building society with the converted cash, which now totalled £26,697.

The following day, Hickey met the gang leader in the Cat and Cage pub in Drumcondra and explained the trouble he had had lodging the stolen money. The bagman was told that the gang leader himself had travelled to Newry the same day and had opened an account with another building society in the town. He showed Hickey his lodgement book. He had opened the account with a lodgement of £1,372.

The following day, Sheridan was instructed to deliver £40,000 to Hickey. Hickey took the money to Newry to carry out his latest instructions. His first call was to the building society, where he withdrew £26,000 from the account he had set up two days earlier. The cash was in the form of a sterling bank draft made out to the gang leader. Hickey then went to another building society and lodged the £40,000. That evening, in Dublin, he handed over the bank draft.

On Monday 9 February, Hickey picked up another £40,000 from Sheridan. In Newry, the bagman converted it into sterling and lodged it into the fast-growing building society account. The balance now stood at £75,279.

In the meantime, however, the investigation team in Raheny had received information that Sheridan was moving large amounts of cash from the Marino Mart heist. On the Monday an undercover team tailed him to the house in Drumcondra, where he handed over the cash. The following morning, Sheridan received another phone call. The operation was to be stepped up, and Sheridan was instructed to bring £80,000 in cash to Hickey. At 8.25am the undercover team tailed him in his Volkswagen van to the Drumcondra house. Hickey was waiting in his car. Hickey walked over to the driver's window and Sheridan handed him a large bag. Hickey went back to his car and threw the bag on the passenger seat.

Two minutes later, Detective Sergeant Willy Ryan and his team swooped on Hickey. He tried to drive away but was blocked by an unmarked squad car. Ryan opened the bag and found the cash hidden underneath clothes in plastic wrappings. He arrested Lonan Hickey under Section 30 of the Offences Against the State Act. Five minutes later, another team arrested Sheridan on Gracepark Road in Drumcondra as he drove home.

Sheridan was brought to Whitehall station. Detective Sergeant Ryan showed him the bag of cash he had found with Hickey and asked whether it was from the Marino Mart job. Sheridan replied yes. When asked if he could help the investigation any further, the bagman admitted that he had more money in the attic of his house in Swords.

'I will bring you there and get it for you,' he offered. In a search, the detectives found two large bags containing a total of £129,361, and an additional £1,600 was hidden in Sheridan's sock drawer. They also recovered a box of rubber bands and plastic bags which he had used to pack the money before delivering it to Hickey.

At the same time, Hickey's home was being searched in Drumcondra. Detective Garda Christy Pentony found two building society books. Later, both men claimed to the detectives that they had been working for Gerry Hutch but stated that they were afraid of him. They made full statements outlining their involvement with Hutch. The Gardaí obtained a order in the Belfast High Court, freezing The Monk's account in Newry. On 11 February Sheridan and Hickey were brought before the Dublin District Court, where they were formally charged with the Marino Mart robbery and with receiving the proceeds. The charges were later amended to receiving the money traced and recovered by the police. The sterling bank draft which Hickey had handed over was also cancelled. The Gardaí were jubilant. They prepared a file for the Director of Public Prosecutions, recommending that Hutch be charged. However, the DPP decided that there was not sufficient evidence to proceed with the case.

Hutch was not giving up without a fight. He applied to the Belfast High Court for the return of the frozen cash in Newry. But the court refused his application after a drawn-out legal battle, on the grounds that the money in the account was the proceeds of the Marino Mart heist. Hutch threatened to bring the case to the European Court, but eventually dropped the appeal. £1 million from the Marino Mart job was never recovered. Sheridan and Hickey subsequently pleaded guilty and were each sentenced to twenty-one months in prison. In the Circuit Criminal Court their defence counsel claimed that they had been used by 'dangerous and ruthless men'. The gang leader was referred to during the case as 'Mr X'.

The Marino Mart robbery had given him a formidable reputation. In the underworld he was celebrated and respected. He moved up the police's list of most-wanted gangsters. Hutch decided to do the sensible thing and keep his head down.

One of those suspected of being part of the Marino Mart gang was Thomas O'Driscoll, who was originally from St Mary's Mansions on Railway Street. In the early 1980s, he was inside at the same time as Hutch, having been jailed for an armed robbery from a department store on North Earl Street. Despite the windfall from the security van job, he and two other members of the gang were planning other heists of their own. In September 1987, they decided to hit the North Cumberland Street labour exchange, where they collected their unemployment assistance each week.

Shortly after 10am on 1 September, O'Driscoll and an accomplice burst into the building. O'Driscoll, armed with a sawn-off shotgun, covered his partner, who smashed the glass partition at Hatch 33 with a sledgehammer, vaulted the counter and began scooping cash into a bag.

Detective Garda Dominick Huthcin from Fitzgibbon Street station, who was on duty inside the partition, heard the commotion. Pulling his .38 revolver, he ran out into the public area to confront the raiders. He pointed his weapon at O'Driscoll and ordered him to drop the shotgun. The raider pointed the shotgun at the policeman, who again ordered him to surrender. O'Driscoll grabbed a pistol from his accomplice and handed him the shotgun. He moved towards the detective and fired twice, narrowly missing him. O'Driscoll's partner, who had jumped back out into the public area, also fired at Detective Garda Hutchin, hitting him in the face and body. The injured detective fired all six rounds in his revolver at O'Driscoll, hitting him five times. The robber fell back into a sitting position, still pointing the handgun at Hutchin, who retreated back inside the staff area to reload his gun and raise the alarm.

Clutching the bag of money, O'Driscoll was helped by his partner to get outside. The third robber was waiting down the street in a stolen getaway car. O'Driscoll leaned against a parked car while his partner, armed with the handgun, took up a covering position in the middle of the street. A squad car, responding to the alarm, screeched around the corner at the bottom of Cumberland Street and drove towards the raiders. The robber in the road pointed his gun at the squad car, forcing the unarmed officers inside to duck down. At the same time, the getaway car drove up behind them.

The armed raider helped O'Driscoll into the car, which then sped off. As it went towards Mountjoy Square, another uniformed officer tried to smash the windshield by throwing his baton at it. The squad car gave chase but lost the raiders, whose car, a Lancia, was much more powerful. A few blocks away, the three robbers abandoned the car. The two other raiders dragged O'Driscoll, who had been seriously injured, to a Toyota Starlet and drove north.

At Roseglen Avenue in Kilbarrack, O'Driscoll's partners decided that he would slow down their escape. They stopped the car and pushed him out onto the side of the road. They reckoned that by leaving him behind O'Driscoll would get medical attention, when the police found him. O'Driscoll tried to get up but couldn't. He was moaning and calling for help. A few minutes later, he died from his injuries. The other two raiders got away with £25,000 in cash. Detective Garda Hutchin recovered from his wounds and was awarded a bronze Scott Medal for bravery, one of the highest honours the force can bestow for courage in action. The brave detective refused to accept the medal, however, on the grounds that he was unhappy about his treatment by his own authorities after the incident.

Laurence Alford, a thirty-four-year-old dock worker from East Wall, was charged with the robbery, but later acquitted. He had provided the Toyota Starlet used by the two surviving members of the robbery team to make their getaway. He made a full statement, outlining how he had handed the car over to the getaway driver. This man, from the North Strand in Dublin, was an associate of Gerry Hutch. The twenty-one-year-old robber was charged with robbing the labour exchange, but was eventually acquitted and released. Subsequently, Alford was given a severe beating for telling the police about his role in the robbery. Alford died some time later from an unrelated illness.

In the meantime, The Monk had moved into the property business. Those who know him well say that Hutch has a keen business sense and has invested his money well. In August 1989, he bought two houses on Buckingham Street, for a total of £20,000. He already owned a house on this street, which he had bought in 1981, when he was eighteen years old. He converted the new houses into rental accommodation for recipients of Eastern Health Board housing assistance. Although he had never been employed, Hutch had a legitimate explanation for where the money had come from – in 1988 he had received £25,000 compensation from the Department of Justice, as a result of a fall he had suffered while serving a sentence in Mountjoy prison.

In 1993, he bought a fourth house on Buckingham Street. In the same year he decided to go legitimate with his landlord business and availed of a controversial tax amnesty, designed to give tax dodgers a clean slate and bring them into the tax net. Hutch did not have to disclose how he had made his money in the first place. He claimed that he had earned just over £30,000 renting out his properties between 1991 and 1994. He paid a total of £9,000 in back tax, after signing a declaration that his statement was true and accurate. There was no mention of Marino Mart.

At the same time, Hutch invested money with Paddy Shanahan, the armed robber-turned-builder who was to be assassinated in October 1994. Shanahan had refurbished the Buckingham Village complex and had also begun a number of major building projects in the city centre. He and Hutch became good friends, and Hutch was later reported to have confronted the man who ordered the builder's killing. At the time of Shanahan's murder, Hutch was not having a good time. He had been wrongly accused of involvement in the murder of The General, who had been whacked the previous August. For a time police feared that The Monk might get involved in a gang war, but he pulled back from the brink. The General's men and the Gardaí were satisfied that he had had nothing to do with the hit.

As the dust settled again, Hutch decided to move house. The following year he paid £100,000 for a comfortable four-bedroom house, in the leafy coastal suburb of Clontarf in County Dublin. He started sending his children to private fee-paying schools in the upmarket south side of the city. Hutch is a dedicated family man who, according to his associates, wants to give his children a crime-free upbringing. Hutch still enjoyed relative anonymity, and his upmarket neighbours knew nothing of his life. But all of that was about to change with one of the biggest and most spectacular armed robberies ever carried out in Irish criminal history.

At 6.30pm on the evening of 24 January 1995, five armed and masked men took off with £2.8 million from the Brinks-Allied security company's cash-holding depot in north Dublin. The level of planning and precision in the 'job' placed every previous heist – including The General's most celebrated 'strokes' – in the shade.

The Brinks-Allied job was the culmination of several months of surveillance and plotting by the close-knit gang. The hood who helped plan the robbery is the same man who was the getaway driver in the robbery at the Cumberland Street labour exchange. He had also been involved in the Marino Mart heist. In January 1992 – three years earlier – he was suspected of masterminding a daring robbery from an Allied Irish Bank cash-holding centre in Waterford. A number of months before that the Gardaí in the area had mounted a surveillance operation after an amateur radio enthusiast taped the gangster's voice sending messages to an accomplice on a two-way radio. He was clearly staking out the cash centre and noting the movements of security personnel and Gardaí at the building. When the heat died down, a team of armed and masked men breached a weak spot in the centre's tight security and made off with an estimated £2 million in cash. No-one was ever charged with the job.

The Brinks-Allied depot was another tough nut to crack. Since 1993, the depot had been housed in a specially-converted factory in Clonshaugh Industrial Estate in Coolock, on the edge of the city. The estate is bordered by roadways. To the north is Turnapin Lane; to the west, across two fields, is the M1 Motorway. The Oscar Traynor Road is to the south and Clonshaugh Road to the east. The depot was equipped with a state-of-the-art security system.

In the summer, the gang began formulating their plan. Their first objective was to find a safe location to store their transport for the job. On 16 October, a businessman who was working with them rented a disused shed in north County Dublin. The businessman told the owner that he needed a discreet location to store cars which were being repossessed on behalf of a finance company. He agreed a weekly rental of £50 per week and paid the owner £600 in cash for three months in advance. The businessman used a false name and address. Up to Christmas, the shed was used to store eight to ten different cars. In the meantime, the gang carried out surveillance on cash vans as they made collections around the city and transported money back to the depot.

On Saturday 26 November, Gardaí spotted a member of the gang watching a security van at the North Side Shopping Centre in Coolock. At a security conference in the Dublin Metropolitan Area HQ, it was decided to mount surveillance on The Monk and his associates. It was thought that the gang were planning a job similar to the Marino Mart job, by hitting a cash van in transit. The operation was code-named 'Operation Liffey'. Surveillance teams, backed up by the Emergency Response Unit (ERU) and the Serious Crime Squad, kept the suspects under constant watch for almost two months.

Just before Christmas the operation was scaled down, because it was felt that the gang had abandoned their plans and were not going to make a move. Since the 1987 robbery, security vans carrying more than £1 million in the city were accompanied by an escort consisting of two armed detectives. Vans travelling throughout the country had even heavier security, with Garda and Army protection. The escort was made up of ten or more soldiers in two or three jeeps and a squad car manned by two uniformed policemen.

On the night of 1 December 1994, two Mitsubishi Pajero jeeps were stolen from a garage compound. The jeeps were driven to the rented shed. On 11 December, two more jeeps were purloined, from Dalkey and Herbert Place. Ironically, one of the jeeps had belonged to Hutch's friend, Paddy Shanahan. He had been driving it on the night he was murdered, three months earlier. A second jeep belonged to world-famous musician Phil Coulter. The four jeeps were fitted with false number plates, which had been ordered through a north inner-city garage.

On 17 January the Garda Criminal Intelligence section sent an urgent circular to stations across the north city. The document named twelve people from the north city. Under the heading 'Information on proposed armed robbery by Dublin criminals' it alerted all uniformed and detective units to monitor the gang's movements. The document also referred to the incident in November which sparked off Operation Liffey. The document stated: 'Information to hand suggests that a number of prominent criminals are planning a major armed robbery. The likely target is money in transit by a security company. Keep a special lookout for the criminals listed inside and monitor and record movements of same.' Photographs of the hoods accompanied descriptions, ages, addresses and types of cars used by the twelve suspects. Within a week, at least five of those faces in the intelligence bulletin were to cause major embarrassment to the Government and the police.

On the morning of 24 January, a security van with radio call sign Yankee 29 left the Brinks-Allied depot at Clonshaugh and drove to the main AIB Bank Centre in Ballsbridge. Yankee 29 was allocated to 'Run 16', collecting cash from banks in the south-east. At the Bank Centre it met with its Army and Garda escort. Around 6.25pm the van returned to Clonshaugh Industrial Estate from its run, still under escort. It had collected almost £3 million in used notes from the various banks. The security van drove through the front gate of the Brinks-Allied complex, around to the the rear of the building and into bay number three for unloading. The police and troops, having concluded their duty, turned and drove away. Two other vans and their escorts had arrived earlier and entered the complex. The gang knew that Yankee 29 was to be the last van back to the depot that evening.

They had been organised and ready to move for several days. Their plan was to strike at the rear of the building just as the last cash van was returning, approaching through the fields from Turnapin Lane, which had been blocked off due to road works on a motorway extension. The area provided perfect cover for the gangsters. It was unlit and there was no traffic. In the days before the robbery, a section of perimeter fence, erected to block off the fields between the industrial estate and the motorway, had been removed.

At 5.30pm, five men in a Pajero jeep were spotted driving up Turnapin Lane. They drove through the hole in the fence and joined a second jeep which had already been brought into the field. Again they had done their preparatory work. They had breached a ditch to allow them to drive through to the second field. They were now able to drive up to the perimeter fence at the rear of the warehouse adjoining the Brinks-Allied depot. Outside, the fence was bordered by a six-feet-deep dyke. The clever crooks had already bridged it over the weekend, by laying railway sleepers and sheets of fibreboard across it. The top portion of the makeshift bridge had even been painted green to camouflage it. Strips of timber had also been fastened to the top sheets to improve the grip of the jeeps when driving across it.

The perimeter fence at the warehouse had also been loosened and took only seconds to remove. The two jeeps drove across the bridge and through the fence into the warehouse yard. All that separated them now from the cash-loading bay was a simple steel fence. The gang had already weakened it by cutting the support bars.

At 6.27pm Yankee 29 drove into the loading bay. The roller shutter doors lowered and locked automatically. Eye witnesses would later report seeing three flares being fired into the night sky, as the Army and Garda escort went out of view. It was the gang's signal to move. The first jeep was driven at speed through the weakened fence between the warehouse and the Brinks-Allied depot. It then rammed the shutter door, pushing it inwards and up, leaving a gap large enough on either side for the raiders to get in. The shutter door was hit with such force that it also shunted the security van forward.

Three gang members, all armed, ran in under the door and threatened the startled staff, who were in the process of unloading the cash into the depot's vaults. The raiders fired a number of shots and then began grabbing the cash-bags. They carried them to the second jeep, which had reversed up to the dividing fence between the warehouse and the cash depot. In under ten minutes the gang were finished. They jumped into the jeep and drove out through the hole in the warehouse fence, across the makeshift bridge and down through the adjoining field. A reflective road sign, from the motorway construction site, had been left at the breach at the ditch bordering the second field, to indicate where the hole was in the dark.

The gang drove at speed onto Turnapin Lane and across the now-disused motorway flyover towards the industrial estate on the Swords Road. From there they drove across the road to a field off Barberstown Lane, where they had parked the second pair of stolen jeeps. They transferred the loot and drove off in different directions. Later that night, one of the gang was arrested under Section 30 of the Offences Against the State Act, near his house on the North Strand. A search of his car revealed a number of traffic cones and wet and muddy overalls and boots. He was held for forty-eight hours and then released, having refused to open his mouth.

The Brinks gang, as they became known, had exposed glaring weaknesses in the security at the depot. The perimeter fences were not alarmed and the security shutter to the bay was not strong enough to resist ramming. When detectives studied the security video footage, they found it to be of such poor quality that they could not even make out descriptions for the raiders. It also transpired that, due to bank cutbacks, the raiders had probably got more money than they should have within the few minutes that they were grabbing the cash-bags. The banks, who were charged for each bag they handed to Securicor, had doubled the amount of cash stuffed into each bag.

In the days after the extraordinary heist, The Monk and his cronies kept a very low profile. Within a week, Hutch and a number of others left the country to go on holiday. Sparks were flying in the Dáil, with predictable demands from the opposition benches for a crackdown on the big criminals. There was also considerable embarrassment when the intelligence document of 17 January was published. Meanwhile, another associate of the gang was given the job of disposing of the two jeeps used to transport the gang and the money from Barberstown Lane. Late one night they were both driven into the Liffey near the Point Theatre. Commercial divers discovered the jeeps on the river bed on 12 July 1995.

An intensive investigation was carried out into the Brinks-Allied robbery but, because of the gang's in-built security system of absolute silence, no clues ever leaked out about the whereabouts of the cash. None of the stolen money was ever traced, nor is it known how it was laundered, although it is suspected that four businessmen, from Dublin, Northern Ireland and England, played a part in its disposal.

On the morning of 26 September 1995, Gerry Hutch and four well-known criminals were arrested and questioned for forty-eight hours. Some of them, including The Monk, never spoke during the two days. They were released without charge.

In December 1995, Gerry Hutch gave the police some cause for concern, when he was seen looking suspiciously at Securicor's main cash depot on Herberton Road in Rialto. A massive security operation was put in place for over three months. Some of The Monk's associates say he did it purely to get the cops in a panic. The large team of detectives, enjoying plenty of overtime just before Christmas, were not necessarily complaining.

In 1996 The Monk was back in the spotlight again. Gerry Lee, from East Wall, was reported to be a member of the Brinks gang. He had been arrested at the same time as Hutch. On 9 March 1996, a lone gunman shot him twice in the chest, as he was celebrating his thirty-first birthday in a house in Coolock. He died instantly from his wounds. At first it was thought that Lee had been whacked because he had moved into the drug business with proceeds from the Brinks job. But detectives later discovered that it was the result of a dispute over a woman.

A team of *Sunday World* photographers watching Lee's funeral were the first to picture the elusive bogeyman of organised crime who had everyone talking. The following week, the paper ran a story about The Monk's bizarre tax affairs, accompanied by a picture with his eyes blacked out. As a result of the story, he agreed to give an interview to *Sunday Independent* journalist Veronica Guerin. She had been shot in the leg at her home a week after the Brinks-Allied heist. The day before the incident, she had revealed details of how The Monk had availed of the tax amnesty. The shooting incident, which came so soon after the robbery, added to the furore and for a short time the finger of suspicion pointed at The Monk. However, detectives soon discounted Hutch from their enquiries. The shooting had been the work of a south-side criminal, who would also play a role in the journalist's murder in June 1996.

In his interview at the time, Hutch wanted to make it clear that, whatever else he was up to, he was not involved in the drug rackets. He also had something to say about the Brinks-Allied job. 'The Brinks was a brilliant job. The best of luck to whoever done it,' he declared. He also explained his insistence on loyalty among friends and associates. 'My philosophy in life is simple enough – no betrayal. That means you don't talk about others, you don't grass and you never let people down.'

On 26 June 1996 a gunman stepped off the back of a motorbike on the Naas road and callously murdered Veronica Guerin. A greedy, dangerous drug baron had decided that she would probe into his business no more. The horrific murder was to result in a sequence of events which would turn gangland upside-down, as police instigated the toughest and most comprehensive investigation ever carried out into organised crime in Ireland.

To an ODC like Hutch, the murder was a despicable act. He was horrified by the crime. He had no real love of journalists, but he did have respect for Guerin. Hutch had known too many people who had perished at the point of a gun. It was, say his associates, the final straw. He wanted nothing more to do with crime. The Guerin murder caused a public outcry about how powerful the godfathers had become. There was widespread anger against the State and the Gardaí, and demands that action finally be taken. A few days after the murder, Gerry Hutch walked into the front offices of Independent Newspapers, on Middle Abbey Street in the city centre, to sign a book of condolences. Even that simple act of registering his sympathy almost descended into farce of the cops-and-robbers variety. He was accompanied by three associates and at least three more detectives, who were making no secret that they were on his tail. The entourage piled into the front lobby. The detectives stood over The Monk's shoulder as he signed his name. A month later he was arrested and held for two days for questioning about allegations of attempts to intimidate Gardaí. He was released without charge.

During that long, tension-filled summer, the people of the inner-city renewed their campaign against the dealers who were destroying their children. They were targeting the likes of Thomas Mullen, who had brought despair and suffering to his own neighbours by supplying heroin. Gerry Hutch also threw himself into the campaign. Hutch claimed that he wanted to put something back into his community. In August he appeared at a public meeting in Rutland Street school in his old neighbourhood to show his support. He was photographed and identified in several newspapers as The Monk. He no longer cared about the reports identifying him as a bank-robber. It was a damn sight better than being involved in the filthy business of drugs. Hutch demanded to know why no-one had come to him to seek his help in ridding the dealers from the area. He was warmly applauded by the locals. When Detective Sergeant John O'Driscoll, the head of the local drug unit which had been hugely successful in tackling the drug dealers, got up to speak, Hutch folded his arms. Clapping for a cop was not his thing.

In the raft of anti-crime legislation introduced after the Guerin murder, the establishment of the Criminal Assets Bureau was probably the most significant development. Within a few months of its mobilisation in the Summer of 1996, it had become one of the most powerful crime-busting weapons ever used in a European country. The CAB are empowered to take literally every penny and every piece of property from a suspected criminal if he is unable to explain the source of his wealth. They do not require the same levels of proof as are required in criminal prosecutions. They have the power to raid the offices of accountants and solicitors and to seize any documents relating to their dodgy client's affairs. The bureau has direct legal access, on demand, to all accounts held by suspected criminals in financial institutions. By the beginning of October 1998, the CAB had seized millions of pounds worth of criminals' property and they are in the process of going after many more. Millions of pounds have also been frozen in bank accounts both here and abroad.

In the Spring of 1997, Ireland's modern version of the untouchables turned their attentions to Gerry Hutch. They raided his home in Clontarf and the offices of an accountant and a solicitor. In June of that year, he received a tax demand for £385,000 by registered letter. The Criminal Assets Bureau say that is just what he owes for one year – 1987. They are still assessing how much he owes them as a result of his criminal activities since then.

In October 1998, the Monk was still appealing the decision to the Revenue Commissioners. The hearings were being held in secret in a modern office block in south Dublin. Unlike many others who have fled the country with their ill-gotten-cash, Hutch is going nowhere. He has decided to stay put in his native town and sort out his differences with the CAB, before settling into a legitimate hassle-free life. Or so his friends claim. Gardaí and criminals alike say that he is clever enough to know when to quit. So has The Monk finally retired?

ALSO FROM PAUL WILLIAMS

THE GENERAL
GODFATHER OF CRIME
Paul Williams

In a twenty-year career marked by obsessive secrecy, brutality and meticulous planning, Martin Cahill, aka The General, netted over IR£40 million. He was untouchable – until a bullet from an IRA hitman ended it all. A compelling read, this book reveals Cahill's bizarre personality and the activities of the *Tango Squad* – the special police unit that targetted him.

Paperback €9.95/STG£7.99/$11.95